T0309214

The SME Business Guide to Fraud Risk Management

All organisations are affected by fraud, but disproportionately so for SMEs given their size and vulnerability. Some small businesses that have failed to manage business fraud effectively have not only suffered financially but also have not survived. This book provides a guide for SMEs to understand the current sources of business fraud risk and the specific risk response actions that can be taken to limit exposure, through the structured discipline of enterprise risk management.

The book provides:

- **A single-source reference**: a description of all of the common fraud types SMEs are facing in one location.
- **An overview of enterprise risk management**: a tool to tackle fraud (as recommended by the Metropolitan Police Service and many other government-sponsored organisations).
- **Illustrations of fraud events**: diagrams/figures (where appropriate) of how frauds are carried out.
- **Case studies**: case studies of the fraud types described (to bring the subject to life and illustrate fraud events and their perpetrators) enabling readers to be more knowledgeable about the threats.
- **Sources of support and information**: a description of the relationship between the government agencies and departments.
- **What to do**: 'specific actions' to be implemented as opposed to just recommending the preparation of policies and processes that may just gather dust on a shelf.

The book gives SMEs a much better understanding of the risks they face and hence informs any discussion about the services required, what should be addressed first, in what order remaining requirements should be implemented and what will give the best value for money.

Robert James Chapman is an established author and has provided risk management services for over twenty years across eight countries and within fourteen industries. He was elected and is a Fellow of the UK IRM, APM and ICM for his contribution to the field of risk management. He is the author of *Simple Tools and Techniques for Enterprise Risk Management*, now in its second edition.

The SME Business Guide to Fraud Risk Management

Robert James Chapman

Routledge
Taylor & Francis Group

LONDON AND NEW YORK

Cover image: © Getty Images

First published 2022
by Routledge
4 Park Square, Milton Park, Abingdon, Oxon OX14 4RN

and by Routledge
605 Third Avenue, New York, NY 10158

Routledge is an imprint of the Taylor & Francis Group, an informa business

© 2022 Robert James Chapman

British Library Cataloguing-in-Publication Data
A catalogue record for this book is available from the British Library

Library of Congress Cataloging-in-Publication Data
A catalog record has been requested for this book

ISBN: 978-1-032-05547-3 (hbk)
ISBN: 978-1-032-05546-6 (pbk)
ISBN: 978-1-003-20038-3 (ebk)

DOI: 10.4324/9781003200383

Typeset in Adobe Garamond Pro
by codeMantra

Kay, Dominic and Gemma

Contents

SECTION I   BACKGROUND

SECTION 2   EXTERNAL 'ACTORS'

SECTION 3   INTERNAL 'ACTORS'

SECTION 4   ADDITIONAL INFORMATION

Figures

Tables

Case studies

Foreword

The raison d'etre of the UK's Institute of Directors (IoD) is to support business leaders, through world-class professional development and guidance, to stimulate the growth, prosperity and longevity of their businesses. At the heart of the IoDs counselling and guidance is recognition of the constantly evolving business landscape and the need for businesses to both recognise and respond to emerging risks. Within its guidance and 'Fact Sheets' designed for businesses of all sizes, it has highlighted the need for businesses to be alert to both fraud and cybercrime. Hence there is a clear synergy between the work of the IoD and this book.

This book makes explicit the types of fraud small and medium enterprises (SMEs) may encounter and, in many instances highlights cybercrime as the common catalyst. The book advocates the adoption of risk management as a structured approach to understanding and responding to fraud. Risk management is now recognised as a mature discipline embedded within many industries as an indispensable tool to unearth, capture, describe, assess and manage threats to business prosperity, sustainability and survival. While the book incorporates a risk management approach to fraud management it is simply intended to provide a logical structure rather than attempt to turn readers into dedicated risk managers. A key message of the book reflects the essence of risk management. The pro-active intervention and management of potential threats is far preferable to fighting a rear-guard action against problems that have already materialised. Once they have occurred these problems may impact a business minute by the minute, not hour by the hour or day by day. The practice of developing proactive preventative measures means there is time to consider what safeguards to adopt as well as when, how and in what sequence.

The author has extensive knowledge of the subject of risk management as well as an in-depth experience of its application, gained in the UK as well as in Europe, Africa, the Middle East and Asia. The author's books have made a significant contribution to the field of risk management, which are on sale in forty countries and recommended reading in universities worldwide. The practical experience of delivering risk management services combined with the previous authorship of risk management texts is clearly evident in the layout and content of this book. Dr Chapman's book describes twelve different types of fraud that SMEs may be exposed to. Each chapter examines a different type of fraud. They are structured in an identical way to support ease of navigation. The author recognises that a director's scarcest resource is time. His book is unique in that each fraud is examined from the perspective of the pattern of the fraud, the mechanics of implementation, previous incidents (case studies), red flags (alarm bells), the risks that may be encountered and specific response actions.

One of the salient points of the book is that the success of SMEs is of paramount importance to the UK economy when considering the extent of their contribution to: innovation; job creation; opening new markets; supporting local communities; and the national GDP. The prosperity of SMEs is vital for governments, national and regional economies as well as local communities. The importance of SMEs is highlighted by BEIS's action plan[1] which states the UK's 5.7 million SMEs make a huge contribution to the economy employing 16 million people and accounting for £1.9 trillion of turnover. However, a single fraud event can leave an SME struggling for years or even bring about its collapse. It is their very size that leaves SMEs the most vulnerable within the business community and the least equipped to combat fraud.

This book will raise the awareness of SME directors and managers alike to the common forms of fraud and seeks to equip them with an understanding of their own business's vulnerabilities and potential responses. The ability of SMEs to survive and prosper will have a positive ripple effect across all aspects of our economy and hence should be important to us all.

Dr. Roger M. Barker
Director of Policy and Corporate Governance,
Institute of Directors
116 Pall Mall, London SW1Y 5ED

Note

1 "BEIS Small and Medium Enterprises (SME) Action Plan" published by the UK's Department of Business, Energy, & Industrial Strategy in 2019.

Preface

Glossaries and definitions

A glossary of risk management terms and definitions is included in **Appendix 1** to support those readers new to the field of risk management.

A comprehensive glossary of terms and definitions relating to information security and cybercrime is included in **Appendix 2**, however, it should be noted that cybercrime is an umbrella term used to describe two closely linked, but distinct ranges of criminal activity. The Government's National Cyber Security Strategy defines these as:

- **Cyber-dependent crimes** – crimes that can be committed only through the use of Information and Communications Technology (ICT) devices, where the devices are both the tool for committing the crime, and the target of the crime (e.g. developing and propagating malware for financial gain, hacking to steal, damage, distort or destroy data and/or network or activity).
- **Cyber-enabled crimes** – traditional crimes which can be increased in scale or reach by the use of computers, computer networks or other forms of ICT (such as cyber-enabled fraud and data theft).

SMEs need to be constantly vigilant for criminals who have:

- Cloned the websites of legitimate businesses to ensnare their victims.
- Taken receipt of goods with no intention of paying.
- Sought 'up-front' payment for goods that do not exist.
- Created false invoices to secure an SME's bank details.
- Created false email addresses to avoid being detected.
- Created false identities to secure employment to commit a crime.
- Planted malware to facilitate ransomware demands.
- Visited websites, professional media sites and social media platforms to glean information to support Business Email Compromise attacks.

- Stolen director's identities or created false director identities to steal from business bank accounts.
- Bought products to reverse engineer them, breach intellectual property legislation and flood the market with counterfeit products.
- Used phishing emails to steal usernames and passwords, and hack business email accounts.
- Advertised anti-virus software packages on the internet which are actually malware. There are over 100 fake anti-virus software packages in existence which are regularly given a new name to give them a new lease of life. One product may have over 20 aliases.
- Instigated mass-marketing frauds, including but not limited to: Phishing scams which are a particular kind of mass-marketing fraud and Pharming scams where computer users are directed to a fake website, sometimes from phishing emails, to input their employee details.

Acknowledgements

I thank the following organisations for providing permission to reference their reports and include their case studies to illustrate the different types of fraud that individuals and organisations perpetrate.

- **Beazley PLC (Beazley.com)**. Approval granted by Mairi MacDonald – Media Relations and Content – to include Case Study 6.2.
- **Crown Prosecution Service**. Their material is subject to Crown copyright under the terms of the Open Government Licence v3.0. See www.nationalarchives.gov.uk/doc/open-government-licence/version/3/.
- **Department for Digital, Culture, Media and Sport**. Their material is subject to Crown copyright under the terms of the Open Government Licence v3.0. See www.nationalarchives.gov.uk/doc/open-government-licence/version/3/.
- **Department for Business, Energy and Industrial Strategy**. Their material is subject to Crown copyright under the terms of the Open Government Licence v3.0. See www.nationalarchives.gov.uk/doc/open-government-licence/version/3/.
- **East Sussex County Council**. Approval granted by Karen Bowles -Senior Media and Content Officer-to include Case Study 12.2.
- **HM Treasury**. Their material is subject to Crown copyright under the terms of the Open Government Licence v3.0. See www.nationalarchives.gov.uk/doc/open-government-licence/version/3/.
- **National Crime Agency** (non-ministerial department). Their material is subject to Crown copyright under the terms of the Open Government Licence v3.0. See www.nationalarchives.gov.uk/doc/open-government-licence/version/3/.
- **National Cyber Security Centre** (part of GCHQ). Case Study 8.3. Their material is subject to Crown copyright under the terms of the Open Government Licence v3.0. See www.nationalarchives.gov.uk/doc/open-government-licence/version/3/.

- **National Fraud Authority**. Case Study 16.1. Their material is subject to Crown copyright under the terms of the Open Government Licence v3.0. See www.nationalarchives.gov.uk/doc/open-government-licence/version/3/.
- **Northumberland County Council**. Approval granted by Andrew Ward, Communications Business Partner, Communications Team-to include Case Study 12.1.
- **Serious Fraud Office**. Approval to include Case Studies: 11.2, 14.1, 14.2, 14.3, 15.1 and 15.2. Their material is subject to Crown copyright under the terms of the Open Government Licence v3.0.
- **Interpol**. Permission to reproduce INTERPOL case studies granted by Carolyn Oxlee, Head of Corporate and Internal Communication, INTERPOL General Secretariat, subject to INTERPOL copyright being recorded against the case studies. See Case Studies 5.1 and 8.2.
- **Wokingham Borough Council**. Approval granted by Lucy Hindmarsh-Communications Engagement and Marketing Specialist-to include Case Study 12.3.

Reviewers

Reviews: I thank the following individuals for their comments on the text during its preparation. The views contained in this book are entirely those of the author and are in no way attributable to the reviewers. Responsibility for the information and guidance incorporated in the book rests with the author and not the reviewers.

- Matthew Collantine is the Chief Information Security Officer at the Nuclear Decommissioning Authority. Matthew is a Chartered Engineer, a member of the British Computer Society, and has degrees in Software Engineering and Strategic Management. He has spent much of his career working in the nuclear sector in a variety of roles including software development and IT management.
- Teresa Noon is the Managing Director of Indigo Tax and Accounting Limited, which is an award-winning firm of Chartered Accountants, specialising in supporting SMEs. Teresa is both a Chartered Accountant and a Chartered Tax advisor who previously worked as an accountant for KPMG. As owner and founder of Indigo Tax & Accountancy Limited, Teresa is responsible for the overall management and development of the company. For the last 15 years, Indigo has embraced technology and is now striving to ensure that its clients embrace it too, not only to meet HMRC requirements of 'Making Tax Digital' but to ensure small businesses are keeping

their records in real-time to allow them to monitor and react to how their business is performing. Indigo recognises that for SMEs, this digital transformation must but be accompanied by a constant awareness of the evolving threats from both cybercrime and fraud.

■ Dr Gavin Ellis is a cyber security specialist at Atkins (a member of the SNC-Lavalin group), which describes itself as a 'market-leading design, engineering and project management consultancy'. Atkins are a major supplier of cyber services to the defence and national security sectors, as well as providers of technical cyber vulnerability investigation services to the UK defence market.

Fraud Specialist

Comments: I thank the following individual for his comments on the subject of fraud and in particular ransomware, which is seen to continue to be a significant threat.

■ Andrew Penhale is the Head of Division, Specialist Fraud Division, Crown Prosecution Service.

Audience

This book is written specifically for small and medium enterprises with less than 250 employees and a turnover of less than €50 million who are seeking to combat business fraud. As businesses strive for growth through the pursuit of increasing market share, penetrating new markets, developing new technologies, acquisitions or enhancing their use of the internet, their exposure to fraud increases disproportionately. More importantly, the impact of a future fraud event would be far more damaging if it coincided with initiatives to drive expansion through say increasing market share, securing funding or enhancing reputation. Hence this book is for those business owners and managers who have recognised their current fraud risk management practices are immature and are seeking guidance for improvement. In addition, it is for those owners and directors who have come to the realisation that, given the rapidly evolving changes in cybercrime and the increased demands on businesses to demonstrate the suitability of their corporate governance and fraud risk management practices, pressure is mounting to improve awareness and demonstrate resilience. These demands are emerging from an array of sources such as prospective lenders, joint venture partners, shareholders, clients, buyers and suppliers, who all have expectations that the businesses they deal with will protect confidential information, intellectual property, details of sensitive contracts and or finance arrangements. It should be noted that the book is not for those seeking to understand which criminal offence would be prosecuted under which legislation or how the legal system prosecutes offenders.

Aim of the book

The primary aim of the book is to provide in one place key details of all of the main types of fraud affecting SMEs so that they do not have to carry out their own extensive and very time-consuming research. Case studies are provided to give real-life instances of fraud events to provide a window into the world of crime and its perpetrators. The book is structured in such a way as to make navigation easy and enable readers to quickly find the general guidance they are looking for in terms of specific actions or the organisations to contact for more information. As a considerable number of the types of fraud commence with an unwitting and unintentional cyber breach, many SMEs have reached out to a Managed Service Provider (MSP) for IT support. However, there is a myriad of organisations delivering outsourced IT each offering a varied array of services and all working to different pricing structures. Hence if an MSP is the chosen route for supporting risk management, the starting point for any SME must be 'what do I want to achieve?' 'what are my priorities?' and 'what is my budget?'. This book will provide SMEs with a much better understanding of the risks they face and hence inform any discussion about the services required, what should be addressed first, in what order should remaining requirements be implemented and what will give the best value for money. While the human behaviour underlying fraud and criminal behaviour has been with us for centuries, developments in information technology and the sophistication of fraud attempts appear to be moving at what sometimes feels like a heart-stopping pace. So SMEs cannot afford to be complacent and must be conversant with the type of fraud events which if they were to occur, would be highly disruptive, stressful and financially debilitating all at the same time and may even pull the rug from under their feet. The book is also written for members and students of the professional bodies supporting businesses such as the Institute of Directors, the Institute of Risk Management, the Federation of Small Businesses, the Chartered Institute of Management Accountants and the Institute of Chartered Accountants England and Wales.

About the author

Robert Chapman CFIRM, FAPM, FICM is an international risk management specialist. He has been a Director of Risk Management at Dr Chapman and Associates, AECOM Middle East, Hornagold & Hills, Capro Consulting and Osprey Project Management. He was the Programme Lead for risk management on the HMG joint venture in South Africa, supporting the Parastatal Transnet and has supported rail projects like HS2, the East London Line, the Digital Railway and the West Coast Main Line. He has provided risk management services in England, Holland, Ireland, France, South Africa, Qatar, UAE, Singapore and Malaysia to companies within the rail, pharmaceutical, highways, aviation, marine, broadcast, heritage, water, energy, sport, nuclear, oil and gas, property development, construction and transportation industries as well to central government and local authorities in the public sector. He has been providing risk management services for over 20 years.

Dr Chapman has provided IT risk management guidance to the Chartered Institute of Accountants England and Wales in the form of a risk management handbook. His book *Simple tools and techniques for enterprise risk management* was first published in 2006. It was followed by a second edition in 2011 and a paperback version in 2013. It is on sale in forty countries around the world and recommended reading in universities internationally (including the USA, UK, Canada, Malaysia, Malta, India, Holland, Singapore and Australia). His next book entitled: *The rules of project risk management, implementation guidelines for major projects*, was published in 2014. The second edition of this title was published in 2020. These books are recommended reading by the UK's Institute of Risk Management. Dr Chapman was a contributory author of the Office of Government Commerce's 2007 publication *Management of risk, guidance for practitioners*, which supports the Prince2 Project Management Methodology.

How to read this book

Time is precious. Founders, directors and senior managers are typically under constant time pressure to perform day-to-day activities to deadlines. Hence how much time do we ever have in any one day to reflect on what we are doing, how we are doing it and whether there is a better approach? Hence this book is purposefully written in such a way that it is hoped that readers can quickly find and focus on the subjects that interest them, rather than having to carry out an extensive search for the instructive guidance they seek. The appropriate approach to reading this book will depend on your exposure to and experience of fraud risk management and where your specific interests lie. The intention is that by dividing the book into a number of identically structured chapters, readers can read single chapters in any order without having to read them sequentially. This had led to a degree of repetition to avoid the need to refer back and for, to previous or subsequent chapters.

SECTION **I**

BACKGROUND

Introduction to Section 1

The premise of this book is that the best way for SMEs to combat fraud is by establishing a structured approach to understanding, defining and responding to business vulnerabilities, through the development and implementation of a tailored risk management process. Hence before describing individual types of fraud, an introduction to fraud is provided, followed by an overview of the risk management process and a description of the business context or setting.

The chapters included in Section 1 are as follows:

Chapter 2 provides a definition of fraud and the drivers behind why individuals commit fraud. It also describes the nature of SMEs and their importance to the UK's economy together with the types of external and internal fraud.

Chapter 3 describes a high-level overview of the steps in the risk management process. Its goal is to provide those new to the subject with an outline description of the steps involved in its implementation. In simple terms, risk management centres on identifying potential problems (threats), assessing them, planning and implementing response actions, and monitoring if the responses have been

DOI: 10.4324/9781003200383-1

effective. Risk management has developed as a discipline over the last 20 years, now has a very broad base and there is a proliferation of detailed guidance on the subject. So it should be emphasised that Chapter 3 provides overview only. For those wishing to learn more about the discipline of risk management, further guidance can be obtained from the following structured texts, also by the author of this text.

Enterprise risk management

Simple tools and techniques for enterprise risk management, 2nd edition, published by John Wiley and Sons Limited, UK in 2011. ISBN 978-1-119–98997-4 (hbk).

Project risk management

The rules of project risk management, implementation guidelines for major projects, 2nd edition, published by Routledge, UK in 2020. ISBN 978-0-367–30932-2 (hbk).

Chapter 4 describes the operating context of SMEs in terms of the external business environment within which they strive for sustainable growth, such as the social, legal, cybersecurity and technology elements of society. In addition, it describes the business processes they implement to achieve their objectives while at the same time responding to both constraints and opportunities within the industry and sector(s) within which they operate.

Chapter 1

Layout of the book

Section 1 Background

Introduction to Section 1

Chapter 1 describes the **layout** of the book as a navigational aid.

Chapter 2 provides an introduction to the **exposure of SMEs** to fraud.

Chapter 3 describes an **overview of the risk management process** to provide those new to the subject with an outline description of the steps involved in its implementation.

Chapter 4 describes the **context** of enterprise risk management for businesses to 'set the scene' in terms of the operational environment of SMEs looking at cyber-crime in general and the myriad of government organisations involved in both combatting fraud and supporting businesses.

Section 2 External 'actors'

Describes the types of fraud committed by third parties or 'actors' outside of the business which require a specific action to limit their occurrence. Criminals rely on the internet and email as the 'entry gate' to businesses to commit the majority of these frauds.

DOI: 10.4324/9781003200383-2

Introduction to Section 2

Section 3 Internal 'actors'

Describes the types of fraud committed by employees and directors of a business ('insiders' or internal 'actors') which require a different approach to the fraud committed by external 'actors' or 'outsiders'. Individuals inside a business commit fraud by exploiting weaknesses in business processes and systems which permit the ready concealment, at least in the short term, of activities pursued for personal financial gain.

Introduction to Section 3

Section 4 Additional information

Three separate glossaries are included as appendices, as listed below. The book navigates across risk management, cyber security and the government's response to fraud, and hence the glossaries are aimed at supporting readers unfamiliar with one or more of these key subject areas.

Introduction to Section 4

Chapter 2

Introduction

Fraud today

Fraud is omnipresent and highly corrosive. It can result in losses which include customers, market share, reputation, funds, and/or staff. A serious fraud event can result in a business struggling to recover for years, or even lead to its collapse. It surfaces in a myriad of business functions and its perpetrators are constantly evolving new ways to search out company vulnerabilities. Fraud can arise for instance from the flooding of the market with counterfeit goods, the theft of intellectual property or the non-delivery of pre-paid goods. It can be perpetrated by both external 'actors' and employees (sometimes referred to as internal 'actors' or 'insiders'). According to Action Fraud,[1] nearly one in five small businesses have been defrauded by an employee at some point during their trading history. The growing prominence of state-sponsored fraud is even more insidious and is often more debilitating.[2] Fraud is a problem for all companies irrespective of size. Given the time and resources needed to minimise fraud, as a consequence of their size, small and medium-sized enterprises (SMEs) are particularly vulnerable. All businesses have to be very vigilant. They have to be aware of the known methods of fraud, the government agencies providing advice as well as the organisations to turn to in a time of crisis. This book aims to provide a structured risk management approach to tackling these burgeoning crimes.

Definition of fraud

The term 'fraud' commonly includes activities such as theft, corruption, false representation, conspiracy, embezzlement, money laundering, bribery and

DOI: 10.4324/9781003200383-3

extortion.[3] Action Fraud (the UK's national reporting centre for fraud and cyber-crime) defines fraud as 'trickery [...] used to gain a dishonest advantage, which is often financial, over another person'. While definitions vary, they generally centre on these themes. Action Fraud lists many of the common words used to describe fraud as scam, con, swindle, extortion, sham, double-cross, hoax, cheat, ploy, ruse, hoodwink and a confidence trick.[4] In essence, fraud might be described as using deception to bring about a personal gain for oneself dishonestly and or to create a loss for another.

Fraud Act 2006

The Fraud Act 2006 (the Act)[5] came into force on 15 January 2007 and applies in England, Wales and Northern Ireland.

The Act repealed the following Theft Act offences (offences which were considered to be too specific, overlapping and outdated):

- Obtaining property by deception[1] (Theft Act 1968, section 20 (3));
- Obtaining a money transfer by deception (Theft Act 1968, Section 15A);
- Obtaining pecuniary advantage by deception (Theft Act 1968, Section 16);
- Dishonestly procuring the execution of valuable security (Theft Act 1968, Section 20 (2));
- Obtaining services by deception (Theft Act 1978, Section 1);
- Securing the remission of an existing liability to make a payment (Theft Act 1978, Section 2 (1) (a));
- Dishonestly inducing a creditor to wait for payment or to forgo payment with the intention of permanently defaulting on all or part of an existing liability (Theft Act 1978, Section 2 (1) (b)); and
- Obtaining an exemption from or abatement of liability to make a payment (Theft Act 1978, Section 2 (1) (c)).

The general offence of fraud, as described under the Act, is as follows[6]:

- Section 1 of the Act establishes a new general offence of fraud, which can be committed in three ways: fraud by false representation; fraud by failing to disclose information; and fraud by abuse of position. These are set out in Sections 2, 3 and 4 of the Act respectively.
- There are two basic requirements which must be met before any of the three limbs of the new offence can be charged. First, the behaviour of the defendant must be dishonest. Second, it must also be his intention to make a gain, or cause a loss to another. However, there is no need to prove that a gain or loss has been made, or that any victim was deceived by the defendant's behaviour. Each of the three limbs of the offence carries a maximum sentence of ten years.

- Section 2 makes it an offence to commit fraud by false representation in any form. For a representation to be false, the representation being made must be wrong or misleading, and the person making it must know that it is, or might be, wrong or misleading. For example, a Section 2 offence would be committed by a 'phisher', i.e. a person who sends emails to large groups of people falsely representing that the email has been sent by say a legitimate financial institution. The email prompts the reader to provide information such as credit card and bank account numbers so that the 'phisher' can gain access to their assets.
- Section 3 makes it an offence to commit fraud by failing to disclose information; meaning if a person dishonestly fails to disclose to another person information which he is under a legal duty to disclose, and intends, by failing to disclose the information: (a) to make a gain for himself or another, or (b) to cause loss to another or to expose another to a risk of loss.
- Section 4 makes it an offence to commit fraud by abuse of one's position; meaning taking advantage of a position where one is expected to safeguard another's financial interests. The offence can be committed by omission or by a positive action, including a failure to act in the interests of another. It covers, for example, a case where an employee of a software company uses his position to clone software products with the intention of selling the products to make a profit for himself, or a case where an employee copies his employer's client database for the purpose for setting up a rival company.
- Section 7 makes it an offence to supply articles for use in fraudulent activity. The defendant: makes, adapts, supplies or offers to supply any article for use in the course of or in connection with fraud, knowing that it is designed or adapted for use in the course of or in connection with fraud (Section 7 (1) (a)) or intending it to be used to commit or assist in the commission of fraud (Section 7 (1) (b).

As summarised by the Crown Prosecution Service (CPS)[7]:

Section 1 creates a general offence of fraud and introduces three ways of committing it as set out in Sections 2, 3 and 4.

- Fraud by false representation (Section 2);
- Fraud by failure to disclose information when there is a legal duty to do so (Section 3); and
- Fraud by abuse of position (Section 4).

In each case:

- the defendant's conduct must be dishonest;
- his/her intention must be to make a gain; or cause a loss or the risk of a loss to another;

- no gain or loss needs actually to have been made; and
- the maximum sentence is ten years' imprisonment.

Drivers behind fraud

There is no single reason behind why individuals commit fraud. A useful model is the fraud triangle which is based on the premise that fraud is likely to result from a combination of three factors: motivation, opportunity and means. See Figure 2.1.

- Motivation: typically based on lifestyle changes, significant personal debt (such as mortgage arrears, overdrafts, loans), addiction issues (such as alcohol, drugs or gambling), pressure to meet targets, a sense of grievance (such as being made redundant, passed over for promotion, receiving a reduction in salary, not receiving a bonus or criticised for poor performance), or entitlement (such as unrewarded commitment, loyalty or hours worked).
- Opportunity: for employees where there is a lack of controls, system weaknesses, concentration or too much responsibility in one role or little fear of exposure or likelihood of detection. For external 'actors' opportunities are represented by system vulnerabilities and poor awareness training.
- Means: typically, where employees (often referred to as 'insiders'), have access to and the ability to manipulate financial information or retrieve sensitive data, or where external 'actors' have the computer skills and tools to pursue financial gain.

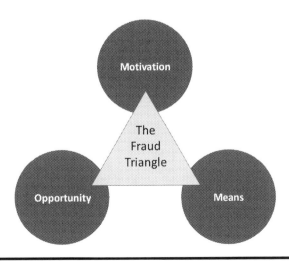

Figure 2.1 The fraud triangle

The Chartered Global Management Accountant (CGMA) report[8] refers to 'rationalisation' as one of the 'legs' of the fraud triangle whereby perpetrators excuse their behaviour because they consider it is harmless (as the impact will be minimal due to the business being very wealthy), or justify it due to a grievance or a necessity to be able to cope with personal financial problems. Given the similarity of the behaviours described, this 'leg' would appear to be an overlap with 'Motivation'.

What are SMEs?

SMEs are more commonly defined by the number of their personnel rather than by any measure of annual turnover or capital assets. The abbreviation 'SME' has been widely adopted and is used by international organizations such as the European Union, the World Bank, the World Trade Organization and the United Nations. The significance of SMEs to national economies is well understood. Several of the organisations mentioned actively support their development and growth. The European Union is a good example. Due to their size, SMEs are heavily influenced by their Chief Executive Officer (CEO) as they are often the founder, owner and manager all rolled into one. While aimed at companies with a premium listing, The UK Corporate Governance Code[9] provides instructive guidance on establishing sustainable businesses. Reflecting on this guidance, CEOs of SMEs must provide entrepreneurial leadership of their company within a framework of prudent and effective controls to ensure longevity. Hence essential activities are the identification, assessment and management of the risks that their business faces. The chapters that follow provide a map for addressing the ever-evolving risk of fraud.

The importance of SMEs

SMEs account for 99.9% of the UK business population (estimated to be 6.0 million).[10] According to the Department for Business, Energy and Industrial Strategy, at the start of 2020, these 6.0 million private sector UK businesses were subdivided as described below.[11] A policy paper entitled 'Department for International Trade (DIT) small and medium enterprises (SME) action plan' published by the DIT on 5 January 2021 provides a turnover value for the SMEs.

- Small businesses, also referred to as micro businesses (with 0 employees, just the owner), representing 76% of the total business population.
- Small businesses (with 1–49 employees and a turnover of under €10 million) including micro businesses representing 99.3% of the total business population. Small businesses represented 23.3% of businesses had 1–49 employees.

- Medium businesses (with 50–249 employees and a turnover under €50 million), representing 0.6% of the total business population.
- Large businesses (with 250 plus employees) representing 0.1% of the total business population.

The significance of SMEs to the UK economy was readily understood when it was recognised that small businesses make up almost the entire business population.[12] Given that SMEs are the engine of the UK economy, a clear objective of Her Majesty's Treasury (HM Treasury) is to support their development to achieve sustainable growth. HM Treasury describes itself as the government's economic and finance ministry, maintaining control over public spending, setting the direction of the UK's economic policy and working to achieve strong and sustainable economic growth.

Vulnerability of SMEs

Often with limited resources, working to challenging deadlines in volatile economic conditions, SMEs typically prioritise winning new business, enhancing their reputation and managing income against expenses, ahead of establishing internal controls and risk management practices. While it is a fallacy, these practices are commonly seen as time-consuming as well as bureaucratic and burdensome. The result, as identified by the CGMA, is that 'despite the serious risk that fraud presents to business, many organisations still do not have formal systems and procedures in place to prevent, detect and respond to fraud'.[13] Hence responses to fraud tend to be reactionary rather than proactive. Unfortunately, this leaves SMEs highly vulnerable. Many organisations that have failed to manage business fraud have not only suffered financially but also not survived. On a positive note, most research shows that organisations which actively manage their fraud risk reap the benefits of reducing fraud incidents and the negative impact arising from a fraud event.

Exposure to fraud originating from cybercrime

The Chartered Institute of Management Accountants' (CIMA) Corporate Fraud report[14] highlighted that fraud is an issue that all organisations may face regardless of size, industry or country. The Department for Digital, Culture, Media and Sport's 2020 cyber security survey[15] (and its predecessors) have consistently shown that almost all UK organisations grapple with cyber security risks involving fraud due to the fact that almost all have email addresses, online bank accounts and social media pages and the vast majority (81% of businesses) have a website.

Emails can be used to target victims, across the world more than 9 billion emails are sent every hour.[16] If a business has valuable property (either money, goods, information or services), then fraud may be attempted. As it is commonly the high-profile frauds committed within the large multi-national organisations that dominate the media headlines, smaller organisations misguidedly feel they are unlikely to be a target for fraudsters. However, according to the 2020 Association of Certified Fraud Examiners (ACFE) report,[17] small businesses (which it defines as having less than 100 employees) suffer higher than average losses. When small companies are hit by large fraud losses, they are less likely to be able to absorb the damage than a larger company and even may struggle to survive. This is particularly true of businesses such as solicitors that are responsible for large sums of customers' money. Examples of fraud originating from cybercrime include Business Email Compromise,[18] theft of intellectual property[19] and identity fraud.[20]

Ability of SMEs to manage cybercrime

According to the 'March 2020 Cyber security skills in the UK labour market 2020' survey report prepared for and published by the Department for Digital, Culture Media and Sport, approximately 653,000 businesses (48%) have a basic skills gap. This 'gap' is defined by the report as individuals in charge of cyber security (within the businesses examined) lacked the confidence to carry out the types of basic tasks laid out in the government-endorsed Cyber Essentials scheme,[21] as well as not getting support from external cyber security providers. The report states: 'the most common of these skills gaps are in setting up configured firewalls, storing or transferring personal data, and detecting and removing malware'. Within the cyber sector as a whole, there is a general skills shortage. The report highlights 'technical skills gaps are relatively high in each of the following areas: threat assessment or information risk management; assurance, audits, compliance or testing; cyber security research; implementing secure systems; and governance and management'. Outside the cyber sector, organisations' in-house cyber teams are typically very small. As illustrated by Figure 2.2, the report records 50% of all businesses have just one person running cyber security in-house and it highlights even larger businesses typically have just two to three cyber specialists.

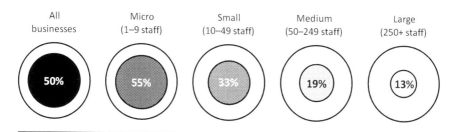

Figure 2.2 Percentage of businesses with just one employee responsible for cyber security

External fraud

Today's criminals can commit fraud from anywhere in the world, communicating covertly through encrypted services and moving illicit finances at speed. Given the reach of the internet, businesses face a constant myriad of external fraud attempts from across the globe as illustrated in Figure 2.3. Examples of frauds typically committed by those residing outside of the UK include theft of intellectual property, Business Email Compromise and identity theft.

Advancing technology gives fraudsters new tools to communicate and to commit and hide their crimes. Criminals increasingly use encryption tools, the dark web and virtual assets such as cryptocurrencies, a well-known example being Bitcoin. Hacking tools are ubiquitous and readily available. The dark web offers a range of tools and techniques for a range of capabilities. Hackers fall into three

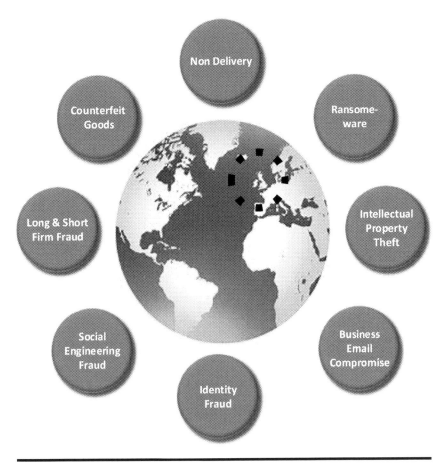

Figure 2.3 External sources of fraud

broad categories: those that are able to apply the off-the-shelf tools openly available on the internet which are pre-written, easy-to-use and specifically designed for malicious purposes; the tool creators; and lastly the exploit developers who spend time to make a tool suitable for multiple tasks and reliable, making them far more valuable commercially. This latter group have specialist knowledge and are able to use tools and techniques that may include malicious code ('exploits') which can take advantage of software vulnerabilities (or bugs) that are not yet known to anti-virus vendors, often known as 'zero-day' exploits.

Internal fraud

Apart from fraud committed by unknown individuals or organised gangs, fraud is committed by directors and employees from within businesses themselves. These can be more damaging financially as they can be perpetrated over a number of years slowly undermining the viability of a business until its very existence is in question. Figure 2.4 illustrates the commonly recognised types of internal fraud. The figure is based on the GCMA 2012[22] and ACFE 2018[23] reports.

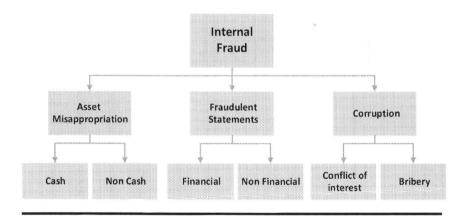

Figure 2.4 Internal sources of fraud

The cost of fraud to businesses

As identified in CIMA's and the CGMA's fraud risk management guides,[24] surveys are regularly carried out in an attempt to estimate the true scale and cost of fraud to UK businesses. These and subsequent guides highlight that survey findings vary and it is difficult to obtain a precise picture as to the full extent of the country's exposure to fraud. However, these guides all paint a consistent picture; that fraud is ubiquitous and remains a very serious and costly problem. According to the National Crime Agency (NCA), fraud is the most common crime type in England and Wales.[25] The NCA has reported that there were an estimated 3.8 million incidents of fraud in the year ending September 2019, a third of all estimated crime, and an increase of 9% on the previous year. The cost of business disruption, including diminished employee productivity and business process failures (which occur after a cyberattack), continues to rise at a steady rate. According to the National Fraud Intelligence Bureau (NFIB), reported losses in the UK increased by 38% in the financial year 2018/2019, to £2.2 billion. This may be a very conservative figure, for according to 'The Financial Cost of Fraud Report' (published in 2019 by the independent consultancy firm Crowe in conjunction with the Centre for Counter Fraud Studies at the University of Portsmouth[26]), fraud is costing businesses and individuals in the UK a colossal £130 billion each year.

Escalating exposure to fraud

The extent of criminal activity is highlighted by the NCA[27] who, based on their improved understanding (following their most comprehensive assessment yet), now estimate there to be at least 350,000 individuals in the UK engaged in serious and organised crime. However, this is the tip of the iceberg when considering UK businesses are exposed to criminal activity from all over the world. The number of cyberattacks with the purpose of committing fraud is on the rise. The UK government survey titled 'Digital Cyber Security Breaches Survey 2020' published in March 2020[28] found that the majority of SMEs surveyed experienced cyber security breaches or attacks in the last 12 months (43% of micro firms, 62% of small firms and 68% of medium firms). As illustrated in Figure 2.5, the survey discovered that for the following categories, medium-sized firms had suffered breaches or attacks in the following percentages.

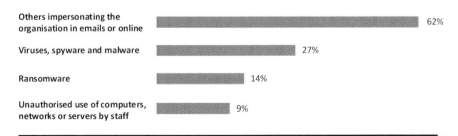

Figure 2.5 Cyber security breaches and attacks suffered by medium-sized firms in the 12 months prior to March 2020

Data obtained under the Freedom of Information (FOI) Act has shown that for the first eight months of 2020 the British Broadcasting Corporation (BBC) on average blocked 18,662 malware attacks such as viruses, ransomware and spyware.[29] Although new information technologies offer entrepreneurial organisations new opportunities to innovate and grow; unfortunately, they also offer criminals new ways of targeting businesses for personal gain. It is now recognised that while organisations face a myriad of evolving challenges, the threat from fraudsters seeking to exploit new technology is now ever-present. In addition, although new tools have and continue to be developed to combat fraud, new threats are emerging at an even faster pace. The National Crime Agency's National Strategic Assessment of Serious and Organised Crime 2020 report describes how the UK is 'confronted with a rapidly evolving threat that is increasingly driven by technology as criminals exploit the fast expansion of encryption to conduct their business'. The use of encryption within criminal communications ranges from using popular apps that embed end-to-end encryption as standard (such as WhatsApp and Telegram) to using criminally dedicated secure communication platforms. The dark web continues to enable a range of criminality that threatens the UK. The extent of criminality appears to be unaffected by the increased presence of law enforcement on the dark web. As identified by a study undertaken by Accenture Security[30] almost 80% of organizations are introducing digitally fuelled innovation faster than their ability to secure it against cyberattacks. Exposure to fraud is further exacerbated by periods of economic difficulty, increased exposure to pandemics, more competitive markets and increased connectivity. According to the *Telegraph*[31] 'modern fraudsters have evolved their ability to detect vulnerabilities in systems, and are shifting their targets to those weak links. They have elevated their game by targeting areas such as payments, account opening and applications'. The NCA considers the threat is continuing to grow in scale and complexity. Respondents to a survey conducted by the World Economic Forum have included data fraud or theft within their top ten list of long-term risks.[32] According to the Department of Culture, Media and Sport (DCMS) 'Cyber Security Breaches Survey 2020', almost half of businesses (46%) reported having cyber security breaches or attacks over a 12-month period.[33] Of the 46% of businesses that identified breaches or attacks one in five (19%) have lost money or data and in 2020 are experiencing breaches or attacks at least once a week.

State-sponsored fraud

While organised criminal groups embark on fraud for financial gain, there is growing evidence of state-sponsored fraud. It is suspected, for instance, that China's first stealth jet named J-20 is based on the stolen designs of the USAF's all-weather F-22 stealth tactical fighter aircraft. During the UK Home Secretary's speech of

11 April 2018 (describing the government's crackdown on the exploitation of the anonymity of the Dark Web for illegal activities[34]), Amber Rudd advised that the UK government was aware that there were several 'capable states (countries) seeking to exploit computer and communications networks to gather intellectual property from [...] industrial targets'. The UK's Crown Prosecution Service is explicit in categorising the theft of intellectual property as fraud. She went on to say that 'hostile states, groups and individuals are using cyber tools to commit crimes [...] in a manner which makes definitive attribution difficult'. From more recent reports it is clear the threat of intellectual property theft is escalating. A recent UK government report[35] records that state threats to the UK are growing and diversifying as systemic competition intensifies. The report states 'States are becoming increasingly assertive in how they advance their own objectives and, in their willingness to undermine ours'. It goes on to say, 'state threats are persistent and take many forms', one of which it describes as 'intellectual property theft'.

A risk management approach

According to the CGMA

> despite the serious risk that fraud presents to business, many organ- isations still do not have formal systems and procedures in place to prevent, detect and respond to fraud. Yet, most research shows that organisations which actively manage their fraud risk reap benefits in terms of reducing the negative impact of fraud.

As highlighted by HM Treasury's policy paper,[36] a risk-based approach is central to the prevention of economic crime. It considers that 'when undertaken effec- tively, it enables firms and supervisors to focus their efforts and resources where the risks are highest, creating a robust regime at a proportionate cost'. These organisations contribute to the weight of opinion recommending the adoption of risk management to reduce exposure to fraud. Other organisations advocating its implementation are the Metropolitan Police Service, CIMA, the Institute of Risk Management (IRM), the Chartered Global Management Accountant (CGMA), the Organisation for Economic Co-operation and Development (OECD), the Chartered Institute of Internal Auditors (IIA), the Chartered Institute of Public Finance and Accountancy (Cipfa), the Financial Conduct Authority (FCA) and the Institute of Directors (IoD). This book provides a guide for SMEs to under- stand the current sources of business fraud risk and the specific risk response actions that can be taken to limit exposure, through the structured discipline of enterprise risk management. The use of risk management is described in a methodical way, to aid a comprehensive understanding of the sources of exposure, capturing the planned responses and monitoring their implementation and effectiveness. The appropriateness of risk management is emphasised as business fraud is not a static problem but a fast-moving dynamic one that requires regular re-evaluation and often amendment of planned responses. Criminals use sophisticated tools which are both regularly supplemented or amended and agilely applied to capitalise on business vulnerabilities. This book recommends that a risk management strategy[37] is developed which is integrated within the entire operation of any business. Business fraud risk management is described as an essential element of a business's culture (this is the way we do things here), to a point where it becomes part of an organisation's DNA. It must permeate all activities from recruitment to dealing with customers, suppliers and contractors, company policies, IT protocols, virus protection, use of email, payments and managing the bank account.

Government response to combatting fraud

On first inspection, there appears to be a myriad of disparate and siloed UK government organisations involved in tackling business fraud, from providing advice, collecting data to hunting down the perpetrators of fraud. These organisations, their role and their relationship are examined within the chapter headed 'Establish the context'. The UK government has made a concerted effort to coordinate the many departments and agencies that have been established over time to tackle specific emerging issues whose activities now increasingly overlap.

The government, led by HM Treasury[38] has developed an Economic Crime Plan which it considers is a step-change in its response to economic crime. It believes the actions of the plan 'set out an ambitious agenda to strengthen our whole-system response for tackling economic crime'. In addition, that collectively these actions will

> provide a greater understanding of the threat, improved transparency of ownership, and better sharing and usage of information will enable the public and private sectors to more efficiently and effectively target their resources. They will also strengthen the resilience of the UK's defences against economic crime through enhanced management of economic crime risk in the private sector and the risk-based approach to supervision.

The plan defines economic crime as 'a broad category of activity involving money, finance or assets, the purpose of which is to unlawfully obtain a profit or advantage for the perpetrator or cause loss to others'. It considers that economic crime poses a threat to the UK's economy and its institutions and causes serious harm to society and individuals. The term includes criminal activity which poses a risk to the UK's prosperity, national security and reputation, and more specifically fraud committed against the individual, private sector and public sector. With the goal of increasing its capability to respond to the threat of economic crime the government has introduced what it describes as 'world-leading reforms', including: the creation of the National Economic Crime Centre (NECC); establishing the Government Counter Fraud Profession; reforms to its policy and legislative framework; and the launch of dedicated public–private initiatives such as the Joint Money Laundering Intelligence Taskforce (JMLIT) and the Joint Fraud Taskforce (JFT). The National Crime Agency (NCA) leads and coordinates law enforcement's response to serious and organised crime in England and Wales and hosts the UK Financial Intelligence Unit (UKFIU), the NECC and the National Assessment Centre (NAC).

National Economic Crime Centre

The NECC is a collaborative, multi-agency centre that was established on 31 October 2018 to deliver a step-change in the response to tackling serious and organised economic crime. The NECC brings together law enforcement agencies, including the NCA, the Serious Fraud Office (SFO), Her Majesty's Revenue and Customs (HMRC), the Financial Conduct Authority (FCA), the Crown Prosecution Service (CPS) and the City of London Police, as the national police lead for fraud in England and Wales. It also houses government departments, regulatory bodies and the private sector to create a shared response to driving down serious and organised economic crime across the whole community. The NECC works in partnership with the 43 English and Welsh police forces and the nine Regional Organised Crime Units, as well as Action Fraud and the National Fraud Intelligence Bureau hosted within the City of London Police.

National Cyber Security Centre

The National Cyber Security Centre (NCSC) provides a Board Toolkit to support the integration of cybersecurity within organisations including SMEs. As with all threat management, it advises that good cyber security is all about managing risks. It states: 'the process for improving and governing cyber security will be similar to the process you use for other organisational risks'. It describes three simple stages as part of a continuous, iterative process as described below.

1. Get the information you need to make well-informed decisions on the risks you face.
2. Use this information to understand and prioritise your risks.
3. Take steps to manage those risks.

An infographic produced by the NCSC on the subject can be downloaded from: www.ncsc.gov.uk/collection/board-toolkit.

Whilst improvements have been made, the scale of cyber-related crime in the UK still exceeds available law enforcement capabilities. Globally police forces are grappling with cyber-enabled crimes including international law enforcement agencies such as Europol and Interpol.

Police Scotland

In September 2020, Police Scotland announced that it would be establishing a National Centre of Excellence and boost the number of specially trained officers to tackle the rise in cybercrime, as part of its Cyber Strategy 2020. It outlined the plan 'to tackle the threat, risk and harm from digitally-enabled crimes such as fraud'. Deputy Chief Constable Malcolm Graham, lead for Crime and Operational Support, said: 'The nature of crime is changing and Police Scotland needs to change with it. The online space is becoming a bigger part of the frontline of policing every day'.

Case studies

A number of short case studies have been included within the chapters that follow to provide real-world examples of fraud events that have impacted businesses (and individuals) where business performance has been detrimentally affected. Fraud events are costly, disruptive and stressful. In addition, while difficult to measure, fraud may also impact customer confidence, impair an organisation's reputation and reduce market share, at least in the short term.

Looking to the future

The World Economic Forum has described Artificial Intelligence (AI) as the next digital frontier. While AI provides significant tools to combat fraud, it also presents multi-faceted risks. AI requires a need for a common set of global protocols. China has strongly encouraged its companies to invest in AI, making it a national security priority.[39] According to a recent article in the *Telegraph*, three key factors are driving artificial intelligence (AI) applications for payments and transaction processing[40]:

■ As technology rapidly evolves, online fraud is becoming more prevalent and damaging;

- Financial services and e-commerce companies are especially vulnerable to sophisticated new cyber-attacks;
- Machine learning is helping organisations combat fraud in ways that were unattainable in the past.

The article considers that machine learning (ML), a branch of AI, offers real solutions for fraud management as it supports systems that automatically learn, predict, act and explain. In particular ML-driven tools can help organisations to replace high-maintenance, rules-based fraud management tools with self-learning algorithms. It goes on to say that the main advantage of these tools is that they afford businesses the ability to utilize the power of big data, performing analytics and delivering risk scores very efficiently, in real time, and with far greater accuracy. A cautionary note is that AI solutions are likely to be many years away and may not be available to SMEs at least in the short term.

Appendices

A number of Appendices are included which provide an explanation of terms and definitions to aid readers new to risk management and cybercrime, together with more detailed advice on intellectual property crime.

Summary

SMEs are recognised as the engine of the UK economy as they are for many European economies. Hence their protection is in the interests of the UK government and the wider economy. All organisations are affected by fraud, but disproportionately so for SMEs given their size and vulnerability. Their exposure is compounded by the myriad of fraud types. Given the reach of the internet, external fraud attempts emanate from all over the world. The scale of fraud for the year 2018/2019 has been estimated to exceed £2 billion and hence is a very onerous threat. When perpetrated, fraud can cause SMEs to suffer a loss of customers, market share, reputation as well as operating capital. In severe cases, recovery can take many years and for some it forces closure. Fraud can be perpetrated by external actors, commonly through breaches in cyber security, or by employees. Given their size, many SMEs have limited experience in risk management, fraud management and combatting cybercrime. There is a weight of opinion, based on the number of organisations recommending its adoption, that risk management should be implemented to reduce exposure to fraud. These include the Metropolitan Police Service, CIMA, IRM, CGMA, OECD, IIA, Cipfa, FCA and the IoD.

According to CGMA despite its seriousness, many businesses still do not have formal processes to combat fraud despite research which shows those that actively manage their fraud risk, reap the benefits of reduced exposure to the negative impact of fraud.

Notes

1 Refer to: https://www.actionfraud.police.uk/know-your-employees.
2 On the premise that the theft of intellectual property for financial gain is fraud, then according to the FBI, China has been engaged in state-sponsored fraud for competitive advantage. See: FBI (2020) "The China Treat". 10 July 2020. https://www.fbi.gov/investigate/counterintelligence/the-china-threat.
3 CIMA (2009) Corporate fraud, Topic Gateway Series No. 57.
4 Action Fraud. "What is fraud and cyber crime?" https://www.actionfraud.police.uk/what-is-fraud.
5 Legistlation.gov.uk, Fraud Act 2006, UK Public General Acts, 2006 c. 35, Fraud. https://www.legislation.gov.uk/ukpga/2006/35/section/2.
6 UK Government (2006) "The Fraud Act 2006: repeal of the deception offences in the Theft Acts 1968–1996". https://www.gov.uk/government/publications/the-fraud-act-2006-repeal-of-the-deception-offences-in-the-theft-acts-1968-1996#_ftn4.
7 https://www.cps.gov.uk/legal-guidance/fraud-act-2006.
8 CGMA Report (2012) "Fraud risk management. A good practice guide".
9 The UK Corporate Governance Code July 2018 published by the Financial Reporting Council.
10 Department for Business, Energy and Industrial Strategy (2020) "Business population estimates for the UK and regions 2020: statistical release (HTML)", October.
11 Ibid.
12 HM Treasury (2018) "Small and medium enterprise action plan". https://www.gov.uk/government/publications/small-and-medium-enterprise-action-plan.
13 Chartered Global Management Accountant (CGMA) report "Fraud risk management, A guide to good practice" 2016.
14 CIMA (2009) Corporate fraud Topic Gateway Series No. 57.
15 Department for Digital, Culture, Media and Sport (2020) "Official Statistics, Cyber Security Breaches Survey 2020", Updated 26 March 2020. https://www.gov.uk/government/publications/cyber-security-breaches-survey-2020/cyber-security-breaches-survey-2020.
16 National Audit Office (2017) "Online Fraud". https://www.nao.org.uk/wp-content/uploads/2017/06/Online-Fraud-Summary.pdf.
17 ACFE (2020) "Report to the nations 2020 Global study on occupational fraud and abuse".
18 https://www.interpol.int/en/Crimes/Financial-crime/Business-Email-Compromise-Fraud.
19 IP Crime Group 2020 (2020) "Crime and IP enforcement report, 19/20". https://assets.publishing.service.gov.uk/government/uploads/system/uploads/attachment_data/file/913644/ip-crime-report-2019-20.pdf.

20 Action Fraud. https://www.actionfraud.police.uk/a-z-of-fraud-category/other.

21 See https://www.cyberessentials.ncsc.gov.uk/advice.

22 CGMA Report (2012) "Fraud risk management. A good practice guide".

23 ACFE (2018) "Report to the nations 2018 global study on occupational fraud and abuse".

24 CIMA (2008) "Fraud risk management, a good practice guide", and CGMA (2016) the Chartered Global Management Accountant's report "Fraud risk management, a guide to good practice".

25 NCA (2020) "The National Crime Agency's National Strategic Assessment of Serious and Organised Crime".

26 The report considers and analyses 690 loss measurement exercises which have been undertaken around the world during the last 20 years to accurately measure the financial cost of fraud. The exercises took place across 40 different types of expenditure in 49 organisations in ten countries. https://www.crowe.com/uk/croweuk/-/media/Crowe/Firms/Europe/uk/CroweUK/PDF-publications/The-Financial-Cost-of-Fraud-2019.

27 NCA (2020) "The National Crime Agency's National Strategic Assessment of Serious and Organised Crime".

28 Department for Digital, Culture, Media and Sport (2020) "Official Statistics, Cyber Security Breaches Survey 2020", Updated 26 March 2020. https://www.gov.uk/government/publications/cyber-security-breaches-survey-2020/cyber-security-breaches-survey-2020. Micro firms are defined as having 1–9 employees, small 10–49 and medium 50–249.

29 Enterprise Times (2020) "BBC hit with 250,000 email attacks daily", Roy Edwards, 3 November 2020. https://www.enterprisetimes.co.uk/2020/11/03/bbc-hit-with-250000-email-attacks-daily/.

30 Accenture Security and the Ponemon Institute (2019) "Ninth annual cost of cyber-crime study unlocking the value of improved cybersecurity protection".

31 The *Telegraph*, Business Reporter (2017) "Fraud management, AI and machine learning: a primer". https://www.telegraph.co.uk/business/business-reporter/fraud-management-ai-machine-learning/.

32 World Economic Forum (2020) The Global Risks Report 2020, Insight report, 15th edition.

33 Department for Digital, Culture, Media and Sport (2020) "Official Statistics, Cyber Security Breaches Survey 2020", Updated 26 March 2020. https://www.gov.uk/government/publications/cyber-security-breaches-survey-2020/cyber-security-breaches-survey-2020.

34 "Law enforcement crackdown on dark web". Speech delivered by Amber Rudd (when Home Secretary) on 11 April 2018 at the National Cyber Security Centre's annual conference.

35 HM Government (2021) "Global Britain in a competitive age, The Integrated Review of Security, Defence, Development and Foreign Policy", March.

36 HM Treasury (2019) "HM Treasury Policy paper, Economic Crime Plan, 2019 to 2022". https://www.gov.uk/government/publications/economic-crime-plan-2019-to-2022/economic-crime-plan-2019-to-2022-accessible-version#fnref:6.

37 The term "strategy" is adopted here to describe a plan of action designed to achieve a long-term goal.

38 HM Treasury (2019) "HM Treasury Policy paper, Economic Crime Plan, 2019 to 2022". https://www.gov.uk/government/publications/economic-crime-plan-2019-to-2022/economic-crime-plan-2019-to-2022-accessible-version#fnref:6.

39 Allen, G.C. (2019) "Understanding China's AI Strategy: Clues to Chinese Strategic Thinking on Artificial Intelligence and National Security". Washington, DC: Centre for a New American Security. https://s3.amazonaws.com/files.cnas.org/documents/CNAS-UnderstandingChinas-AI-Strategy-Gregory-C.-AllenFINAL-2.15.19.pdf?mtime=20190215104041.

40 The *Telegraph*, Business Reporter (2017) "Fraud management, AI and machine learning: a primer". https://www.telegraph.co.uk/business/business-reporter/fraud-management-ai-machine-learning/.

Chapter 3

Approach to fraud risk management

Overview

Given the seriousness of business fraud, it requires a structured methodical approach to combat it. A recommended approach is fraud risk management (FRM). There is broad recognition of the enormous value of the effective management of risk. Risk management is now a mature discipline as demonstrated by its widespread application across many industries and UK government departments as well as the creation of an international standard, the availability of university degrees (to PhD level), training courses, journal articles and books, the formation of the UK Institute of Risk Management and careers in what is now a recognised profession.

The fraud risk management (FRM) approach

The nucleus of the FRM approach is the risk management process itself. It provides a road map of how risk management will be implemented. Risk management is an iterative process and hence is illustrated in Figure 3.1 as a continuous loop. As more information becomes available, steps in the process are repeated. Business vulnerabilities never remain static due to (for instance) changes to the organisational structure, the market, business policies and processes, the behaviour of criminals (threat actors) and developments in information technology (such as software and data backup options). As a consequence, businesses need to regularly review and amend assessments and planned response actions as required.

DOI: 10.4324/9781003200383-4

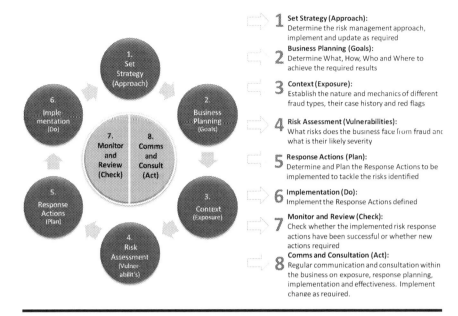

Figure 3.1 Overview of the fraud risk management process

Steps in the process

The following sections provide a high-level overview of each of the steps within a formal risk management process (as illustrated in Figure 3.1) aimed at tackling business fraud. The description of each step is deliberately brief to aid assimilation. Subsequent chapters examine individual fraud risks to guide specific responses. Included within Table 3.1 is a short summary of each of the steps in the risk management process and should be read in conjunction with the glossary of terms and definitions contained in Appendix 1.

Step 1: Setting the strategy

While the risk management strategies of different companies have common elements there is no 'one-size-fits-all' approach to implementation. The purpose of the strategy is to describe how the business intends to manage risk. A strategy is typically the umbrella term for the individual aspects of risk management which when combined describe the overall approach that will be adopted to manage risk. These aspects or components include the policy, the definition of the business's risk appetite, risk management process, the definition of the roles and responsibilities, budget, risk categories, scales of impact and probability, reporting requirements and the terms that will be used and their definition (so there is a common language).

Table 3.1 Steps in the risk management process

No	Step	Description
1	Set the strategy	The risk management strategy reflects the business's view on how it intends to manage risk.
2	Business planning	Refers to establishing those aspects of the business plan that would be impacted by a fraud event.
3	Establishing the context	Over and above recognition that businesses have an internal and external context, for fraud risk management there needs be an understanding of the pattern (or nature) and mechanics of the different types of fraud together with case histories and red flags so that businesses can determine where their vulnerabilities (risk exposure) may lie.
4a	Risk identification	Identification and recording of both threats and opportunities. Issues may be captured and managed as part of the same process.
4b	Risk analysis	Assessment of the likelihood, impact and proximity of the threats and opportunities.
4c	Risk evaluation	When appropriate, the completion of a study of the aggregate net effect of the threats and the opportunities when combined together. This study may also include the assessment of assumptions, dependencies and issues.
5	Response actions (risk treatment)	The development and implementation of responses to the identified threats and opportunities.
6	Implementation	Implementation of the agreed response actions in a timely manner to protect the business.
7	Monitoring and review	The continual process that a business undertakes to understand the risk exposure and the success or otherwise of the implemented responses.
8	Communication and Consultation	The continuous process carried out to engage the business in the assessment and communication of risk exposure, response planning and monitoring of effectiveness.

Step 2: Business planning

Refers to establishing those aspects of the business plan that would be impacted by a fraud event such as the business goals, the business products or services, business processes, organisational structure, finance, marketing and supply chain.

Step 3: Establishing the context

When considering the overall context for enterprise (business) risk management, the context is recognised to have two components, external and internal. For completeness these are discussed in turn below; however, for fraud risk management it should be borne in mind the focus should be on the fraud types and how they are perpetrated.

External

The external context for a business is multi-faceted. Aspects of the external context in the main are not controllable and have to be responded to as and when they materialise. Examples include the: economy; taxation; composition of the market including competitors; regulatory regime; supply chain; manufacturing processes; logistic infrastructure; labour market; information technology, artificial intelligence and cybercrime; use of the internet as a business tool; patterns of crime; and existing legislation.

Internal

Likewise, the internal context of a business is also multi-faceted. Given that the internal context is under the control of a business, steps can be taken to remove or significantly reduce the risk of exposure to internal threats. Aspects of the internal context relate to the business management mechanisms such as the business: objectives, governance, plan, processes, dependencies, decision-making mechanisms, organogram, compliance mechanisms, procurement methods, financial management procedures, stakeholders, contingency planning and approach to joint ventures/partnerships. This is not an exhaustive list. Typically, they are not set-in-stone at business formation but (by necessity) develop over time. The important factor to remember is that any change in these management mechanisms may have a major impact on a business's risk exposure profile.

The sources of threats

Understanding the context of a business is a precursor to understanding the internal and external sources of fraud risk, as described in Figures 2.3 and 2.4. The pattern, mechanics, case studies and red flags for individual risks (see Figure 3.2) need to be understood to gain an appreciation of the vulnerabilities of the business to incidents of fraud. The context step (in the risk management process) informs risk identification.

Pattern: Describes the steps in a fraud attack or event.

Mechanics: Describe the tools used by criminals to implement a fraud attack.

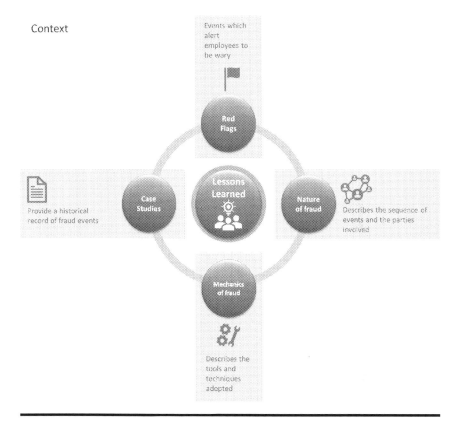

Figure 3.2 Characteristics of individual frauds

Case studies: Provide a historical record of fraud events and in particular provide information on aspects such as method, mechanics, the scale of financial impact, perpetrators, changes in modus operandi, the malware used, resilience (or otherwise) of backed-up data, exfiltrated data and resolution.

Red flags: Events that should they materialise should alert employees, managers or directors to a fraud attempt.

Step 4a: Identification

The identification step requires the identification of issues, threats and opportunities as illustrated in Figure 3.3. The polarity is used to illustrate the positive or negative (adverse) nature of these relevant events. Issues are relevant events that have already occurred and require management. Threats are knowable adverse events that may or may not materialise. Opportunities may or may not be realised depending on whether they can be successfully exploited.

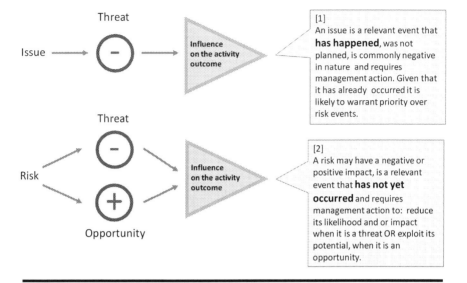

Figure 3.3 Identification of issues, threats and opportunities

Source: *The Rules of Project Risk Management*, 2nd edition, published by Routledge 2020

Comprehensive identification

The goal of the identification step is, as far as practicable, to identify all of the knowable threats and opportunities to a business's objectives. However, it is not possible to identify all of the threats and opportunities at the outset. Over time as the business matures and knowledge of the context expands, new threats and opportunities will be identified and the nature of known risks will change as a result of new information, decisions made or actions previously taken. It is common for the number of threats identified to significantly exceed the number of opportunities identified.

Collaborative approach

Identification requires a collaborative approach whereby the collective knowledge and experience of the entire organisation is harnessed to think through the threats and opportunities relevant to a business. A department or discipline not consulted during the identification step will potentially leave a critical gap in the schedule of risks and opportunities captured. For SMEs, it is common to include external consultants in the identification process to provide facilitation capabilities or bring in external expertise.

Threat information capture

To maintain a live record of the threats and opportunities identified requires a spreadsheet (referred to as a register or a log) or a database. Without capturing the information in this way, it will not be possible to track for instance:

- new threats or opportunities;
- closed threats or opportunities;
- cause and impact descriptions;
- identification dates;
- changes in risk owner or actionee;
- changes in likelihood, impact or proximity;
- response categories;
- response descriptions;
- the success or otherwise of the response actions.

An extract of a simple threat register is included in Figure 3.4. Only the financial impact is included in the figure however there are typically multiple impacts from a threat materialising such as business interruption (time), loss of reputation and

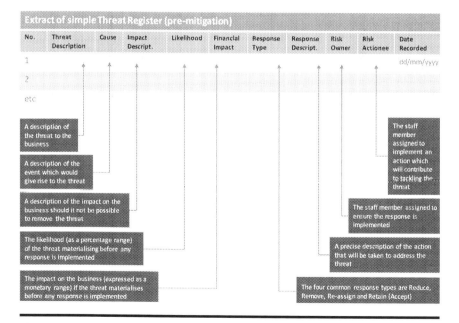

Figure 3.4 Extract of a simple threat resister

reduction in sales. The heading of the spreadsheet is 'pre-mitigation'. This spread-sheet would capture the 'Likelihood' and 'Financial impact' before any mitigation actions were defined and implemented.

Threat descriptions

Threat descriptions need to be clear and unambiguous so that they are readily understood by the whole business and not just by the author. Without clarity, it is not possible to define threat response actions that would reduce or remove the threat or enable it to be re-assigned to a third party. All too often a threat description is a jumble of the cause, threat, impact as well as background activity information. Experience has shown that if threat descriptions are confined to a single sentence it forces the author to articulate the threat more clearly. Equally, it is important that descriptions are not so short, such as two or three words, so the threat becomes open to interpretation (or the author cannot recall what prompted recording the threat when questioned about it at a later date). Threat authors often require coaching in writing threats so that they can be readily understood by the business as a whole and can actually be responded to. If a threat description is too broad and at a high level it will not be possible to assign it to a single Risk Owner or determine a response action. To provide a simple example, in Figure 3.5 threat descriptions A, B and C are imprecise whereas description D is readily understood and can be responded to.

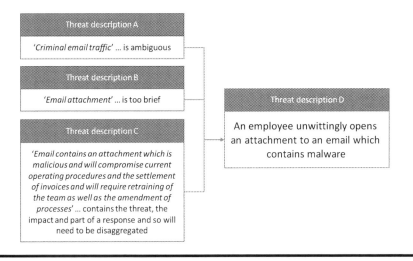

Figure 3.5 Refinement of the threat description

Relevance

Issues, threats and opportunities are only of interest if they have a direct bearing on one (or more) of the business's objectives which underpin the organisation's business case.

Cause→Threat→Impact

There are trigger events, 'causes', which may give rise to 'threats'. Should these threats materialise they will have an 'impact' on the business objectives. Hence as a *consequent of* some event, a *threat* may become apparent which should it materialise, would have a detrimental impact on one or more of a business's objectives.

Identification techniques

There is a wide range of techniques available to support the identification of risks. The most common identification technique is 'brainstorming' used in a workshop setting. Routinely techniques may be used together such as 'lessons learned', 'risk breakdown structures', 'SWOT analysis' and 'decision-trees'.

Risk Owner

An individual Risk Owner is typically assigned to each threat or opportunity who is responsible for managing the implementation of the response (or responses) in liaison with the appropriate manager.

Risk Actionee

When appropriate, the Risk Owner will assign individual threat responses to Actionees who will be responsible for defining and implementing a specific response (which when combined with the actions of other Actionees) will remove or reduce the threat to an acceptable level.

Timing

It is important to record when a threat or opportunity was captured on a spread-sheet or database and when a risk owner was assigned so that in the event a major risk materialises, an audit can trace what was captured, when was it captured, who it was assigned to and when response planning was instigated.

Step 4b: Analysis

The analysis step involves an assessment of the impact of issues and the likelihood, impact and proximity of threats and opportunities as illustrated in Figure 3.6. As an issue is an event that has already materialised, the analysis examines the known or anticipated impact. While analysis is highly subjective, even when based on events that have occurred on concurrent or completed activities, it enables threats in particular to be compared (in terms of their potential detrimental impact on the business's objectives) to assist in the prioritisation of response actions. An assessment of impacts will also provide a business with a sense of urgency where threat events can be very damaging. The term proximity relates to when a threat may materialise. A threat may relate to a potential problem moving hardware during an office move. The proximity relates to the dates assigned to moving the hardware.

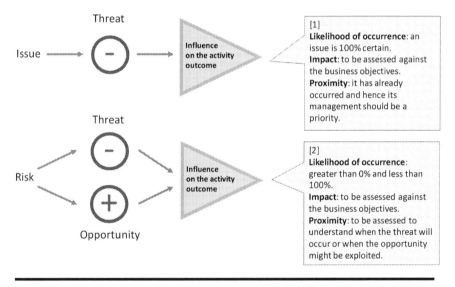

Figure 3.6 Analysis of issues, threats and opportunities in terms of their likelihood, impact and proximity

Source: *The Rules of Project Risk Management*, 2nd edition, published by Routledge 2020

Threat characteristics

For any threat, it is important to understand how *likely* is it, what will be the *impact* if it materialises, *when* will it occur and is it *related* to any other threat. Table 3.2 looks at each of these characteristics in turn.

Opportunity: Opportunities typically have a limited window in which they may be introduced as they are commonly tied to a specific business activity.

Table 3.2 Analysis of threats

Likelihood	Impact	When	Relationships
Estimating probability	*Estimating impact*	*Estimating proximity*	*Estimating interdependencies*
In simple terms, if a threat has a 0% chance of occurring then it is not of concern, and if a threat has a 100% chance of occurring then it is certain to occur and should be treated as an issue. So, assessments are concerned with events that have a likelihood of occurrence of between 1% and 99%. Common good practice recommends defining a probability band for a threat rather than say a single percentage due to the inability to be precise about future events.	A business is only concerned about the impact on its objectives. Hence any risk assessment must be clear about what a specific activity's objectives are and how they would impact the business as a whole if they were not to be achieved. To be of value, impact statements, rather than being qualitative like high, medium and low, need to be a range of weeks (or months) for time or a range of costs (thousands or millions) for expenditure.	Threats have what might be termed a 'risk window'. Threats commonly relate to existing activities (now), planned activities (in the short term) or activities that will be engaged in as part of say entering new supply agreements producing new products, or entering new markets (in the long term).	Not all threats act independently. It is important to understand whether a specific threat will generate a secondary threat if it materialises. In addition, whether a threat will diminish or exacerbate other threats already identified and recorded.

It may be disruptive and the costs of implementation may exceed the perceived benefits if an opportunity is exploited and implemented too late in a planned schedule or programme. For instance, if pursuing an opportunity requires changing a supplier, changing a material's specification or re-tendering a contract.

Concurrent schedule threats

When assessing the impact of threats on a schedule/programme it is important to understand what activities would be affected by each threat and whether a single activity could potentially be impacted by multiple threats. If these multiple threats were to materialise concurrently, consideration must be given as to whether only the threat with the largest time impact should be included in an evaluation.

Step 4c: Evaluation

The evaluation step involves the aggregation of the identified threats and opportunities for a business activity, project, or sub-project to understand their combined net effect on the overall activity or project objectives. This step is only warranted for large investments to support decision-making. It is not suitable (value-for-money) for very small businesses with a low turnover.

Simulation

The objective of simulation is to obtain a distribution of the possible outturn costs and or the schedule duration based on the combination of the input variables (threats, opportunities, assumptions, costs and durations). Each input variable is represented by a distribution for both probability and impact. The simulation takes account of and models the known relationships between the threats and between the opportunities.

Monte Carlo simulation

Monte Carlo is a simulation technique which provides a means of evaluating the effect of uncertainty on an activity or project. In summary, it looks at a large number of what-if scenarios for say, the cost of a project by accounting for a large number of possible values that each variable could take and weighting each by the probability of occurrence. In operation, Monte Carlo simulation generates a number at random for each risk item within the constraints of the impact distribution assigned to it and weights this number in accordance with the distribution of the probability of the risk occurring.

Sensitivity analysis

This technique involves taking a single variable (a threat for example) and examining the effect of changes in its values on the simulation results. By examining the impact of the changes it is possible to arrive at an assessment of how sensitive they would be to the activity or project outcome. Although only one variable is examined at a time, a number of variables considered important to the performance of an activity (in satisfying its objectives) may be examined consecutively.

Scenario analysis

This technique helps risk managers and project managers gain a feel for the effect of potential forecast inaccuracies by examining different 'states' or scenarios for an activity or project by (for instance) looking at more pessimistic or optimistic outcomes for a group of identified threats and opportunities.

Step 5: Response actions (treatment)

The treatment step uses all of the preceding risk management efforts to produce responses in terms of specific action plans to address the threats and opportunities identified. If risk management is to be effective this step is crucial.

Risk response strategies

The four threat response strategies adopted here (and shown in Table 3.3) are Risk Reduction, Risk Removal, Risk Reassignment and Risk Retention. The primary opportunity response is exploitation.

Risk reduction: The majority of threats will be treated in this way. This strategy is commonly adopted for what might be termed unavoidable threats where the activities attracting the threat have to be undertaken to maintain the business. The purpose of reduction is to reduce the threat as far as possible while ensuring that the cost of a response does not exceed the cost of the threat should it materialise. Reduction means only partial success is anticipated. Hence there must be a clear understanding of the percentage of the threat that remains (as far as can be judged) and the potential impact for the business.

Table 3.3 Risk response categories

Risk response strategies (summary statements)			
Reduction	*Removal*	*Re-assignment*	*Retention*
Partial removal of the threat as total removal is just not viable.	Removal of the threat altogether typically through taking a different path to activity implementation.	Re-assignment is commonly achieved through the transfer of the threat to a third party under certain circumstances.	Removal, reduction or re-assignment are not viable or where the cost of removal would be greater than the potential impact.

Risk removal: The threat response called removal is also known as termination, avoidance, elimination and exclusion. The greatest opportunity to remove a threat is at the commencement of an activity. Removal is typically achieved by removing the aspect of the activity attracting the threat by (for instance) adopting a less aggressive schedule, removing scope or adopting a different procurement strategy.

Risk reassignment: This risk response is also known as transfer and deflection. For some threats, the best response may be to transfer them. Reassignment is the strategy adopted to move a threat onto another organisation. This might be achieved by conventional insurance, by paying a third party to accept the threat or by transfer through a contract or supply agreement. When transferring a threat through insurance, the threat is rarely transferred in its entirety as policies typically include excess clauses. When transferring a schedule threat to a contractor, it should be borne in mind that if the contractor fails to manage the threat the business may still suffer a delay. When transferring a risk consideration should be given to four tests.[1]

> Objectives of the parties: What is a party's motivation for transferring or accepting a threat and is it transparent.
> Ability to manage: Transfer can only ever be effective if the party that accepts the threat, the recipient, has the ability to manage the risk. In other words, has the ability to devise and implement response actions that will directly reduce or remove the threat.
> Risk volatility: The ability of the party to effectively manage a threat that it has accepted (through transfer) will to a degree depend on whether the source of the threat remains static or is volatile. The degree of fluctuation will impact the ability to contain the threat.
> Cost effectiveness: It is usual for a 'premium' to be charged by the party accepting the transferred threat.

Risk retention: In the instance where the exposure from a threat may be tolerable without any further action being taken, where the cost of taking action may be disproportionate to the potential benefit gained or where a response is not viable, the solution may be to retain the threat.

Exploitation: Where an opportunity has been identified a course of action is defined to exploit the opportunity to say for instance reduce the cost, shorten the schedule, modify the scope or alter the procurement route. A workshop is typically held to assess the benefit and viability of the opportunity and how it may be translated into a change to the business activity.

Step 6: Implementation of the response actions

Once the response actions have been determined a decision needs to be made regarding the typical questions of 'who', 'when' as well 'is there sufficient budget' and 'what procedures need updating', as illustrated in Figure 3.7.

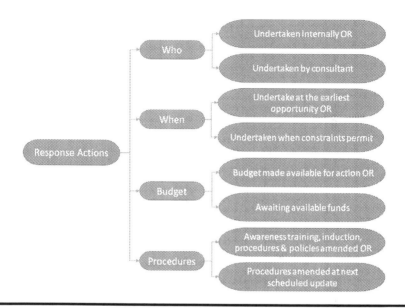

Figure 3.7 Considerations for the implementation of response actions

Step 7: Monitor and review

The primary process goal of Monitoring and Review is to monitor the success of implemented risk response actions to inform the department concerned as to whether there is a need for further proactive risk management intervention or to modify or accelerate already approved responses.

Reacting to early warning indicators: This process step requires the business to react to early warning indicators that have highlighted where activity performance has fallen short of recorded targets and if left uncorrected will put the activity objectives in jeopardy.

Registering changes: The internal and external contexts of a business activity require monitoring to understand if any of the currently identified and recorded threats and opportunities require revision or closure or if new threats or opportunities need to be recorded.

Recording emerging threats and opportunities: Not all threats and opportunities are identified at the first pass and new threats in particular emerge over time. Hence the risk identification process is iterative and should be updated on a regular basis. In addition, as business information is developed, the nature of assumptions and dependencies may change and the scope of business activities may be modified.

Reviewing response implementation: Regular risk meetings should review whether: risk responses have been implemented, responses have been successful, further actions are required, 'deteriorating' threats should be escalated to senior management, the risk managers have adequate control or the contingency for specific major threats is adequate.

Risk reporting: Risk reporting forms an integral part of 'Communication and Consultation' discussed below. Senior management needs to understand on a regular basis 'are we going to achieve our business targets' or (for instance), what is going to potentially delay the business activity, increase the costs, prevent part of the scope being delivered or induce operational constraints.

Contingency revision: The business's contingency (especially for time and cost) needs to be routinely reviewed at pre-determined intervals for comparison against activity performance to-date and its adequacy.

Step 8: Communication and consultation

Communication is carried out continuously throughout the risk management process. This is driven by the fact that any activity's risk exposure is never static and that effective risk management is dependent on a collaborative approach across all of the contributing business departments.

Communication is required for all of the following activities:

- Understanding the benefits of risk management and more importantly the downside if risk management is not undertaken.
- Capturing, disseminating and acting upon lessons learned from completed activities.
- Understanding the organisation's risk capacity, risk tolerance and risk appetite.[2]
- Understanding the risk policy, plan, process and probability impact grid.
- Discerning the level of risk management maturity and the deficiencies to be focussed on initially.
- Understanding of the terms and definitions being used.
- Understanding the risk management requirements of any audits or reviews.
- Understanding how risk management is to be integrated across all business functions.

- Escalating on a regular cycle the most serious threats, their assessment, planned or implemented responses and the residual risk.
- Escalating emerging risks which staff consider warrant the immediate attention of the senior management team.

Summary

This chapter has described the common steps in a risk management approach, namely: setting the strategy; establishing those aspects of the business plan that would be impacted by a fraud event; establishing the context; risk identification, analysis, evaluation and treatment; monitor and review; and lastly communication and consultation. How well threats are identified and responses defined and implemented will determine how well the business protects itself from fraud. This approach is tried and tested and has been seen to deliver clearly identifiable benefits.

Notes

1 See within "Risk Treatment" within *Simple tools and techniques for enterprise risk management*, 2nd edition, published by John Wiley and Sons.
2 Refer to "Risk Appetite", Chapter 12, within *Simple tools and techniques for enterprise risk management*, 2nd edition, published by John Wiley and Sons.

Chapter 4

Establish the context

Introduction

As described in Chapter 3 and depicted in Figure 4.1, establishing the context is the third stage in the overall eight-stage process of enterprise risk management described here. Establishing the context is concerned with gaining an understanding of (1) the *external* business environment or setting and (2) the specific *internal* business activity (or activities) under examination tailored to reflect it. This stage provides the foundation for everything that follows.

How well this stage is completed will determine the quality of the remainder of the risk management process. The object of this stage is to obtain relevant, current and accurate information. The three most important aspects of risk management are preparation, preparation and preparation.[1] Before data gathering can commence a decision must be made as to the approach to be adopted and the information to be gathered. This will largely be dictated by the focus of the risk process, such as whether it will examine all processes or target prioritised areas, such as:

- cyber security
- procurement processes
- payment processes
- IT protocols
- employee selection and training.

External business environment

As described in Chapter 3 there are numerous aspects of the external business context (sometimes referred to as the business environment) that need to be

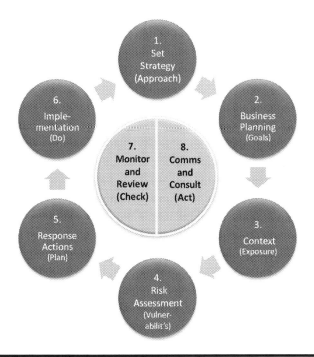

Figure 4.1 Eight-stage process of enterprise risk management

examined for sources of risk exposure. A description of each of these aspects is described elsewhere.[2] Of specific interest in understanding fraud risk are social context, the legal framework, technology and cybercrime.

Social context: The social context of a business is multi-faceted however what is of interest here is the prevalence of crime and its nature. Due to the scale of business conducted over the internet, UK businesses are exposed to individuals from a diverse range of cultures with different social norms, patterns of behaviour and perspectives on crime. Given the prevalence of crime committed by certain nationals, clearly in some parts of the globe crime is not seen as morally reprehensible and no thought is given to the victims. For those subjected to crime, it can be life changing.

Legal framework: The primary Act of Parliament in the UK relating to fraud is the Fraud Act 2006 (the Act) which came into force on 15 January 2007 and applies in England, Wales and Northern Ireland. Its component sections were discussed in Chapter 2.

Cybercrime: The risk to information and computer assets comes from a broad spectrum of threat actors with a broad range of capabilities. The impact (and therefore the harm) to an SME will depend on the opportunities it presents to an attacker (in terms of the vulnerabilities within its systems), the capabilities of the attackers to exploit them, and ultimately their motivation for attacking a business. There are two common forms of cybercrime tools, those that are commodity tools (referred to as off-the-shelf) which are openly available on the internet and relatively simple to use and those that are bespoke and have been 'built' for a specific purpose. An example of a commodity tool is described in Case Study 4.1. Bespoke tools the National Crime Agency (NCA) advises may include malicious code ('exploits') that take advantage of software vulnerabilities (or bugs) that are not yet known to

Case Study 4.1: Malicious software

Cybercrime

A website selling a commodity hacking tool which allowed cyber criminals to steal data and spy on victims through their webcam was taken offline in a major international effort. The Imminent Monitor Remote Access Trojan (IM RAT) could be obtained for as little as $25 – just under £20 – and was purchased by 14,500 people in 124 countries, according to the National Crime Agency (NCA). With the malicious software covertly installed on a victim's computer, hackers could take full remote control, giving them the power to disable antivirus software, steal data or passwords, record keystrokes and view footage from webcams. A total of 21 search warrants were executed across the UK targeting suspected sellers and users of the tool. Searches were carried out in Greater Manchester, Merseyside, Milton Keynes, Hull, London, Leeds, Walsall, Lancashire, Nottingham, Surrey, Essex and Somerset, leading to nine arrests and the recovery of more than 100 exhibits. 'The IM RAT was used by individuals and organised crime groups in the UK to commit a range of offences beyond just the Computer Misuse Act, including fraud, theft and voyeurism',[3] said Phil Larratt, from the NCA's National Cyber Crime Unit. He went on to say 'Cyber criminals who bought this tool for as little as 25 dollars were able to commit serious criminality, remotely invading the privacy of unsuspecting victims and stealing sensitive data'. An international effort led to the takedown of the site. The North West Regional Organised Crime Unit (NWROCU) took charge of the UK investigation, which was led internationally by the Australian Federal Police (AFP). Countries including Belgium, Sweden, Czech Republic, Poland, the Netherlands, Spain and Colombia also took part, resulting in 85 warrants executed worldwide, with 14 people arrested and more than 400 items seized. The authorities were able to take down the website selling the software, which subsequently stopped the cyber-stalking tools from working.

Source: Adapted from the NWROCU[4] (https://www.nwrocu.police.uk/news/2019/ 11/29/64/cyber-crime-site-selling-hacking-tool-taken-down-following-international-operation), the *BBC* (https://www.bbc.co.uk/news/technology-50601905), the *Metro* (https://metro.co.uk/2019/12/02/hacking-tool-allowing-cybercriminals-spy-webcams-taken-offline-11252463/) and the *Belfast Telegraph*.

vendors or anti-malware companies, often known as 'zero-day' exploits. Appendix 2 contains common cybercrime terms and definitions.

Technology: Advanced technology projects are prime targets for cyber criminals. As illustrated in Figure 4.2, projects undertaken by businesses may suffer security breaches and the exfiltration, deletion or corruption of data directly or through breaches suffered by an organisation that they have engaged with to support them. They may be sponsors, partners, suppliers, contractors, sub-contractors or consultants. Businesses supporting the UK government's scientific agency called the Advanced Research and Inventory Agency (ARIA),[5] will look to assist in preventing national and international cyberattacks.

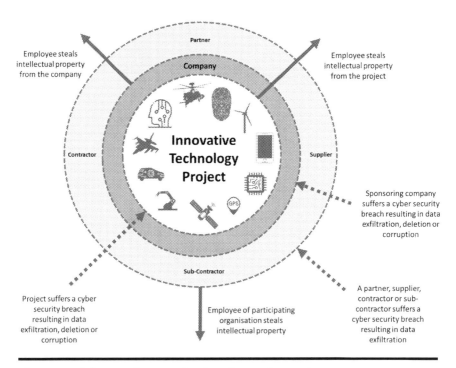

Figure 4.2 Cyberattacks on technology innovation projects

Specific business activity

As illustrated in Figure 4.3, examination of specific business activity typically entails examining (in a logical sequence) the Business Objectives, the Business Plan and the Business Setting together with the Business Processes and the Organisational Structure to support the business case. It also examines

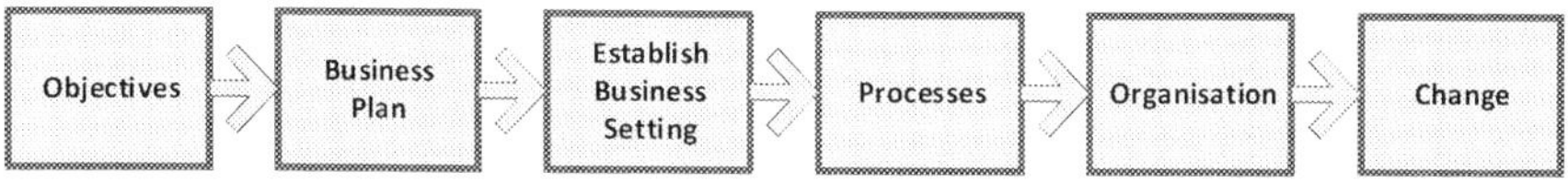

Figure 4.3 Linear development of a business

the Change Management processes established to bring about organisational change, from say introducing a new database, to developing a new product or restructuring to reflect market changes. Each of these aspects of the context are examined below.

Business objectives

Revisiting and understanding the business objectives is a prerequisite to understanding the threats and opportunities arising from these objectives. The business objectives will be the criteria against which the success of the business strategy will be measured, the business strategy being the overall plan aimed at achieving sustainable competitive advantage to produce healthy profits.[6]

Business plan

The goal of the business plan is to explain how the business will achieve its objectives in a coherent, consistent and cohesive manner. The plan should identify the market, its growth prospects, the target customers and the main competitors. It should identify the risks facing the business, their likely impact should they materialise and the actions planned to reduce or remove the risks. Given the rise in cybercrime and fraud, these subjects must be addressed.

Business setting

The business setting refers to a vast range of interfaces such as the economy, interest rates, the market, existing competitors, the cost of market entry, legislation, taxation, the employment market, technology, the IoT and levels of crime.

Business processes

A way for businesses to question and fully understand their vulnerabilities is to understand their processes at a low level of granularity. Process mapping is recognised as a proven analytical and communication tool to improve comprehension of a business's existing processes and understand those that require amendments to reduce fraud. A business process is a series of steps designed to produce a product or service. A business's processes are highly influential in determining entrepreneurial success. Process mapping provides a proven tool with which to understand business processes to help guard against criminal activities. Without knowing the current 'as-is' it is not possible to discern the target destination. There needs to be recognition that people are the weakest link in all processes. Databases, spreadsheets and payment schedules do not populate themselves.

The common business processes undertaken to enable a business to operate are illustrated in Figure 4.4.

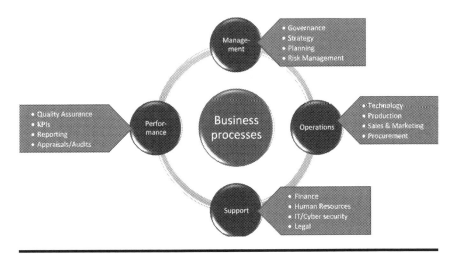

Figure 4.4 Common business processes

Organisation

Another way of analysing a business is to identify its resources and how they are used to competitive advantage. Generally, businesses that allocate and deploy their resources in the most efficient manner are likely to achieve a greater return on capital employed. However, the examination of resources when focussed on combatting fraud requires a specific approach in terms of the resources themselves, the configuration of the resources and ongoing assessment.

- *The resources themselves.* The management of information technology and financial resources in particular will impact both the day-to-day running of a business and its longevity. The resources assigned to the management of receiving payment and paying suppliers, contractors, consultants, government agencies and staff will be significant in reducing exposure to fraud.
- *The configuration of the resources.* For SMEs given the number of employees, the configuration can be very simple; however, for medium-sized organisations, the configuration needs to satisfy the operational requirements established to prevent fraud perpetrated internally or externally.

■ *The resource audit.* Resource audits typically cover operational, human and financial resources. For fraud prevention, the focus needs to be on recruitment, training, IT resources, operational procedures and adherence to those procedures.

Change management

Combatting fraud commonly requires implementing changes to current methods of working and specific practices. The changes may require changes to job descriptions and or the recruitment of additional staff. To be effective, these changes need to be introduced through a well-planned and orchestrated change management process. The process needs to be tailored to the extent of the change planned. The introduction of change needs to be managed as a project in its own right. Ad-hoc changes poorly communicated can lead businesses into a false sense of security with disastrous consequences.

UK organisations combatting fraud

There are now a myriad of organisations within the UK either purely gathering data, investigating and or prosecuting fraud or providing guidance on how to limit it (see Figure 4.5). Collectively they provide a wealth of information. Businesses need to 'mine' the readily available guidance. In particular, businesses need to understand which organisations they need to turn to, to:

■ gain information on setting up robust processes;
■ understand the methods adopted by criminals;
■ report fraud incidents;
■ report attempts to gather data (phishing);
■ understand why organisations have been prosecuted and specifically where their processes have failed;
■ obtain guidance on safe and unsafe anti-virus software;
■ obtain business insurance.

The UK government's survey of 2020[7] discovered that the most common sources of information and guidance for businesses are:

■ external cyber security consultants, IT consultants or managed service providers (mentioned by 27% of businesses);
■ general online searching (9% of businesses);
■ any government or public sector source, including government websites, regulators and other public bodies (6% of businesses);
■ trade associations (4% of businesses).

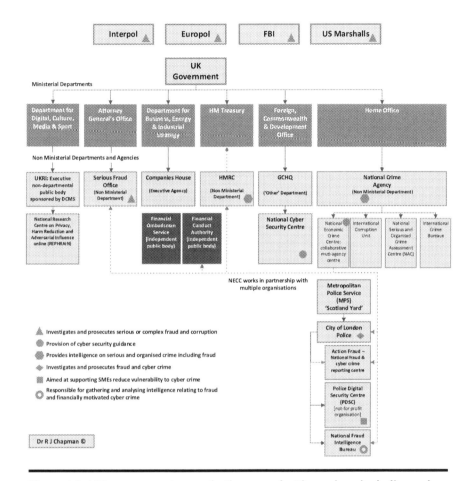

Figure 4.5 UK government organisations combatting crime including cyber-crime and providing the infrastructure for governance. The organisations referred to in the figure are included in Appendix 3 – a glossary of government departments, agencies and external organisations together with their roles, terms and acronyms

Summary

Assessment of the business context will be vital in acting as a prompt to interrogate the sources of risk, determine the participants (subject matter experts) required in any risk identification process and ascertain the subjects that warrant closer inspection. Any context assessment must be tailored to suit the objectives of any risk management study. The context step is likely to examine the business plan and objectives, in-house resources and capabilities and how any changes would be implemented through change management. In simple terms it is an examination of: what are we trying to achieve? what is occurring in the marketplace? what are our current fraud management capabilities? what guidance is readily available? and who can we turn to for support?

Notes

1 Chapman, R.J. (2011) *Simple tools and techniques for enterprise risk management*, 2nd Edition, John Wiley and Sons.
2 These aspects of context are discussed in *Simple tools and techniques for enterprise risk management*, 2nd Edition published by John Wiley and Sons Limited, 2011 and *The rules of project risk management*, 2nd Edition published by Routledge, 2020.
3 Techmonitor "RAT Bought by 14,500 People Taken Down in International Operation" https://techmonitor.ai/techonology/software/im-rat-nca
4 "Cyber crime site selling hacking tool taken down following international operation" https://www.nwrocu.police.uk/news/2019/11/29/64/cyber-crime-site-selling-hacking-tool-taken-down-following-international-operation
5 The planned launch of ARIA was announced by the Department for Business, Energy & Industrial Strategy on 19 February 2021. It will be a 'high-risk, high-reward' scientific agency aimed at providing rapid funding for UK inventors and researchers. The goal is for it to be fully operational by 2022. The ARIA is modelled on America's long-running Defence Advanced Research Projects Agency (DARPA), which aims to make pivotal investments in breakthrough technologies for national security. The new body will complement the work of UK Research and Innovation (UKRI) while building on the government's ambitious R&D Roadmap published in July 2020. In November 2020, the Spending Review set out the government's plan to cement the UK's status as a global leader in science and innovation by investing £14.6 billion in R&D in 2021–2022, putting the UK on track to reach 2.4% of GDP being spent on R&D across the UK economy by 2027.
6 Chapman, R.J. (2011) *Simple tools and techniques for enterprise risk management*, 2nd Edition, John Wiley and Sons.
7 Department for Digital, Culture, Media & Sport (2020) "Cyber Security Breaches Survey 2020", Updated 26 March 2020. https://www.gov.uk/government/publications/cyber-security-breaches-survey-2020/cyber-security-breaches-survey-2020.

EXTERNAL 'ACTORS'

Introduction to Section 2

As explained in Chapter 1 'Layout of the book', Section 2 describes the types of fraud committed by third parties or 'actors' outside of the business which require specific action to limit their occurrence. Criminals rely on the internet and email as the 'entry gate' to businesses to commit the majority of these frauds. The chapters included in Section 2 are as follows:

DOI: 10.4324/9781003200383-6

Structure of the chapters within Section 2

Each chapter is structured in an identical way for both ease of navigation and the ease of comprehension of each fraud type. They describe the risk management steps 4 to 6 (Risk Assessment through to Implementation) sequentially, as illustrated in Figure 3.1 in Chapter 3 and repeated below for ease of reference. Step 4 is expanded to show three elements: Lessons Learned, Risk Identification and Risk Analysis (Figure S2.1).

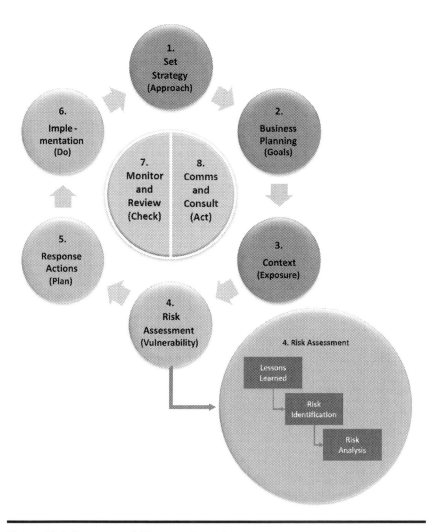

Figure S2.1 Structure of Chapters 5 to 12

Content of the chapters within Section 2

Steps in the risk management process are adopted to describe the unique characteristics of each fraud type and develop tailored responses to improve the capabilities of a business to combat it. Each business needs to learn lessons from its own processes together with external case studies. In addition, they should follow government guidelines where appropriate and seek consultancy support as required. Each chapter contains a description of the steps described in Figure S2.2.

Home office assessment of online crime against different commercial sectors

All of the subjects addressed by Chapters 5 to 12 listed above are affected to some degree by online crime. The extent of online crime against specific business sectors has been captured by annual Home Office surveys. The surveys have consistently shown that businesses under 50 personnel have been more vulnerable to and suffered more from online crime than larger organisations.

The Home Office publication 'Crime against businesses: findings from the 2018 Commercial Victimisation Survey', published on 5 September 2019 presents findings from the 2018 Commercial Victimisation Survey (abbreviated to CVS), a sample survey that examines the extent of crime against business premises

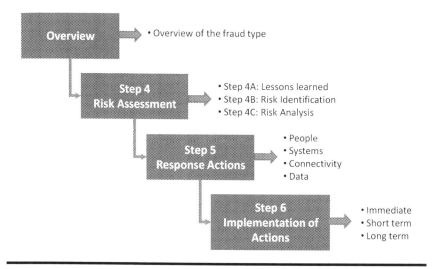

Figure S2.2 Content of Chapters 5 to 12

in England and Wales. The CVS was previously run in 1994, 2002 and then each year since 2012. The survey was paused for 2019 while a review has been undertaken to consider whether changes were needed to better meet user needs. The CVS looks at the following sectors:

- wholesale and retail
- accommodation and food
- transportation and storage
- manufacturing
- agriculture, forestry and fishing
- arts, entertainment and recreation
- construction
- information and communication
- administrative and support services.

Online crime

One of the areas of crime that the CVS examines is Online Crime. Online crime covers a range of crime types carried out over computer networks. The CVS asked respondents who used computers at their premises about their experience of the following types of online crime:

1. **Hacking:** having a computer, network or server accessed without permission.
2. **Online theft of money:** having money stolen electronically (e.g. through online banking).
3. **Phishing:** having money stolen after responding to fraudulent messages or being redirected to fake websites.
4. **Online theft of information:** having confidential information stolen electronically (such as staff or customer data).
5. **Website vandalism:** having a website defaced, damaged or taken down.
6. **Viruses:** having computers infected with files or programs intended to cause harm.
7. **Denial of service attack (extortion):** having a website shut down through targeted request overloads.
8. **Ransomware:** having computer access illegally blocked until a ransom is paid.
9. **Unlicensed software downloads:** having unlicensed or stolen software downloaded from the organisations' computers or network.

10. **Intellectual property theft:** the organisation having experienced theft of intellectual property (Information and Communications sector only – not surveyed in 2018).
11. **Other online crimes:** Any other online crimes which do not fall into the above categories.

Vulnerability by the size of organisation 2014 (wholesale and retail)

According to Home Office's official statistics contained within its publication 'Crimes against businesses findings 2014', published on 23 April 2015, businesses with under 50 employees are more vulnerable within the wholesale and retail sector for instance. Historically the wholesale and retail sector has been singled out repeatedly as it has been one of the more exposed business sectors (Table S2.1).

Table S2.1 Extract of "Crimes against businesses findings 2014": Table 1.7: Numbers of online crime per 1,000 premises in the last 12 months, by number of employees at premises, wholesale and retail sector, 2014 CVS

Crime type	1–9 employees	10–49 employees	50+ employees	All premises
Hacking	22	6	13	19
Phishing	2	67	0	15
Theft of money (online)	2	67	4	15
Theft of information (online)	0	5	0	1
Website vandalism	7	12	5	8
Computer virus	417	240	126	373
All other online crime	449	398	148	430

Vulnerability by the size of organisation 2016 (wholesale and retail)

According to Home Office's official statistics contained within its publication 'Crime against businesses: findings from the 2016 Commercial Victimisation Survey', published on 4 May 2017, businesses with under 50 employees are more vulnerable within the wholesale and retail sector for instance (Table S2.2).

Table S2.2 Extract of 'Crimes against businesses findings 2016' Table 1.8: Number of online crimes per 1,000 premises in the 12 months by number of employees at premises, wholesale and retail sector, 2016 CVS

Crime type	1–9 employees	10–49 employees	50+ employees	All premises
Hacking	17	51	10	23
Phishing	…	…	…	…
Theft of money (online)	20	…	31	17
Theft of information (online)	5	11	4	6
Website vandalism	39	5	19	31
Computer virus	42	193	291	78
All other online crime	811	…	…	638

Notes:
- '…' indicates that there were no respondents in the category shown.
- Columns related to victims do not sum to the totals shown for all online crimes. This is because one premise can be a victim of more than one type of crime. Other columns may not sum exactly to the total shown due to rounding off.

General guidance

Employees business travel and working from an overseas location

When working in a foreign country on behalf of the business, employees should be given clear guidance on how to protect the business. Suggestions are indicated below. As this guidance applies to some degree to all of the chapters in this Section it is included here rather than repeating it each time.

- **Secure Wi-Fi:** Employees should only use a secure Wi-Fi connection that they have in their accommodation (i.e. they should not be using open access Wi-Fi in a public area. Using a company mobile as a hotspot would be preferred).
- **Physical security:** Employees should stay in accommodation with secure doors and windows and where they have the only key to one of the lockable habitable rooms. The aim is to prevent unauthorised access – If this is not possible due to staying with family, a lockable cabinet where the employee holds the sole key would suffice. Employees should seek advice from the individual or consultant acting as the head of physical and personnel security regarding physical security during the stay and travelling to and from the accommodation.
- **Home office:** Employees should work in a room within the accommodation that is not overlooked and does not allow conversations to be overheard. When a laptop is not being used it should be locked away out of sight.
- **Access to information:** All information must be in an electronic format. Employees must not print business documentation or connect any company equipment to a printer or any other equipment whilst abroad.
- **Portable devices:** There is no requirement for the business documents to be transferred electronically via a USB stick or a portable hard drive. All information would be solely contained on the business laptop.

Specific instructions should be given to employees with regard to the business laptop when travelling and working overseas on behalf of the business:

- Be fully powered down for the duration of your travel to your secure location.
- Be protected by a strong passphrase.
- Be secured, out of sight and powered down when not in use or sleeping.
- Be powered down before approaching Border Control/Customs.
- Be powered up if requested by Border Control/Customs but refuse to enter a password and login to the business account.
- Be kept in your possession at all times. Report to the business immediately if it is removed or taken away by Border Control/Customs, and should be considered compromised.
- Not to be used while in a public place (e.g. coffee bars; restaurants; in hotels).
- Not be connected to any insecure Wi-Fi networks. Note: Public Wi-Fi connections are almost always unencrypted, allowing attackers to redirect

employees' browsing requests to a malicious website and then run malware on the device.

- Have Wi-Fi and Bluetooth services on the laptop turned off when not in use, ensuring that the device's 'autoconnect' settings are turned off.
- Have a privacy screen fitted at all times when working on the laptop where you could be overlooked.

Chapter 5

Non-delivery fraud

Structure of Chapter 5

Chapter 5 is subdivided into the following four sections. An overview of the fraud type is provided followed by an assessment of the threat posed by the fraud, suggested response actions and their implementation (Figure 5.1).

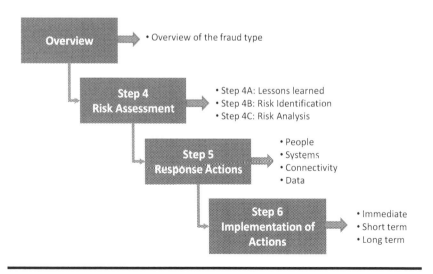

Figure 5.1 Structure of Chapter 5

DOI: 10.4324/9781003200383-7

Overview

Non-delivery fraud describes the fraud perpetrated by criminals who promise the supply of highly sought-after goods (such as during the coronavirus pandemic), collect the payment but default on delivery. While the principle is simple, the fraudster's schemes are often sophisticated yielding huge profits. Criminals can adapt a well-established method of working to suit any product from electronics to everyday items. These types of fraud are not carried out by lone criminals but by organised criminal groups (OCGs) who have gone to considerable lengths to set up a sophisticated operation, involving websites, email addresses, salespeople, intermediaries and bank accounts. These frauds often involve more than one country in order to make victims feel helpless and complicate investigations. In 2020, the world was gripped by the COVID-19 pandemic, leading to an unprecedented demand for personal protective equipment (commonly abbreviated to PPE) and medical equipment such as ventilators. INTERPOL reported in March 2020[1] that they had assisted with some 30 COVID-19-related fraud cases with links to Asia and Europe, leading to the blocking of 18 bank accounts and the freezing of more than $730,000 in suspected fraudulent transactions.

Step 4: Risk assessment

The Risk Assessment step consists of a sequence of activities which answer the questions: what are the possible problems my business may face? How likely are they? What impact will they have? And how soon will they impact? How well these questions can be answered depends on the research undertaken. A starting point is undertaking lessons learned. For large businesses operating over a number of years, they may have developed a database of events, recording how they were managed and what degree of success was achieved. However, for SMEs, they typically have to look outside of their business for lessons learned. In addition, as technology is moving so rapidly and cyber criminals are constantly evolving their approach and developing new malware, monitoring external sources of information has assumed greater importance.

Step 4A: Lessons learned

Lessons learned are typically drawn from a combination of a business's own experiences and those of other companies. Given that non-delivery fraud is not industry-specific and all businesses can fall foul of this type of fraud, lessons can be drawn from a broad range of businesses and law enforcement agencies here and abroad. A key lesson is to plan ahead so that the business is not exposed to having to order parts or components at very short notice. This will afford the business the time to follow procurement processes and the normal careful selection and appointment of suppliers. In the event that a fraud is detected and as time is of the essence in contacting the bank with the aim of stopping payments, staff must be clear who to contact, when, in what sequence and with what information. To appreciate the vulnerabilities of a business to non-delivery fraud requires an appreciation of the sequence or pattern of these fraud events, the tools and techniques employed (described here as the mechanics), historical events (captured in case studies) together with 'red flags' or the 'alarm bells' over potential exposure, as illustrated in Figure 5.2. These activities contribute to Lessons Learned which in turn assist in deciding on the actions to be implemented, to thwart non-delivery fraud.

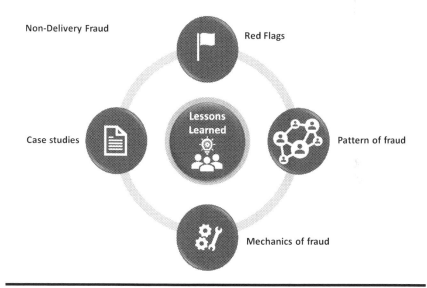

Figure 5.2 Lessons learned from non-delivery frauds

 Understanding the pattern of non-delivery fraud: There are usually five steps to a sophisticated non-delivery fraud as described below and illustrated in Figure 5.3.

Establish 'company': OCGs will establish a website, email addresses, phone numbers and bank accounts as well as organise 'sales people' and 'intermediaries' all with the intent of creating the deception of a legitimate business operating in the field of the specialist goods they are pretending to sell.

Advertising: The fraudsters advertise their 'goods' on their websites which typically have names very similar to well-known legitimate businesses which

Step 1: Organised Crime	Step 2: Advertising	Step 3: Sale	Step 4: Create relationships	Step 5: Disapperance
Organized crime groups go to great lengths to set up a sophisticated modus operandi involving websites, salespeople, intermediaries and bank accounts. Scams often involve more than one country in order to complicate investigations by law enforcement agencies.	Glossy advertisements are created. Criminals approach potential buyers online or in person. Fake websites and social media accounts almost identical to those of known businesses are created. Online contact forms, phone numbers and email addresses all give the impression of a legitimate customer service centre.	Once contact is made, the sales process commences. Prices for large orders are negotiated. Fraudsters provide contracts etc, on official letterhead. Fraudsters then ask for an advance payment to secure the goods. The payments are made directly into accounts which have been opened under registered (fake) companies. Tracking numbers are given.	Alleged sellers work hard to create trust with the buyer. The scammer will maintain contact throughout the delivery process and invent as many reasons as possible to obtain extra payments for say customs fees, express delivery, insurance, etc. Contact is maintained until the victim starts to hesitate, becomes irate or accuses the salesperson of fraud.	Once the criminals feel they have been uncovered; they end all contact. Phones are cut off, emails go unanswered and websites are shut down. The criminals move on quickly and start a new fraud with a new product. If one domain is suspended or taken down, other domains are still available to attract new victims. The cycle starts again.

Figure 5.3 Steps in non-delivery fraud

include contact forms for would-be buyers to populate with their details to give the impression of a legitimate business.

Sale: Once contact has been made the fraudsters negotiate prices for large orders taking into account their fictitious packaging processes, transportation logistics, production rates and quality standards. The key to the whole fraud is that the criminals ask for an advance payment to secure the order. When there are worldwide shortages of the product they are purporting to sell, persuading buyers to make an advance payment is that much easier. They issue contracts on printed letterheads they have created using copied logos, as part of the masquerade of being a legitimate business.

Create relationships: The alleged sellers will maintain regular contact with the buyers throughout the process with the primary goal of securing additional payments to overcome say delivery obstacles. They will also strive to switch the country of origin of the goods during the purchasing process to make traceability of payments that much more difficult.

Disappearance: As soon as the fraudsters believe that they have been uncovered, email accounts and phone lines are closed down and the website is terminated. They seek to remove all traces of their existence. They then move on to the next product they want to 'sell' and start the whole process all over again.

Understanding the mechanics of non-delivery fraud

Spoof website. The fraudsters build a hoax website to mislead potential buyers that they are viewing the website of a legitimate business. The criminals may copy the content and style of the legitimate website, complete with images, pictures, forms and text. The URL (Uniform Resource Locator), or web address typically very closely resembles the URL of a legitimate website that a business manager is likely to know and trust. A cursory glance would not pick up the difference. If a manager is not expecting web addresses to be cloned, a hoax website will not be detected. So, a legitimate site established as www.ppemedicalsupplydirect.com may be set up as www.ppemedicalsuppliesdirect.com. The email accounts created are based on the spoofed URL.

Contracts. Care is taken in the preparation of contracts as part of the overall deception to give the impression to potential buyers that they are dealing with a long-established mature business. Contracts are cloned legitimate contracts with amendments made to suit their operation.

Sales staff. Those within the criminal organisation that are designated 'sales staff' are knowledgeable about the products on offer, national or global shortages, logistics and, typical transportation methods. They must seek to secure a large advance payment, upon which the success of the scam hinges. The staff strive to strike a rapport with the buyers and convince them that they are fortunate as they had had a recent cancellation, they had just recently ramped up production to meet demand or new additional plant had just been brought in online. It is a way of explaining why, in a market where there are such pronounced shortages, that they or their affiliated agents have stock for sale.

 Case Study 5.1 provides an example of non-delivery fraud which hinged on the lack of detection by the buyers that the well-produced website that they had visited had been cloned and the business was non-existent.

Case Study 5.1: Non-delivery Fraud

Legitimate website cloned

During mid-March 2020, a number of countries were entering lockdown due to the coronavirus outbreak. German health authorities contracted two sales companies, one in Zurich and the other in Hamburg, to procure face masks valued at €15 million. With a global shortage of medical supplies complicating usual business channels, the buyers followed new leads in the hope of securing the masks. Following research, the buyers discovered a legitimate company in Spain selling face masks. Unfortunately, unknown to the buyers, the company's website had been cloned and their email address compromised. The buyers unwittingly contacted the fake company through the cloned website and commenced an email exchange. The fake company initially claimed to have 10 million masks, however subsequently advised the arranged delivery had fallen through. As a remedy or fall-back, they then referred the buyers to a 'trusted' dealer in Ireland. The Irish middleman promised to put them in touch with a different supplier, this time in the Netherlands. Claiming to have a strong commercial relationship with the company, the man provided assurances that the alleged Dutch company would be able to supply the 10 million face masks. An agreement for an initial delivery of 1.5 million masks was made, in exchange for an up-front payment of €1.5 million. The buyers initiated a bank transfer to Ireland and prepared for delivery, which involved 52 lorries and a police escort to transport the masks from a warehouse in the Netherlands to the final destination in Germany. Just before the delivery date, the buyers were informed that the funds had not been received and that an emergency transfer of €880,000 straight to the Dutch supplier was required to secure the merchandise. The buyers sent the wire transfer but the masks never arrived. It transpired that the Dutch company existed, but their website had also been cloned. There was no official record of the order. When the buyers realised they had been duped, they immediately contacted their bank in Germany, which in turn contacted INTERPOL's financial crimes unit, setting off a race to intercept the funds and follow the money trail. Banks, financial intelligence units and judicial authorities, as well as partner organizations Europol and EUROJUST, joined INTERPOL in pursuit of the money. INTERPOL contacted its National Central Bureau in Dublin as well as the Irish bank. Prompt intervention by the Garda National Economic Crime Bureau allowed them to freeze the 1.5 million in the account and identify the Irish company involved. The Dutch Fiscal Information and Investigation Service quickly tracked down the €880,000 which had been transferred from the German company. Nearly €500,000 of those funds had already been sent to the United Kingdom, all of which was destined for an account in Nigeria. Europol activated its professional networks to reach key contacts in the banking sector. Thanks to an alert raised by investigators, the UK bank was able to recall the full amount. Those funds have now been returned to the Netherlands and frozen by authorities. Two arrests were made in the Netherlands with other arrests anticipated.

Source: Interpol. Subject to Interpol copyright. https://www.interpol.int/News-and-Events/News/2020/Unmasked-International-COVID-19-fraud-exposed.

Red flags: A red flag has been used as a warning of danger for centuries. In business, a red flag is an indicator that there is something wrong with a company, situation, process, salesperson or contract arising from the possible existence of fraud, corruption or unethical practice. When a red flag is spotted, management should take immediate action to investigate and correct the situation. Examples of red flags are:

- Receipt of unsolicited emails offering the equipment your business is seeking.
- The directors or owners of the company are unclear.
- The physical office of the company offering the goods/parts required cannot be verified.
- The business has been in existence for a very short length of time.
- It has not been possible to speak to previous clients or independently check references.
- An explanation of the transportation logistics appears ill-informed.
- If the business is asked to make a payment to a bank account located in a country different from the one where the supply company is located.

Criminals prefer payment to a bank in a different country as it is far more difficult for victims to liaise with a bank abroad once fraud is detected.

- The advance payment(s) requested seems disproportionally high when compared to the total cost.
- The web pages on another company's website are identical.
- The website has not been independently verified.
- The sales agent advises there is a last-minute problem with the supplier and suggests going through an intermediary to establish contact with another supplier in another country.
- The sales agent says the first payment has not been received and to secure the delivery another deposit needs to be paid.
- There is an unexpected request to pay additional sums to overcome problems in transportation or shipment.
- If the urgency for payment seems 'manufactured' and unwarranted.
- There are repeated recommendations to act quickly to secure the supplies due to widespread demand.
- It is not possible to establish their business track record.
- A deep dive on the internet suggests that criminal gangs are trapping businesses into purchasing goods that are never delivered.

Step 4B: Threat identification and impact

Typically, as a consequence of a series of causes, a business may be vulnerable to non-delivery fraud, which should it materialise, may have a series of negative impacts, one of which may be financial, depending on when the fraud is detected (Tables 5.1 to 5.3).

Table 5.1 Non-delivery fraud common causes

Non-delivery fraud threats (Cause → Threat → Impact)	
The **causes** or triggers behind fraudulent activity	
Induction	New employees are not fully inducted into the methods adopted to tackle fraud.
Training	Lack of fraud awareness training and subsequent updates.
Adverts	Staff fall victim to glossy advertisements with high-quality images and brand names which imitate those of trustworthy businesses.
Online approach	Staff are duped by an online approach by a 'sales person' who has infiltrated professional purchasing circles and is knowledgeable about general details of the industry such as the supply chain, transportation, contract terms and the products being sought by the company.

Spoofed website	Staff fail to detect that a website visited is fake as it is almost identical to a known business website. The fake website describes several ways for making contact and includes online contact forms, phone numbers and email addresses which all give the impression of a legitimate customer service centre.
Existence	Lack of assessment as to how long the producer has been in existence.
False legitimacy	Lack of awareness that criminals register their company at Companies House to give it a false legitimacy in the full knowledge that Companies House do not carry out verification checks on businesses.
Companies House check	No check completed at Companies House to determine the opening date of the business, if it was registered in the UK.
Bank account	Lack of verification of how long the producer's bank account has been open, where this is possible to determine.
References	References provided are taken at face value and are not checked.
Payment protocols	Not all employees are aware of the payment protocols and penalties for breach.
Red flags	Lack of development and dissemination of red flag events.
Second authentication	Second authentication of payments is not implemented.
Company review	Lack of a check of online reviews of a company before making a purchase – for example, have there been complaints of other customers not receiving the promised items.
Fake contract	Staff fail to detect a contract provided by criminals as fraudulent due to the presence of the logo of a genuine company and the professionalism of the wording of the contract.
Sales person verification	Staff do not verify the company or the sales person before committing to a purchase.
Advance payment	The criminals create a false legitimacy for one or more advance payments and provide a phony tracking number so that the purchaser can supposedly determine where their goods are at any time.

Table 5.2 Non-delivery fraud common threats

Threats (uncertain events)	
Advance payment	Staff are duped into paying an advance payment to secure urgently needed goods (known to be in heavy demand) to what they believe is a legitimate company but is in fact a criminal organisation which has no intention of supplying the requested goods and whose sole aim is to secure financial gain from susceptible businesses.
Full payment	Staff are duped into paying the full stipulated price to secure urgently needed goods to what they believe is a legitimate company but is in fact a criminal organisation which has no intention of supplying the requested goods and whose sole aim is to secure financial gain from susceptible businesses.

Table 5.3 Non-delivery fraud impact of the threats (based on the common causes)

Impact description (if the threats were to materialise)	
Business interruption and increased costs	The business suffers from non-delivery fraud resulting in the promised goods not being delivered and one or more of the following: lost production, lost planned manufacture, programmed delivery delays, disappointing customers/ clients/end users, tarnished reputation, reduction in market share, or increased operating costs/reduced profitability.

Step 4C: Risk analysis

When examining the characteristics of a potential threat, it commonly involves estimating the likelihood, the impact (in cost and time together with other parameters when appropriate) and the proximity (when is the threat likely to materialise) (Table 5.4).

Table 5.4 Analysis of non-delivery fraud threats

Analysis of non-delivery fraud threats	
Likelihood	As these risks have already been encountered by numerous other firms, the likelihood of their occurrence (in the absence of any mitigation actions being implemented) is very high.
Financial impact	The financial impact, should the risk materialise, will depend on a series of factors such as when the fraud is detected, the value of any advance payments, whether the advance payments have been made, and if so, whether the bank is notified swiftly enough to block the payment if possible.
Proximity	Out of the course assessment of short, medium and long term all of these risks relate to the short term and need to be addressed at the earliest opportunity.

Step 5: Risk response actions

Risk response actions need to be tailored to the fraud type (Figure 5.4).

Step 6: Implementation of actions
Immediate response

A business should immediately notify its bank if it considers it has been the victim of non-delivery fraud as well as the local police. It should document what actions were taken when for future reference (a timeline). A business can report fraud or cybercrime to Action Fraud any time of the day or night using its online fraud reporting tool. Businesses can also report and get advice about fraud or cybercrime by calling (at the time of writing) 0300 123 2040. The Serious Fraud Office can be contacted if it is believed the rogue company is still active, it is perpetrating fraud and millions of pounds are involved.

Your People

Inductions: Ensure all new employee inductions include non-delivery fraud training. Use a specialist provider of E-Learning or in-house training. Update on a regular basis.

CS training: Ensure the delivery of regular ongoing, comprehensive cyber security awareness training to all employees across all business functions, to help employees be alert, wary and vigilant.

Telephone number: Staff should call the seller to see if the telephone number is correct and working. Staff should be very wary of calling mobile phone numbers.

Physical address: Staff should obtain a physical address (street name and district) rather than simply a post office box address.

NTS: Provide guidance on contacting National Trading Standards (who are focused on leading investigations into trading standards offences) to understand if the company proposing to supply goods to your business has already attracted attention for rogue activities.

Your Systems

Free email: Be wary of companies that use a free e-mail service where a business credit card was not required to open the account. Be cautious when responding to special supply offers, especially through unsolicited e-mails.

Test email: Send an email to the company that you believe you are doing business with, other than an email address from their website to verify if the company is legitimate.

Independent references: Where possible, seek independent references for the business that you intend to do business with. Phone the companies that the organisation claims that it has done business with previously.

Foreign bank account: Consider challenging the use of a foreign bank account when called upon to send funds overseas. Ideally call on the supplier to use a UK bank account and ask the bank to verify the account.

Website: Do not base decision making purely on the information included on a visited website regardless of how professional it looks as they can be set up relatively quickly and may contain images or text copied from legitimate websites.

Your Connectivity

Industry: Make contact with industry partners, trade organisations, existing suppliers and/or professional bodies where appropriate to find background information on the company that your business intends to do business with, particularly where large sums of money are involved and/or the parts/goods will form part of an assembly being sold to an important client.

Overseas suppliers: Insist on visiting the factory where the goods will be produced (to, say, carry out factory assessment tests) and previous client's/customer's offices to verify references regardless of whether the seller insists time is of the essence or interest has been expressed by many other buyers

Your Data

Company information: Wherever possible, limit the sharing of company information to companies that your business has not already developed a relationship with.

Sensitive information: As numerous emails are typically received each day from multiple suppliers, communications with legitimate suppliers may be interspersed with emails from fraudsters looking for recipients to open an attachment or click on a link infected with malware, with the ultimate goal of steeling sensitive data. Whatever the circumstances, ensure that sensitive business information is protected and backed up.

Figure 5.4 Response actions to address non-delivery fraud risks

Short-term response

The short-term responses include induction training and ongoing regular training on the risks of non-delivery fraud and the defences that can be put in place to combat it. Regular contact should be made with trade organisations and law enforcement websites to understand any changes in the pattern or mechanics of non-delivery fraud.

Summary

Non-delivery fraud, as with many other fraud types, can have a very severe and long-lasting impact on SMEs that have found themselves falling victim to this crime. This type of fraud is characterised by being typically perpetrated by an OCG whose modus operandi is highly sophisticated. The OGC will have undertaken extensive research and spent considerable time in developing an approach and establishing a website, logo, email address, phone numbers, sales team and contract documents. As soon as an SME believes it has fallen foul of this fraud it must notify its bank, the local police and Action Fraud.

Note

1 Interpol (2020) "INTERPOL warns of financial fraud linked to COVID-19". https://www.interpol.int/News-and-Events/News/2020/INTERPOL-warns-of-financial-fraud-linked-to-COVID-19.

Chapter 6

Ransomware attacks

Structure of Chapter 6

Chapter 6 is subdivided into the following four sections. An overview of the fraud type is provided followed by an assessment of the threat posed by the fraud, suggested response actions and their implementation (Figure 6.1).

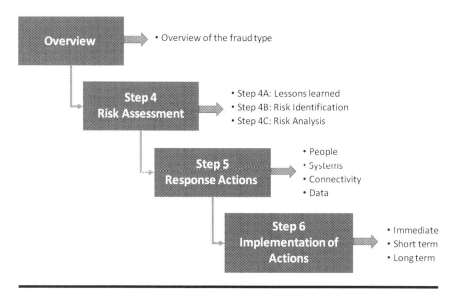

Figure 6.1 Structure of Chapter 6

DOI: 10.4324/9781003200383-8

Overview

Ransomware is a form of malicious software (malware) that enables cyber criminals to remotely lock down, steal, delete or encrypt the files on a business's device. The Cybersecurity and Infrastructure Security Agency (CISA) of the United States defines ransomware as

> an ever-evolving form of malware designed to encrypt files on a device, rendering any files and the systems that rely on them unusable. Malicious actors then demand a ransom in exchange for decryption. Ransomware actors often target and threaten to sell or leak exfiltrated data or authentication information if the ransom is not paid.[1]

Some ransomware will also try to spread to other machines on a network, such as the Wannacry malware that impacted the NHS in May 2017. Criminals use ransomware to extort money from companies (a ransom) and will claim to restore access to a company's files or device once it has paid the ransom. According to research conducted by Google in 2017, cyber-thieves had made at least $25 million (£19 million) from ransomware in the previous two years.[2] More recently, research by Elliptic[3] has shown that the DarkSide ransomware group has received 57 payments following ransomware attacks. The group received $4.4 million alone from the crippling cyberattack on the highly digitised Colonial Pipeline on 8 May 2021, which led to widespread fuel shortages on the East Coast of the United States.[4] The news channel CNN reported that the ransomware attackers had used a compromised password to gain access to the company's computer networks. In its report CNN said:

> the revelation about how the hackers could force a critical supply chain company to its knees with something so simple underscores the grave risks posed not only by the opportunistic cybercriminals but also the lax digital hygiene of some major US businesses.[5]

In June 2021, American-based JBS, reputed to be the largest meat supplier in the world and heavily reliant on IT systems, was subjected to a ransomware attack, suspected to be carried out by a Russian criminal organisation. JBS notified the White House of the attack who in turn contacted the FBI. According to a US Treasury advisory note,[6] many cybercriminals are sharing resources to enhance the effectiveness of ransomware attacks, such as ransomware exploit kits that come with ready-made malicious codes and tools. The note also mentions these kits can be purchased, although they are also offered free of charge. In addition, there is evidence that some ransomware groups are also forming partnerships to share advice, code, trends, techniques and illegally-obtained information over shared platforms. A troubling trend is the emergence of RaaS providers on the Dark Web, where RaaS is an abbreviation for ransomware-as-a-service. According to security specialists

Sophos (www.sophos.com), RaaS providers give their customers fully functional ransomware with a dashboard to track victims and support services should they be required. In return, the authors of the RaaS portal ask for either a percentage of the ransom or a flat fee.[7] On 11 March 2021, Microsoft reported that cyber criminals had exploited vulnerabilities in Microsoft Exchange Servers to install ransomware on a network. Those businesses which suffer an attack are usually asked to contact the criminal via an anonymous email address or follow instructions on an anonymous web page to make payment. The payment is typically demanded in a cryptocurrency such as Bitcoin, in order to unlock computers or access affected data. However, even if businesses pay the ransom, there is no guarantee that they will get access to their computers, or their files. Occasionally malware is presented as ransomware (e.g. NotPetya), but after the ransom is paid the files are not decrypted.

Attacks on small businesses

When commenting on the focus of ransomware, Bill Conner, chief executive at security firm SonicWall said that medium and small companies were now being targeted with ransomware,[8] adding: 'But they are least prepared because they have the least money and they cannot go out and hire cyber-experts'. This visible new direction adopted by cybercriminals was echoed by Philipp Amann of Europol's European Cybercrime Centre in an article by the *NewScientist*: 'As criminals become more adept and the tools more sophisticated yet easier to obtain, fewer attacks are directed towards citizens and more towards small businesses [...] where greater potential profits lie'.[9] While the media continues to focus predominantly on ransomware incidents affecting the larger businesses, given the recognition that SMEs are the engine of the economy, more attention needs to be given to incidents impacting smaller businesses.

Step 4: Risk assessment

As described in the previous chapter, risk assessment consists of a sequence of activities which answer the questions: what are the possible business-critical problems my business may face? How likely are they? What impact will they have? And how soon will they impact? The key point here is that given the limited time and resources typically available to SMEs, the emphasis must be on business-critical issues. How well these questions can be answered depends on the research undertaken. A starting point is undertaking lessons learned. For large businesses operating over a number of years, they may have developed a database of events, recording how they were managed and what degree of success was achieved. However, for SMEs, they typically have to look outside of their business for lessons learned. In addition, as technology is moving so rapidly and cyber criminals are constantly evolving their approach and developing new malware, monitoring external sources of information has assumed greater importance.

Step 4A: Lessons learned

To appreciate the vulnerabilities of a business from a ransomware attack requires an appreciation of the sequence or pattern of these fraud events, the tools and techniques employed (described here as the mechanics), historical events (captured in case studies) together with 'red flags' or the 'alarm bells' over potential exposure, as illustrated in Figure 6.2. These activities contribute to Lessons Learned which in turn assist in deciding on the actions to be implemented, to thwart ransomware attacks.

Figure 6.2 Background to ransomware risk

 Understanding the pattern of ransomware fraud: When ransomware attacks first emerged, there were usually four steps to a sophisticated fraud. While these steps remain largely unchanged, recent attacks have also included the exfiltration of data, as described below and illustrated in Figure 6.3.

- **Installation:** The victim typically opens a malicious attachment to an email or downloads compromised software from a website where the software is offered free or at a discounted price.
- **Contact:** The malware contacts the fraudsters' server.
- **Encryption:** The malware encrypts the victim's files so that they cannot be opened and or takes a copy of the data and threatens to release it to the internet. The data taken can be customers' account details or precious intellectual property.
- **Fraud:** A message is sent to the victim's computer displaying a ransom deadline and the amount to be paid to a cryptocurrency account.

Capitalising on world events. Ransomware attacks typically involve the infection of computers with malicious software, often downloaded by clicking on seemingly innocuous links in emails or other website pop-ups and leaving users locked out of their systems, with the demand of a ransom to be paid to restore computer functions.[10] Emails with malicious embedded links or attachments were perpetuated during 2020 but took on a new dimension. As fraudsters endeavour to take advantage of events occurring on the world stage, they strove to capitalise on the emergence of COVID-19 and subsequent testing and vaccinations. So, individuals within organisations were targeted with emails similar to: 'Someone that you have been in contact with has tested positive. Please click on the link to find out who and the steps to follow'.

 Release of stolen data. The insurance market detected a marked change in the nature of the majority of ransomware attacks in 2020. Today's ransomware incidents are more likely to include a threat to release stolen data as opposed to encryption alone.[11] According to the Risk Insights report issued by specialist insurer Beazley, entitled 'Beazley Breach Insights Q3 2020',[12] during 2020 ransomware attacks 'developed a long way from the early incarnations of ransomware designed to trick an employee into clicking on a bad email that then encrypts a workstation and file shares'. The report considers ransomware attacks 'have reached new levels of complexity' whereby 'cyber extortion events are much more likely to involve threat actors who exploit access to networks, install highly

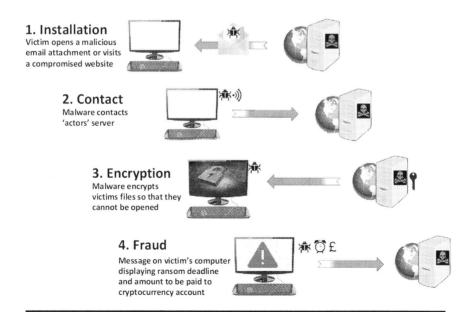

1. Installation
Victim opens a malicious email attachment or visits a compromised website

2. Contact
Malware contacts 'actors' server

3. Encryption
Malware encrypts victims files so that they cannot be opened

4. Fraud
Message on victim's computer displaying ransom deadline and amount to be paid to cryptocurrency account

Figure 6.3 The pattern of ransomware fraud

persistent malware, target backups, steal data, and threaten to expose the compromise'. Threat actors now typically access a network, carry out reconnaissance and examine the data stored on it. Frequently, they are now also exfiltrating data and uploading it to an external site, both to prove that they have access to it and to threaten to release it. It is assumed the criminals believe that the release of the exfiltrated data would be more harmful to a company than just encrypting data.

 Understanding the mechanics of ransomware fraud: Still, the most common method (adopted by fraudsters) to instigate a ransomware attack is by sending a malicious email that has malware attached to a link or an attachment. Ransomware can be delivered in various ways including via attachments in an authentic-looking email purporting to be from a genuine company. According to software company Kaspersky,[13] the two main forms of malware that are currently widespread are:

 Blocker ransomware which locks users out of basic computer functions. For example, it might deny access to a desktop by partially disabling files the computer uses to boot. The victim could still use their computer to pay the ransom, but otherwise, it would be useless. On the upside, locker type malware typically avoids encrypting critical files in favour of simply locking the victim out, and hence there is less chance of total data destruction.

 Crypto ransomware which encrypts a business' critical data such as documents, photos and videos, while leaving more basic computer functions untouched. Crypto creators often include a countdown in their ransom demand.

In 2017, several new ransomware infections spread across the world.

 WannaCry: The most infamous ransomware virus was called WannaCry and infected 200,000 computers in at least 150 countries, including causing notable disruption to the National Health Service in the UK.[14] Among those impacted were Telefonica, the Spanish telephone operator, Renault the French car manufacturer and logistics company FedEx in the US.

 Petya: McAfee advise the ransomware named Petya was first discovered in March 2016 with a variant containing additional capability circulating later in the same year.[15] It was not until June 2017 that the latest variant of Petya emerged which took down organizations across the globe in a matter of hours. The ransomware takes over computers and demands $300, paid in Bitcoin. The malware encrypts the part of the hard drive that manages file location and prevents the computer from booting up, making the computer and its files inaccessible.[16] The malicious software spreads rapidly across an organization once a computer is infected using the EternalBlue vulnerability in Microsoft Windows or through two Windows administrative tools.[17] (Microsoft subsequently released a patch.)

'It has a better mechanism for spreading itself than WannaCry', said Ryan Kalember, of cybersecurity company Proofpoint.

It is clear from the government and other websites there is a proliferation of cybercrime tools with existing tools being modified or updated and new software emerging all of the time.

 Infection 'Vectors': According to the UK's National Cyber Security Centre (NCSC) Cybercrime botnets[18] such as Emotet, Dridex and Trickbot are commonly used as an initial infection vector (communication method), prior to retrieving and installing the ransomware. Cyber security companies have also described Pen-testing tools such as Cobalt Strike being used. Ransomware such as Ryuk, LockerGoga, Bitpaymer and Dharma have been prevalent more recently.

 Bad Rabbit malware gains access to computers when users download what they think is an installer for Adobe Flash. Once it activates, it tries to spread to other devices on the network, guessing passwords to gain access. It draws on a list of usernames and passwords buried inside the malware. Bad Rabbit encrypts both user files and the computer's boot files.[19] It demands in order of $280 in bitcoins to be paid on a website accessible through the Tor browser.

 Case studies: Case studies provide a rich source of information in terms of how entry was gained to a company's systems, the behaviour of the fraudsters, what information was compromised and how the attack was resolved. A reoccurring theme among case studies of cybercrime committed by external actors is the purchase and application of 'off the shelf' tools. These tools allow the less technically proficient criminals to commit cybercrime. Their appeal is growing as awareness of the potential profits of fraud becomes more widespread.

 Case Study 6.1 describes the thwarted ransom attack on the car company Tesla which illustrates that criminals have amended their approach from not only locking files but also to include extracting data and threatening to make the information public. In this instance, the threat actors clearly considered that the release of commercially sensitive information would be more damaging than encrypting files. Exfiltrating data would have been disastrous for Tesla which has developed leading edge battery technology which if made public would undermine their competitive advantage. Over time it would have led to the loss of market share, a fall in sales, a drop in the share price and job losses. This approach provides an additional lever for criminals to extort greater sums from the victim.

 Case Study 6.2 describes a successful cyberattack on another automotive group which not only exfiltrated data but also compromised backup data. In this instance, a ransomware negotiator was engaged with the aim of lowering the level of the ransomware demand, which was successfully accomplished.

Case Study 6.1: Ransomware fraud

Car company Tesla avoids ransomware attack

Elon Musk, the chief executive of Tesla confirmed the electric car maker had been targeted by a ransomware hacker planning to extort money from the company. Tesla attracts considerable attention as it is now reported to have a market capitalisation of around $465 billion. It leads the U.S. in electric vehicle sales and the hackers could have obtained valuable information from battery chemistry to manufacturing techniques and costs. Tesla has reported the factory has cut battery cell costs through innovative manufacturing. A Russian speaking employee at a Tesla factory in Nevada was offered $1 million (as well as an upfront payment of 1 bitcoin, worth some $11,000) to install malware onto Tesla's computer network. However, the employee didn't carry out the plan but instead alerted other Tesla staff who contacted the FBI. On 3 September 2020, a federal grand jury in the District of Nevada returned an indictment charging a 27-year-old Russian national for his role in a conspiracy to intentionally cause damage to a protected computer. The indictment alleged that the Russian citizen attempted to recruit an employee of the car maker located in Sparks, Nevada, with the purpose of introducing malicious software into the company's computer network, extracting data from the network and subsequently extorting ransom money from the company under the threat of making the extracted data public. According to the indictment, from about July 16, 2020, to about 22 August 2020, the Russian citizen conspired with associates to recruit an employee to introduce malware onto the computer network of the employee's company. The malware would purportedly provide the Russian and his co-conspirators with access to the data within the computer system. After the malware was introduced, the Russian and his co-conspirators planned to extract data from the network and then threaten to make the information public, unless the company paid their ransom demand. If convicted, the Russian faces a statutory maximum sentence of five years in prison and a $250,000 fine. He also faces a period of supervised release, restitution, and monetary penalties. (An indictment merely alleges that crimes have been committed. The defendant is presumed innocent until proven guilty beyond a reasonable doubt). The investigation was led by the FBI's Las Vegas Field Office.

Source: Adapted from *Forbes:* "Elon Musk Confirms 'Serious' Russian Bitcoin Ransomware Attack On Tesla, Foiled By The FBI". https://www.forbes.com/sites/

billybambrough/2020/09/01/elon-musk-confirms-serious-russian-bitcoin-ransomware-attack-on-tesla-foiled-by-the-fbi/?sh=4a96e7ff3492; *ABC news:* "Elon Musk confirms thwarted cyberattack at Nevada Gigafactory". https://abcnews.go.com/Business/elon-musk-confirms-thwarted-russian-cyberattack-nevada-gigafactory/story?id=72676615; the Department of Justice, U.S. Attorney's Office, District of Nevada: "Russian National Indicted for Conspiracy to Introduce Malware into a Computer Network". https://www.justice.gov/opa/pr/russian-national-indicted-conspiracy-introduce-malware-computer-network; *BBC News:* "Russian pleads guilty to Tesla ransomware plot"https://www.bbc.co.uk/news/world-us-canada-56469475.

Case Study 6.2: Ransomware fraud

Car company compromised by ransomware attack

An automotive group was attacked with eGregor ransomware. Employee information was encrypted and backup systems were compromised. The threat actor provided proof they had exfiltrated employee data, however they had not exfiltrated any customer data, which was protected on a separate platform. The cyber extortion demand was set at nearly $500K. Forensic investigation revealed the company's ransomware demand was most likely triggered by a malicious email sent from a compromised email account outside the organisation. With their insurer's assistance, the company engaged privacy counsel, forensics and a ransom negotiator. Over the course of several days, the ransom negotiator succeeded in lowering the demand to $50K. Because their backups were compromised, the automotive group made the decision to pay the demand. The threat actor provided the decryption key and confirmed deletion of exfiltrated data, and the automotive group was able to decrypt their data and return to normal operations.

Source: Adapted from: *Beazley:* "Beazley Breach Insights Q3 2020", 16 December 2020. https://www.beazley.com/news/2020/beazley_breach_insights_q3.html.

Case Study 6.3 describes the highly publicised cyberattack on the foreign exchange company Travelex and the subsequent ransom demand. From reports at the time, Travelex had been notified of vulnerabilities to its systems but did not act promptly to address them.

Case Study 6.3: Ransomware fraud

Travelex's websites across Europe, Asia and the US were taken offline due to a ransomware attack

In December 2019 foreign exchange company Travelex which has a presence in 70 countries, was held to ransom by cyber criminals. The criminals demanded $4.6 million to be paid within seven days. The incident reduced the company's share price by almost 20% to a record low. Travelex's websites across Europe, Asia and the US were taken offline. As of 7 January 2020, visitors to Travelex.co.uk were met with a message stating the service 'is temporarily unavailable due to planned maintenance'. Travelex was forced to take down its website after Sodinokibi ransomware took hold on New Year's Eve, which is thought to have been timed while many of the firm's staff were on holiday. Sodinokibi (also known as REvil), first appeared in April 2019 which is ransomware that can be 'rented' and customised by criminals to target their own victims for a cut of the profits. The attackers claimed that on payment of the ransom in Bitcoin (to a domain registered in China) they would restore either Travelex's IT systems or protect its customers' data. The attackers claimed that if they did not receive the ransom by an undisclosed deadline, they would release 5GB of customers' personal information into the public domain, including social security numbers, dates of birth and payment card details. On 17 January 2020, in a video message on Travelex's website, CEO Tony D'Souza announced that the IT systems in-store were now operating but some systems still remained offline. However, this meant that customers were still unable to order currency online, either from Travelex itself or through the network of banks that use its services, including HSBC, Virgin Money, Barclays, Lloyds, RBS, and the finance websites of Sainsbury's and Tesco. Brett Callow of security firm Emsisoft, when contacted by Sky News said 'Ransomware groups are now stealing data prior to encrypting it, meaning that ransomware incidents are now effectively data breaches'. More significantly he said 'The fact that Travelex appears not to have patched servers which it had been notified were vulnerable can only be described as shockingly negligent'.

The Metropolitan Police is leading the investigation into the attack, and claims 'enquiries into the circumstances are ongoing'. The National Cyber Security Centre said it was providing technical support.

Source: Adapted from *ComputerWeekly*: "Cyber gangsters demand payment from Travelex after 'Sodinokibi' attack". https://www.computerweekly.com/

news/252476283/Cyber-gangsters-demand-payment-from-Travelex-after-Sodinokibi-attack; the *BBC:* "Travelex being held to ransom by hackers". https://www.bbc.co.uk/news/business-51017852; *Reuters:* "Forex firm Travelex says ransomware behind last week's cyberattack". https://www.reuters.com/article/us-britain-travelex-idUSKBN1Z62KD, *Evening Standard:* "Travelex 'being held to ransom' by New Year's Eve cyber attackers", https://www.standard.co.uk/news/crime/travelex-website-down-police-hackers-a4328621.html; and *Sky News:* "Travelex down to pen and paper as it suffers ransomware attack". https://news.sky.com/story/police-investigating-ransomware-attack-on-currency-exchange-travelex-11903064.

Case Study 6.4 illustrates the importance of backing up data. Companies are still paying ransom demands as they feel they have no choice if their business is to survive. However, there is no guarantee that a business's computer system will be unlocked if it pays the hackers. Businesses should consider seeking professional help. Refer to the sections below headed 'Risk Process: Response actions' for pre-emptive actions and 'Immediate response' if a ransom demand has been made.

Case Study 6.4: Ransomware fraud

SME is subject to a ransomware attack

A member of staff within an SME opened an email and clicked on a link that in fact contained malware. The malware infected the computer system and encrypted all files so that no access could be gained by members of staff. The criminals contacted the company giving it 24 hours to pay £300 in Bitcoin to unlock their system. The company was particularly vulnerable as they had not backed up their files. They had not heard of Bitcoin or how to source them and had to employ a computer consultant at short notice to enable them to make the payment. Once the Bitcoins were obtained payment was sent to the criminals who then provided access to the system.

Source: The Little Book of Big Scams, business edition. Published by the *Metropolitan Police Service*. https://www.met.police.uk/SysSiteAssets/media/downloads/central/advice/fraud/met/little-book-of-big-scams-business-edition.pdf.

Red flags: Sometimes the way people or organisations behave might suggest they are committing a fraud. The signs are referred to as 'red flags'. Defending against ransomware attacks as with other frauds requires employees to be *constantly* wary and vigilant. Regardless of whether they receive over 100 emails a day, they must slow down and think before responding, opening attachments or clicking on links. Attackers expect staff, particularly those under time pressure, to take action before considering the risks. Consequently, employees need to do the opposite.

Here are some of the ransomware attack red flags businesses need to be aware of. They relate to how the business is managed and how employees behave in terms of not taking proactive steps to limit their exposure to ransomware attacks.

- Lack of understanding of the consequences of an incident and how it will affect the business in the future. Lack of recognition that these attacks are not just about loss of data, there can be real disruption and significant impacts.
- System updates not installed on all devices as soon as they become available.
- Anti-virus software not installed on all devices and kept up to date.
- Regular backups of important/business-critical files are not created and uploaded to a device that is not left connected to the network.
- Lack of prevention of the delivery of malicious files being sent via phishing emails, typically achieved by restricting the file-types permitted by email and web filtering tools.
- Not restricting access to social media sites and unsavoury websites on workstations or laptops.
- Delaying the deployment of multi-factor authentication on all externally accessible services, critical internal services and services used by managed service providers to access internal systems leading to the abuse of compromised credentials.
- Failing to restrict membership of local administrator groups.
- Failing to set up unique random passwords on default local administrator accounts.
- Not insisting on the use of strong passwords to protect typically highly privileged service accounts to prevent hackers from logging in interactively.
- Not limiting the ability for attackers to gain access to sensitive data which could be achieved by restricting access to open network shares and other potentially sensitive data stores (e.g., Intranet and file servers).
- Not limiting the ability for attackers to exploit vulnerable systems by not adopting patches and accepting software upgrades.
- Not improving the ability to detect and respond to attacker activity by deploying additional security tooling, notably Endpoint Detection and Response technology or anti-virus products which interface with Microsoft Windows.

Step 4B: Risk identification

Any business should look for potential weaknesses that may undermine its security and provide opportunities for fraudulent activity. The 'four steps in an attack' provides a high-level vehicle for examining any vulnerabilities in the business. The actual vulnerabilities of any business will be dependent on the actual nature of its business, its maturity, its day-to-day processes, its policies and the awareness training provided to staff. A threat is broken into several components, how these components are articulated is critical to how that risk is viewed, understood and managed. 'Because of a [cause], a [threat event] may occur, which should it materialise would lead to an [impact] on the business's objectives'. The common 'cause' is the motivation of individuals to secure financial gain from as many businesses as possible. There is no let-up from the tidal wave of ransom demands. A list of causes is included in Table 6.1. It is not exhaustive and is only intended as a guide. The resultant potential threats are included in Table 6.2.

Table 6.1 Causes behind ransomware attacks

Ransomware attack threats (Cause → Threat → Impact)	
The **causes** or triggers behind fraudulent activity	
Policy	Cyber security policy is not prepared or prepared and signed off but is not disseminated whereby mandated obligations in terms of cyber security are not known and acted upon.
Induction processes	Cyber security is not an integral part of the induction processes relying on the training programme where training is only provided very periodically.
Training	Cyber security training is ad-hoc, not kept up to date and not provided on a regular basis.
Downloads	Employee downloads a software file from a website offering a free download.
Attachment	Employee opens an attachment on an unsolicited email that contains malware.
Firewall	Computers are not protected by a firewall.
Use of firewall	Firewall is switched off, is disabled, contains many exceptions, has open ports or is circumnavigated.
Anti-virus software	An up-to-date, real-time, anti-malware solution from a vendor trusted by the business is not installed.
Fake anti-virus	Fake ant-virus software loaded onto a business computer unwittingly downloads malware. Users operate as computer administrators or local administrators, and are able to install software themselves.

(Continued)

Ransomware attack threats (Cause → Threat → Impact)	
Flash drive	Employee inserts a flash drive found in the office into their computer unwittingly which downloads malware.
Software updates	Software updates notified by a software manufacturer are not downloaded immediately and overlooked for a long period, including software from Microsoft, Adobe, Oracle, Java and others.
Data backup	Data is not backed up regularly or not backed up to a remote location that cannot be accessed directly from the business network.
Audits	Cyber security audits are not undertaken on a regular cycle to check for vulnerabilities.
Feedback	Results from cyber security audits are not implemented promptly.
SPF	Strict Sender Policy Framework (SPF) checks for all inbound email messages, verifying the validity of sending organisations, are not enforced.
Email phishing	Employees click on links or open attachments from untrusted sources – malicious emails (phishing) are one of the most common ways staff encounter ransomware.
Malware link delivery channels	Data is not regularly backed up. Cloud storage services such as SkyDrive are not used to safely store data. These services are now fully integrated into Windows 10 and Microsoft Office.
URL phishing links	Employee opens the link to a phishing website delivered in emails, texts, social media messages and online ads. Attacks hide links in hyperlinked text or buttons, using link-shortening tools or deceptively spelled URLs.

Table 6.2 Potential threats arising from the causes

Threats (uncertain events)	
Ransomware attack	An external actor encrypts data (and in some instances exfiltrates data and threatens to sell or leak it).
Backup	Backup files are encrypted (if backups are accessible from the same network without any subdivision or barriers).
Payment	Despite payment, the external 'actor' does not provide decryption keys to decrypt the data.

The impact descriptions below cannot address all possible scenarios and hence are generic in nature and need to be tailored to the business, its context and ongoing operations. A ransomware attack if successful can be very damaging. Its impact will depend on a number of aspects such as whether data has been copied, corrupted, deleted, shared or 'simply' locked and how long it takes to recover (Table 6.3).

Table 6.3 Ransom attack impact descriptions

Impact descriptions (if the threats were to materialise)	
Loss of reputation	While a business may strive to keep the incidence of an attack quiet, it may be leaked by a third party or unwittingly by a member of staff who makes an entry on social media 'friends' saying 'no work today as all of our data has been encrypted and the business is at a standstill'. It is typically one of the consequences of an attack that causes reputational damage rather than the attack itself due to, say, disruption to its operations, late delivery of its services or products, release of its customer or employee details or late payment of its suppliers or staff.
Time	Business interruption can last days, weeks or months depending on whether a ransom is paid and files are decrypted, a ransom is paid but files are not decrypted and stolen data is not returned or the business decides not to pay the ransom and needs to restore systems and data.
Cost	Businesses subject to a ransom demand suffer the cost of the ransom payment (or some lower figure negotiated with the criminals that instigated the attack) or if the ransom is not paid, loss of business, consultancy fees and IT restoration costs. If a ransom is paid, there is no guarantee that there will not be another ransom attack in quick succession by another group before protection can be put in place.
Director stress	A ransomware attack can be highly stressful while determining the course of action to follow, who the attack should be reported to, whether an attempt should be made to use decryption tools, or which consultant or firm to turn to for advice – all the while the ransom payment demands keep increasing and the business is still incurring operational costs while no income is coming in.

Step 4C: Risk analysis

When examining the characteristics of a potential threat, it commonly involves estimating the likelihood, the impact (in cost and time together with other parameters when appropriate) and the proximity (when is the threat likely to materialise). Included in Table 6.4 is a descriptive analysis of the likelihood, impact and proximity; however, where possible businesses need to capture actual figures for the different categories.

Step 5: Response actions

Specific response actions: people, systems, connectivity and data

Included in Figure 6.4 are specific response actions that should be considered with regard to the topics of people, systems, connectivity and data. The actions

Table 6.4 Ransomware attack risk analysis

Analysis of ransom demand risks	
Likelihood	According to UK company JC Cyber Security, some 71% of cyberattacks are on SMEs. According to the BBC, the UK's National Cyber Security Centre has reported that it handled more than three times as many ransomware incidents in 2020 than it had in the previous year. According to the Home Secretary's speech to the National Cyber Security Centre's Cyber UK on 11 May 2021, nearly two out of every five businesses in the UK identified at least one cyber security breach or attack in the last 12 months.
Financial impact	According to the UK's Department for Digital, Culture, Media and Sports Cyber Security Breaches Survey 2021, while ransomware attacks are less common than phishing attacks, the damage they can inflict on organisations is often more substantial.
Time impact	While it has not been possible to verify their website claim, UK company JC Cyber Security says that it is a fact that 60% of SMEs are forced to close down within six months after being targeted by a cyberattack.
Proximity	Ransomware attacks are relentless. While not as frequent as phishing emails, ransomware attacks still represent a significant threat for all organisations to consider.

that a business chooses to adopt will depend on its number of personnel, the number and disbursement of offices and its short-term expansion plans. Over burdensome controls can be counter-productive whereas superficial controls can leave a business vulnerable. One size does not fit all and every approach needs to be tailored to the business's unique circumstances. Increasingly organisations are looking to understand the availability, costs and benefits of insuring against ransomware. The key message is to maintain backups of data as many ransomware variants attempt to find and delete any accessible backups. Maintaining offline and up-to-date backups is critical as it means there is no need to pay a ransom for data that is readily accessible to the business.

Step 6: Implementation of actions

Included in Table 6.5 is a short overview of key information on dealing with ransomware attacks.

Immediate response

Action Fraud provides guidance on the steps to follow if the business has been the victim of a ransom demand:

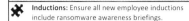

Your People	Your Systems
Inductions: Ensure all new employee inductions include ransomware awareness briefings.	**Hardware and software:** Remove unsupported or unauthorized hardware and software from systems.
Training: Ensure the delivery of regular ongoing, comprehensive cyber security awareness training to all employees across all business functions, to help employees be alert, wary and vigilant. The importance of training cannot be overstated. Consider the Cyber Essentials Scheme - a government-backed, industry-supported scheme to help organisations protect themselves against common online threats.*	**Inventories:** Maintain inventories of hardware and software assets to know what is in-play and at-risk from attack.
Flash drives: Never let staff insert unfamiliar USB flash drives or other removal storage devices into company computers if their origin is not known. Cybercriminals may have infected the device with ransomware and left it in a public space to lure employees into using it.	**Verification:** Enforce strict Sender Policy Framework (SPF) checks for all inbound email messages, verifying the validity of the sending organisations. Filter all inbound messages for malicious content including executables, macro-enabled documents and links to malicious sites.
Passwords: Make sure passwords are hard to guess. Password managers can generate long, complex and random passwords, and remember them for retrieval. Ensure a really strong password is created for the password manager itself so that a criminal cannot gain access to all passwords at once. The NCSC's password guidance is very helpful. Web-accessible services should be supported by two-factor authentication.	**Unsolicited emails:** If SPF is not in place, ensure staff do not open attachments or click on the links within any unsolicited emails the company receives. Spoofed emails purporting to be from a person or company the business regularly trades with can be used to deliver ransomware. Alternatively malicious emails may have come from a trusted supplier who has themselves been compromised.
Tests: Conduct organization-wide phishing tests to gauge user awareness and reinforce the importance of identifying potentially malicious emails.	**Anti-virus software:** Use anti-virus software on all devices, and where possible, configure the software to automatically update.
Phishing: Help employees learn how to spot phishing and malware emails which will empower them to help protect computers and the network.	**Regular scans:** Run a complete scan of the system at regular intervals to check for any malware infections.
Blacklisting: Limit the potential for employees to visit harmful and malicious websites by restricting access through the use of blacklisting software.	**A-V updates:** Immediately install all updates (patches) provided by the anti-virus software supplier as and when they are issued.
Escalation: Have a clear escalation procedure so that employees know where to send a suspicious email, including the wording 'Warning' in the header to avoid the email and suspect attachments being opened inadvertently by another employee.	**Hard drives:** Make sure any USB hard drives are not connected to a business computer when not in use (and ideally kept in a safe). If it is plugged in when the company becomes a victim of a ransomware attack, this data will also be encrypted.
Lessons learned: Maintain awareness of current events related to cybersecurity, using lessons learned and reported events to encourage staff to remain vigilant against the current threat environment and agile to cybersecurity trends. Instruct staff not to enable macros in document attachments received via email. Microsoft deliberately turned off auto-execution of macros by default many years ago as a security measure. A lot of malware infections rely on persuading recipients to turn macros back on.	**System access:** Put in place appropriate measures for general user and system access across the organisation: only provide privileged access for critical assets (servers, end-points, applications, databases, etc.) for those with a specific need-to-know and enforce multi-factor authentication (MFA) where appropriate.

Figure 6.4 Steps to reduce the incidence of a ransomware fraud

Note: *The Government worked with the Information Assurance for Small and Medium Enterprises (IASME) consortium and the Information Security Forum (ISF) to develop Cyber Essentials, a set of basic technical controls to help organisations protect themselves against common online security threats.

Downloads: Ensure staff browse and download only official versions of software and always from trusted websites. Where possible, downloads should be under the strict control of the IT function/department.

Software updates: Install the latest software and app updates on all of your devices. These updates will often contain important security upgrades which help protect your device from viruses and hackers. Remove unsupported software—if this is not possible, isolate the computer from the network.

Public Wi-Fi: When staff use public Wi-Fi, the business computer system is more vulnerable to attack. Staff should avoid public Wi-Fi if at all possible.

Red flag : Establish a red flag notice which is automatically triggered when a member of staff receives an email from outside the organisation. Change it periodically so users don't get used to it and ignore it.

User permissions: Regularly review and remove user permissions that are no longer required, to limit the malware's ability to spread.

Response plan: Create, maintain and exercise a basic cyber incident response plan and associated communication plan that includes response and notification procedures.

Normal activity: Baseline and analyse network activity over a period of months to determine behavioural patterns so that normal, legitimate activity by personnel can be more easily distinguished from anomalous network activity (e.g., normal vs anomalous account activity).

Software: Use application directory allowlisting (such as AppLocker) on all assets to ensure that only authorised software can run, and all unauthorised software is blocked from executing Conduct regular vulnerability scanning to identify and address vulnerabilities.

Administration: Ensure system administrators avoid using their accounts for email and web browsing (to prevent malware being able to run with their high level of system privilege).

Devices: Ensure devices are properly configured and the security features are enabled.

MFA: Use Multi-Factor Authentication (MFA) to authenticate users so that if malware steals credentials, they can't easily be reused

Network segmentation: Employ logical or physical means of network segmentation to separate various business unit or departmental IT resources within your organization as well as to maintain separation between IT and operational technology.

Your Connectivity

Policies: Develop IT policies and procedures addressing changes in user status (transfers, termination, etc.).

Controlled access: Grant access and admin permissions based on need-to-know and least privilege. Ensure unique passwords for all user accounts.

Defence layers : Adopt a 'defence-in-depth' approach. This means using layers of defence with several mitigations at each layer.

Attack plan: Plan for an attack, regardless of whether the business thinks it is unlikely. Develop an internal and external stakeholder communication strategy for prompt notification. Determine how the business will respond to the ransom demand and the threat of the business's data being published. Ensure that incident management guides and supporting resources such as checklists and contact details are available if access to computer systems is unavailable.

Your Data

Standard: Develop a Data Management Standard that describes the requirements for data management.

Encrypt files: When exchanging confidential information outside of the company, consider encrypting files using UK government-recommended software.

Automated backups: Check that any automated backups are actually occurring and undertake test restores to ensure the integrity and validity of the data. Validating backups is just as important as setting them up. Ensure data that is backed up is encrypted.

Regular backup: Maintain offline backups. For micro businesses, back up all important business data (ideally daily) to an external hard drive. Make sure it is not connected to a business computer when not in use. If it is plugged in when the company becomes a victim of a ransomware attack, this data will also be encrypted. If there is concern that a routine backup will be forgotten, then take advantage of automatic cloud backup services or set up calendar reminders for the business.

Figure 6.4 (*Continued*)

Dummy run : Like a fire alarm, test the business's incident management plan. This will assist in clarifying the roles and responsibilities of staff and third parties and to prioritise system recovery. Run the scenario that if a widespread ransomware attack meant a complete shutdown of the network, consideration needs to be given to how long it would take to restore the minimum required number of devices and files for business operation.

Reporting: Identify the business's legal obligations regarding the reporting of incidents to regulators, and understand how to approach this.

Inventories: Maintain inventories of network connections (user accounts, suppliers, business partners, etc.).

RDP: Employ best practices for a remote desk protocol (RDP) and other remote desktop services as recommended by Microsoft. RDP enables the building of safe connections between computers on the internet.

Third parties: Take into consideration the risk management and cyber hygiene practices of third parties or managed service providers (MSPs) your organisation relies on to meet its mission. MSPs have been an infection route for ransomware impacting client organisations.

Third party: When outsourcing the storage of digital data to a third party, check ease of access and retrieval for business purposes as well as for possible audits, litigation defence, response to tax payment enquiries and regulator questions. Speed of retrieval will be vital if the system has been compromised by a ransomware attack. In addition, consideration needs to be given to security of the data, ability to set levels of access and the creation and maintenance of a retrievals log. Access should be via a web browser so that data can be accessed from any location at any time.

Document systems: Use access-controlled document collaboration systems such as SharePoint or OneDrive. Ensure access permissions are maintained and reviewed on a regular basis.

Travel overseas: Ensure staff do not take devices overseas without consent as they could be targeted by criminals.

Scanning: Scan backups for malware before you restore files. Ransomware may have infiltrated your network over a period of time, and replicated to backups before being discovered.

Data compromise: A ransomware infection may be evidence of a previous, unresolved network compromise. For example, many ransomware infections are the result of existing malware infections, such as TrickBot, Dridex and Emotet.

Figure 6.4 ***(Continued)***

Don't pay: Don't pay extortion demands as they only feed into criminals' hands, and there's no guarantee that access to your files or device will be restored if you do pay. Criminals have been known to re-target victims that have already paid a ransom once; paying a ransom only highlights to criminals that you're vulnerable to a ransomware attack. Even after you've paid the ransom, and access to your files is restored, it's possible for criminals to leave a 'backdoor' installed on your device which can later be used to re-infect. As reported by the BBC,[20] Europol's head of the European Cybercrime Centre, Steven Wilson has said 'Companies need to understand that if you pay a ransom it perpetuates the crime. It encourages the criminals to commit further crimes [and] you're fuelling organised crime on a global basis'. All organisations such as the Metropolitan Police Service, Europol and Interpol recommend not paying the ransom as it encourages criminals to perpetuate the crime.

Ransomware removal: Sometimes it's possible to remove a ransomware infection without paying the criminals. 'No More Ransom' (www.nomoreransom.org) has been set up with the goal to help victims of ransomware retrieve their encrypted data without having to pay the criminals. If you are still unable to remove the ransomware, seek professional technical help from a trustworthy

Table 6.5 Short overview of support information

Overview of key support information in tackling ransomware attacks

Report
 	
■ Report cyber security incidents to:
  ■ the NCSC by visiting https://report.ncsc.gov.uk/
  ■ The Action Fraud website
 	
Reporting responsibilities
■ Identify your legal obligations regarding the reporting of incidents to regulators (when required) and understand how to approach this.
 	
Decryption
■ The 'No More Ransom' project provides a collection of decryption tools and other resources from the main anti-malware vendors, which may help; however, resolution of a ransom attack is not guaranteed.
 	
Support
■ The NCSC runs a commercial scheme called Cyber Incident Response, where certified companies provide support to affected organisations.
 	
Remediation
■ The NCSC has jointly published an advisory: Technical Approaches to Uncovering and Remediating Malicious Activity, which provides more detailed information about remediation processes.
 	
Membership
■ The Cyber Security Information Sharing Partnership (CiSP) offers organisations in the UK a safe portal to discuss and share intelligence that can assist the community and raise the UK's cyber resilience.
 	
Certification
■ Consider the Cyber Essentials Certification scheme (which covers a number of these mitigations), so your customers and partners can see that you have addressed these risks.

source. No More Ransom (NMR) is a joint initiative by Europol's European Cybercrime Centre, the National High Tech Crime Unit of the Netherlands' police and McAfee to help victims of ransomware retrieve their encrypted data without having to pay the criminals. According to Europol[21] NMR was launched in July 2016, has assisted more than 200,000 people. It has grown to include over 150 supporting partners from law enforcement, to the private sector and academia. The resources are available in 36 different languages, and it deploys more than 90 tools capable of decrypting over 100 different types of ransomware.

How NMR works:

■ The victim uploads two encrypted files and the ransomware note to the NMR Crypto Sheriff.

- The Crypto Sheriff matches the information against a list of available decryption tools.
- If there is a positive hit, the link to the tools is provided. The victim only needs to follow the instructions to unlock their files.
- If no tool is available at the time of contacting NMR, the victim is advised to continue checking in the future, as new tools are added on a regular basis.

Reporting: If you have been a victim, report it to Action Fraud. Every report made helps Action Fraud build a clearer picture of the threat from ransomware and allows the police to direct the focus of their investigations.

24/7 Reporting for businesses: If your business is currently experiencing a *live* cyberattack (an attack in progress), at the time of writing, Action Fraud request that you call them on 0300 123 2040 to speak with one of their specialist advisors. You should keep a timeline of events and save any information that is relevant to the attack.

Actions to implement in the short term

Lessons learned are drawn from the pattern and mechanics of ransomware fraud together with the case studies and the identification of red flag events.

 Stop hackers getting in: Provide: induction training for new employees, regular awareness training, tests for phishing emails and attach red flag notices to incoming emails from outside the business.

 Deploy blacklisting software: Use browse control web filter software recommended by a trusted source to proactively block high-risk websites to prevent employees from unintentionally infecting the business's network. Specific websites can be blocked such as Facebook as well as categories such as gambling, pornography, weapons and criminal activity. As an example, one supplier of the software is CurrentWare, which it is suggested would need to be validated by an independent third party before an appointment.

 Back up your data: Backing up data is critical for business continuity in the event of a ransomware attack but also in case the office premises are damaged due to: flooding, a fire, gas explosion, malicious employee behaviour, a partial structural collapse or a lightning strike, or deemed unsafe due to the discovery of asbestos, rising damp, settlement or the leaking of methane from the subsoil.

 Consider cloud computing: Data can be backed up using cloud computing services to overcome the limited space and flexibility of a hard drive. Typically, a cloud provider hosts a network of remote servers that store, process and manage huge volumes of data on the internet. Examples of cloud services include Microsoft Azure, the Amazon Cloud Drive, Cisco Cloud Solutions, Dropbox, Apple iCloud (for Apple products) and Google Drive. Key benefits include:

- Reliability: Cloud computing makes data backup, disaster recovery, and business continuity easier and less expensive because data can be mirrored at multiple sites on the cloud provider's network.
- Security: With cybercrime on the rise, there is intense scrutiny of a company's ability to protect its client's details. Many cloud providers offer a broad set of controls that strengthen business security overall, helping protect data, applications, and infrastructure from potential threats. Data that is stored in the cloud is encrypted to block hackers attempting to intercept files. Cloud security commonly exceeds the internal security of most SMEs.
- Cost savings: Cloud computing eliminates the capital expense of buying (and updating) hardware and software and setting up and running on-site servers. It avoids the worry of capacity planning and overloading in-house servers. It reduces space needs and power requirements.
- Speed: Most cloud computing services are provided self-service and on demand, so even large amounts of data can be accessed in minutes, typically with just a few mouse clicks, giving ease of access.
- Flexibility: Business employees can access data from servers remotely that are not hard-wired in-house servers and hence provides greater flexibility through remote working.
- Productivity: Cloud computing removes the need for many of the normal IT administrative tasks releasing employees to deliver the business's core goals.
- Technology: Development in digital technology is moving quickly and SMEs can struggle to keep up. Investment in cloud computing reduces the need to keep updating in-house hardware and software. Cloud computing services are regularly upgraded to the latest generation of fast and efficient computing hardware. This reduces the problem of having to work with legacy systems and can provide greater economies of scale.

Actions to implement in the long term

 Explore organisations that can support decryption: There are file decryption specialists who offer a ransomware recovery service who may also assist with finding a reliable cloud backup solution once the decryption process is complete. An example of a company providing ransom recovery and decryption services is ransomrecovery.co.uk (https://ransomrecovery.co.uk/ransomware/decryption-service/).

Cyber incidence response: Engage a cyber incidence response company on a retainer, based on a defined set of duties or responsibilities.

 Cyber insurance: Consider obtaining cyber insurance. This requires a clear understanding of the conditions of the insurance and what would constitute a breach whereby the policy becomes null and void.

Summary

As the common trigger for ransomware demands is the opening of an attachment to a malicious email a key response to this threat must be exercising extreme vigilance in opening attachments. The common guidance from government agencies together with Interpol and Europol is not to pay ransom demands as it perpetuates the crime. If your business has been the victim of ransomware then in the first instance, contact your IT department or third-party consultant. Then the business needs to contact the insurers if an insurance policy has been taken out. If appropriate, contact 'No More Ransome' for external support and possible decryption. In addition, notify the police and Action Fraud. Data important to the business should be backed up on a regular basis ensuring that it can be readily retrieved when needed.

Notes

1   Cybersecurity and Infrastructure Security Agency (CISA), "Ransomware Guidance and Resources". www.cisa.gov ransomware. CISA describes itself as the US's 'risk advisor, working with partners to defend against today's threats and collaborating to build more secure and resilient infrastructure for the future'.
2   BBC (2017) "Ransomware 'here to stay', warns Google study". Mark Ward, Technology correspondent, BBC News in Las Vegas. Published 27 July 2017. https://www.bbc.co.uk/news/technology-40737060.
3   A boutique company providing blockchain analytics for cryptoasset compliance.
4   Elliptic (2021) "Elliptic follows the Bitcoin Ransoms paid by colonial pipeline and other darkside ransomware victims". 14 May 2021 https://www.elliptic.co/blog/elliptic-follows-bitcoin-ransoms-paid-by-darkside-ransomware-victims.
5   CNN (2021) "Ransomware attackers used compromised password to access Colonial Pipeline network", 4 June 2021. Brian Fung and Geneva Sands.
6   US Treasury Financial Crimes Enforcement Network (FinCEN) (2020) "Advisory on ransomware and the use of the financial system to facilitate ransom payments". Reference FIN-2020-A006. October 1.
7   See "Ransomware as a service: how the bad guys marketed Philadelphia". https://nakedsecurity.sophos.com/2017/07/25/ransomware-as-a-service-how-the-bad-guys-marketed-philadelphia/ and "The dark web goes corporate", Josh Fruhlinger, CSO. 20 July 2017. https://www.csoonline.com/article/3208064/the-dark-web-goes-corporate.html.

8 BBC (2018) "Ransomware tops malicious attack charts". https://www.bbc.co.uk/news/technology-43713037.

9 New Scientist (2019) "Ransomware attacks are on the rise and the criminals are winning". 5 July 2019. Chris Stokel-Walker.

10 Reuters (2020) "Ransomware attacks on the rise even as cyber insurers scale back", 16 December 2020, Noor Zainab Hussain, Carolyn Cohn. https://www.reuters.com/article/us-cyber-insurance-idUSKBN28Q2JD.

11 Beazley (2020) "Ransomware severity and costs increase in 2020", 16 December 2020. https://www.beazley.com/news/2020/beazley_breach_insight_ransomware_severity_and_costs_increase_in_2020.html.

12 Beazley (2020) "Beazley Breach Insights Q3 2020", 16 December 2020. https://www.beazley.com/news/2020/beazley_breach_insights_q3.html.

13 https://usa.kaspersky.com/resource-center/threats/ransomware-threats-an-in-depth-guide.

14 BBC (2019) "How a ransomware attack cost one firm £45m". Joe Tidy, BBC Cyber-security reporter, Published 24 June 2019.

15 McAfee (2021) "What is Petya and NotPetya ransomware?" 1 January 2021. https://www.mcafee.com/enterprise/en-us/security-awareness/ransomware/petya.html#overview.

16 https://mobile.nytimes.com/2017/06/27/technology/ransomware-hackers.html.

17 The Guardian (2017) "'Petya' ransomware attack: what is it and how can it be stopped? Olivia Solon & Alex Hern". https://www.theguardian.com/technology/2017/jun/27/petya-ransomware-cyber-attack-who-what-why-how.

18 A network of private computers infected with malicious software and controlled as a group without the owners' knowledge, e.g. to send spam.

19 Sophos (2017) "Bad Rabbit ransomware outbreak". 24 October 2017. https://nakedsecurity.sophos.com/2017/10/24/bad-rabbit-ransomware-outbreak/.

20 BBC (2019) "How a ransomware attack cost one firm £45m". Joe Tidy, BBC Cyber-security reporter, Published 24 June 2019.

21 Europol: "No more ransom – do you need help unlocking your digital life". Public awareness and prevention https://www.europol.europa.eu/activities-services/public-awareness-and-prevention-guides/no-more-ransom-do-you-need-help-unlocking-your-digital-life.

Chapter 7

Intellectual property fraud

Structure of Chapter 7

Chapter 7 is subdivided into the following four sections. An overview of the fraud type is provided followed by an assessment of the threat posed by the fraud, suggested response actions and timing of implementation (Figure 7.1).

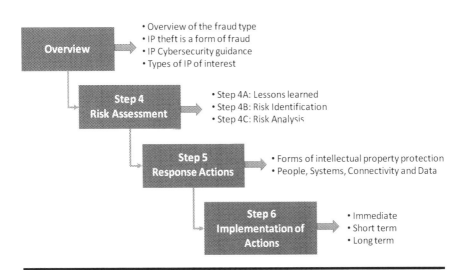

Figure 7.1 Structure of Chapter 7

DOI: 10.4324/9781003200383-9

Overview

Intellectual property (IP) is often described as the lifeblood of many organisations. The significance of IP is described within a recent government report entitled 'Inovation increases productivity, grows markets and creates jobs'.[1] The same report highlights that there is evidence which shows that UK firms that innovate, grow at around twice the rate of those that don't. The importance of IP to the UK economy is underlined by the report's statement 'the UK is a global leader in innovation, ranked 5th in the World Intellectual Property Office's Global Innovation Index 2019'. Intellectual property has been described as something that individuals create using their minds. Intellectual property can: have more than one owner; belong to people or businesses; and be sold or transferred. Having the right type of intellectual property protection helps a business stop other businesses from stealing or copying: the names of its products or brands; its inventions; the design or the look of its products; and the things it writes, makes or produces. Copyright, patents, designs and trade-marks are all types of intellectual property protection. Europol reports[2]: 'IP crime is often seen as a "victimless" crime, causing relatively "little" harm'. However, in addition to causing harm to companies owning IP (particularly SMEs), it is damaging to economies as a whole. Europol also advises that in many cases IP crime is conducted by OCGs (Organised Crime Groups) who can cause damage to the health and well-being of consumers, the environment and society. Given the significance of IP, the CSO (cyber security information) website expressively observes 'now more than ever, it's a target, placed squarely in the cross-hairs by various forms of cyberattack'.[3] Perpetrators of cybercrime are seeking highly prized business secrets (not already disclosed through patents) and proprietary business information that can quickly be translated into financial gain. Proprietary business information may include for example geological survey information of precious metals or details of mergers and acquisitions. Apart from OGCs, IP theft is also sponsored by rival businesses and hostile states seeking prized designs and technology to provide an operational or technological advantage. In a speech at MI5's Thames House headquarters, the head of the Security Service (MI5), Mr Ken McCallum said following hostile state espionage 'we see businesses hollowed out by the loss of advantage they've worked painstakingly to build'. He went on to say

> given half a chance, hostile actors will short-circuit years of patient British research or investment. This is happening at scale.[4] And it affects us all. UK jobs, UK public services, UK futures.

Further reading is included in Appendix 4.

IP theft is a form of fraud. Section 5 of the Fraud Act 2006 defines the meaning of 'gain' and 'loss' for the purposes of Sections 2 to 4 of the Act.

The definitions are essentially the same as those in Section 34(2)(a) of the Theft Act 1968. Under these definitions, 'gain' and 'loss' are limited to gain and loss in money or other property. The definition of 'property' which applies in this context is based on Section 4(1) of the Theft Act 1968. The definition of 'property' covers all forms of property, including intellectual property.[5]

IP Cybersecurity guidance. The UK government has advised that while Intellectual property (IP) crime was traditionally viewed as piracy (illegal copying), cybercriminals are increasingly coming to recognise the value of sensitive information about business operations ('trade secrets and know-how'). It comments that these attacks on confidential data are happening globally with increasing rapidity and ever more complexity. Zero-day vulnerabilities (where hackers have discovered and exploited a software security breach before a fix is available) are increasing exponentially. In response to this IP Wales, an award-winning business support initiative based at the College of Law and Criminology at Swansea University has launched a new online initiative to help SMEs to protect their IP online. A free downloadable copy of the *SME Guide to IP Cybersecurity* is also available. For further information contact Swansea University. See: www. gov.uk/government/publications/topical-issues-for-business-and-consumers/ topical-issues-for-businesses-and-consumers.

Types of IP of interest: The types of IP most likely to be stolen by organised crime cyber criminals, state-sponsored and rival company hackers are initial concepts, designs, specifications, assemblies and process maps together with manufacturing production methods which exist mostly in a tangible form and are of considerable value to a competitor. Examples include research and development outputs; product prototypes; business cases; documents describing unique business process methodologies or corporate strategies and business decision-making; staff details, including personal information, role descriptions and remuneration levels; and where they exist, descriptions of company capabilities and weaknesses. Any associated data breaches can result in significant damage or compromise to long-term strategies and corporate finance.

Step 4: Risk assessment

Risk-taking is necessary for business growth as illustrated in Figure 7.2, however, businesses need to have a clear picture of the risk exposure they are facing and their ability to reduce that exposure. All risks cannot be avoided. Having opened the door to the digital world which presents enormous opportunities, it leaves businesses exposed to unwanted intruders coming back through the same door. Hence there needs to be a holistic approach, recognising both the opportunities and the threats.

The theft of intellectual property is commonly triggered by common events. Hence risk assessment consists of understanding the business vulnerabilities, how

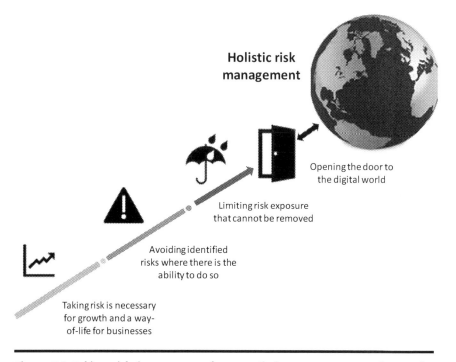

Holistic risk
management

Opening the door to
the digital world

Limiting risk exposure
that cannot be removed

Avoiding identified
risks where there is the
ability to do so

Taking risk is necessary
for growth and a way-
of-life for businesses

Figure 7.2 Taking risk is necessary for growth however exposure has to be minimised

likely are they are, what impact will they have, their proximity and how soon will they impact. How well these questions can be answered depends on the research undertaken. A starting point is undertaking lessons learned. For large businesses operating over a number of years they may have developed a database of events, recording how they were managed and what degree of success was achieved. However, for SMEs, they typically have to look outside of their business for lessons learned. In addition, as technology is moving so rapidly and cyber criminals are constantly evolving their approach and developing new malware, monitoring external sources of information has assumed greater importance.

Step 4A: Lessons learned

To appreciate the vulnerabilities of a business to intellectual property fraud requires an appreciation of the sequence or pattern of these fraud events, the tools and techniques employed (described here as the mechanics), historical events (captured in case studies) together with 'red flags' or the 'alarm bells' over potential exposure, as illustrated in Figure 7.3. These activities contribute to Lessons

Figure 7.3 The lessons learned from prior events

Learned which in turn assist in deciding on the actions to be implemented, to thwart IP theft.

Understanding the pattern of intellectual property fraud: There are a number of scenarios whereby intellectual property theft may occur as illustrated in Figure 7.4 and described below:

- By a departing company employee with the view to use the IP to start up a new company.
- By a departing company employee (or employees) with the view to use the IP, take it to a new employer or to sell it (on the assumption a buyer can be found).[6]
- By an opportunist cybercriminal who will evaluate the data to understand whether they will seek to blackmail the owner of the IP or to sell it: on the underground economy; to a rival company operating in the same market; or to a nation-state.
- By an 'insider', an employee who already had links to an organised criminal group or employed by a nation-state prior to joining the business.
- By nation-state hackers sponsored by their own foreign intelligence service to steal IP to enable the swift accumulation of knowledge at a fraction of the cost normally needed to develop it and for the long-term gain of their country to make it technologically and financially superior on the world stage.[7]

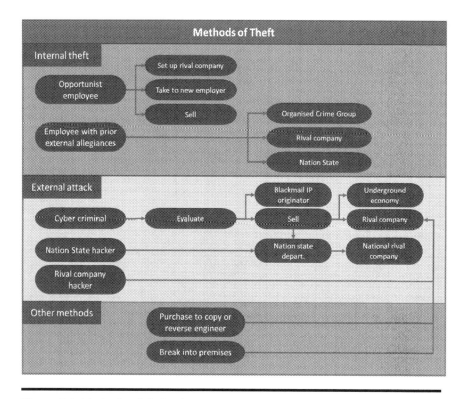

Figure 7.4 Methods of theft of IP

- By an employee of (or a third-party hacker sponsored by) a disreputable but legitimate rival company in the same market who considers the ends justify the means.
- By a person or persons who physically break into the offices or a company car of the business or the home of an employee.
- By buying it (in the case of a product), and then reverse-engineering or copying it.

 Evaluation of stolen IP: Employees and hackers sponsored by rival companies or nation-states already have a good understanding of the value of the IP before commencing their actions whereas cyber criminals on successfully exfiltrating data will assess its value and how they might be able to exploit it. The degree to which the IP can be exploited is likely to depend on a number of situational factors such as:

- the importance of time-to-market for the product, organisation, or industry;
- the level of innovation involved and the subsequent value this adds;

- the level of competition and value within an organisation's industry sector; and
- the potential market for the IP in terms of the ability to 'sell' stolen IP to third parties via the underground economy or to foreign intelligence services.

Exploiting stolen IP: According to a joint Detica and Cabinet Office report,[8] once the IP has been acquired by rival companies, state-sponsored hackers, cyber criminals or other third parties, it can be exploited in a number of ways, including:

- producing a direct replica, which is likely if the IP is not legally protected;
- producing a similar product using the same concept more quickly, which is highly dependent on the complexity of the IP;
- incorporating elements of the IP into an alternative design, which is highly dependent on how closely the original IP fits the alternative design;
- becoming inspired to generate new IP, which is highly situational, and doesn't guarantee the new IP being successful;
- selling the IP to a third party, which is likely if the IP can be commercially exploited by an opportunistic stakeholder; and
- blackmailing the IP-owner by threatening its disclosure, which is highly dependent on the value of the IP to the organisation.

Understanding the mechanics of intellectual property theft: Still, the most common method adopted by cyber criminals and nation-state hackers to instigate an intellectual property theft is by sending a malicious email that has malware embedded in a link or an attachment or by attaching malware to a website.

Case studies of the theft of intellectual property: Case studies provide a contemporary window onto intellectual property fraud and its debilitating effects. Reported case studies addressing intellectual property fraud describe very serious implications for the victim businesses in terms of reduced market share, turnover and profits, resulting in, in some instances, the need to reduce staff numbers. Theft of intellectual property can be perpetrated by an 'insider' supported by an ex-employee as was the case with Case Study 7.1.

Case Study 7.2. China has been accused of turning a blind eye to intellectual property fraud conducted by Chinese registered businesses and sponsoring fraud directly in pursuit of benefits for its national economy. This case study for instance describes the actions of Chinese nationals in their role as state representatives engaged in the theft of intellectual property. In May 2014 a US federal grand jury indicted five uniformed members of the Chinese military on charges of IP theft and conducting economic espionage against large US entities in the nuclear power, metal, and solar energy industries.

Case Study 7.1: IP Fraud

Theft of intellectual property from GE

An investigation by the US Federal Bureau of Investigation (FBI) found that two engineers (an *employee* and a *former employee*) had stolen elements of a computer program and a mathematical model created by the US multinational General Electric Company (GE) used to expertly calibrate the turbines used in power plants. The *former employee* pleaded guilty to conspiring to steal trade secrets and was sentenced in December 2019 to time served and ordered to pay compensation of $1.4 million to GE. The other engineer (*employee*) also pleaded guilty to plotting to steal trade secrets and was anticipated to face up to 87 months in prison in line with the federal sentencing guidelines. According to Special Agent Manglavil of the FBI, the *employee* downloaded thousands of GE proprietary files, including valuable intellectual property and launched a company with the *former employee* to compete against his employer in the belief he would not be discovered. Wayne Myers, the Assistant US Attorney for the Northern District of New York said 'The company [GE] had a skill set and engineering-level details that no one else could offer'. As a consequence of their expertise, power plant operators from all over the world hired GE's performance engineers to help their turbines achieve peak performance for the climate and conditions in which they were installed. The service could increase the efficiency of the turbines enough to substantially lower the plants' operating costs. In May 2012, GE learned they had an unknown competitor on a bid to service a major power plant in Saudi Arabia. The competing bid came in far under what GE had quoted and at a number that was strangely similar to GE's base cost for providing the work. When they looked into their new competitor, GE learned the company had been incorporated in Canada by an *employee*. When confronted the *employee* resigned and the FBI instigated its investigation soon after. The FBI agents examined extensive digital and physical evidence with the help of a team of forensic specialists, intelligence analysts, prosecutors, FBI legal attachés, and partner agencies. GE supported the investigation at every phase. The break in the case came when the *former employee* was intercepted when traveling on company business and carrying a company laptop that had the GE intellectual property on it. The investigation also uncovered evidence that the two business partners had sent the calculations over email and uploaded them to cloud storage accounts for use elsewhere.

Source: FBI: "Trade Secret Theft, Investigation Into theft of Intellectual Property from GE Leads to two guilty Pleas", 29 July 2020. https://www.fbi.gov/news/stories/

two-guilty-in-theft-of-trade-secrets-from-ge-072920 (All information the Bureau provides on its websites [that is not otherwise attributed] is considered public information and may be distributed or copied, subject to Sections 701 and 709 of Title 18, United States Code.)

Case Study 7.2: IP Fraud

State sponsored theft of intellectual property

Intellectual property fraud is also carried out by nation-state actors. The US Department of Justice has pursued charges against nation-state actors engaged in economic espionage through cyber means. In May 2014 a federal grand jury indicted five uniformed members of the Chinese military on charges of hacking and conducting economic espionage against large US entities in the nuclear power, metal, and solar energy industries. The lengthy statement of charges described numerous specific instances where officers of the People's Liberation Army ('PLA') were alleged to have hacked into the computer systems of US victims to steal trade secrets and sensitive, internal communications for commercial advantage or private financial gain. This is an example of state-sponsored theft of trade secrets or other confidential business information, with the intent of providing a competitive advantage to Chinese companies or commercial sectors. This subject was addressed within the bilateral agreement between the US and China in September 2015 and among the G20 at the Antalya Summit in Turkey in November 2015. While computer intrusions by Chinese state-sponsored hackers targeting US firms have decreased since 2015, further incidents have been detected such as those that occurred towards the end of 2017 which were reportedly carried out by Chinese nationals who worked for the Internet security firm known as Boyusec.

Source: The US Department of Justice.

Case Study 7.3. Another example of a Chinese company being involved in IP theft occurred in 2018. In June of that year, the US Department of Justice convicted a China-based manufacturer and exporter of wind turbines for the theft of technology from an American company.

Case Study 7.3: IP Fraud

Theft of intellectual property from a wind turbine manufacturer

The US Department of Justice (the Department) obtained a conviction in January 2018 in the US federal court against a China-based manufacturer and exporter of wind turbines that stole trade secrets from a US-based company. According to the Department, the Chinese company, Sinovel Wind Group Co. Limited, conspired with others to steal proprietary wind turbine technology from the American corporate victim in order to produce its own wind turbines and to retrofit existing wind turbines with stolen technology. These crimes cost the victim more than $1 billion in shareholder equity and almost 700 jobs, over half its global workforce.

Source: US Department of Justice. (See Press Release, "Chinese Company Sinovel Wind Group Convicted of Theft of Trade Secrets," US Dept. of Justice, 24 January 2018. https://www.justice.gov/opa/pr/ chinese-company-sinovel-wind-group-convicted-theft-trade-secrets, last accessed 29 June 2018.)

 Case Study 7.4. Is an example of employees who both stole and utilised their employer's intellectual property for personal gain.

Case Study 7.4: IP Fraud

Theft of intellectual property from a US naval development company

In 2016, the US Attorney for the District of Connecticut announced an indictment against two men relating to the offences concerning the theft of IP from a Connecticut-based defence contractor. The indictment charged the two men, an electrical engineer and an electronics technician, with one count of conspiracy to steal, upload, transmit and possess stolen IP. The indictment also charged the engineer with seven counts of theft of IP, seven counts of uploading IP, two counts of transmission of IP and five counts of possession of stolen IP. The technician was also charged with seven counts of possession of stolen IP. If convicted, the defendants faced a maximum term of imprisonment of ten years. According to court documents the two men both worked at LBI Inc., a Connecticut-based defence contractor which designs and builds unmanned underwater vehicles for the US Navy Office of Naval Research. From 4 January 2010 until 2 December 2011, the engineer was employed by LBI as the Lead Electrical Engineer for design, prototyping and testing for prototypes of unmanned vehicles. From 10 May 2010 until 23 November 2011, the technician was employed by LBI as an Electro-Mechanical Technician tasked with the fabrication, installation, testing and operation of various prototypes of unmanned vehicles. During the course of their employment with LBI, the two men collaborated with employees of Charles River Analytics, a Massachusetts-based software company that developed software to be integrated into LBI's unmanned underwater vehicles. In late 2010 and early 2011, Charles River Analytics sought to expand its business and agreed with the Office of Naval Research that it would complete the testing for a number of unmanned vehicles designed and developed by LBI. However, Charles River Analytics had never undertaken that type of work before and had no staff with the necessary experience. After April 2011, the engineer and technician began exploring employment with Charles River Analytics and were eventually hired in 2011. Information obtained from the execution of search warrants revealed that beginning in May 2011 and continuing until November 2011, the two men, without authorisation, uploaded LBI proprietary information to accounts in Dropbox, a cloud-based storage application. The two men ended their employment with LBI in the winter of 2011 and began working with Charles River Analytics on January 3, 2012. The two men continued to possess stolen trade secrets belonging to LBI after the end of their employment with LBI. During the course of their employment at Charles River Analytics, they both continued to work on at least one of the unmanned underwater vehicles that LBI had designed and developed. At the time of the indictment, U.S. Attorney Daly said Connecticut's defence contractors were critical to the US's national security and the U.S. Attorney's Office was committed to working with law enforcement to ensure that intellectual property was protected and that those who profited from stealing trade secrets were prosecuted. The theft of defence contractors' trade secrets was considered to pose a grave threat to the US's national economic security.

The U.S. Attorney Daly stressed that an indictment is not evidence of guilt. Charges are only allegations, and each defendant is presumed innocent unless and until proven guilty beyond a reasonable doubt. Both defendants had been released on bond pending trial.

Source: Department of Justice, U.S. Attorney's Office, District of Connecticut: "Two Men Charged with Stealing Trade Secrets from Connecticut Defence Contractor". https://www.justice.gov/usao-ct/pr/two-men-charged-stealing-trade-secrets-connecticut-defense-contractor.

Red flags: Sometimes the discovery of goods for sale online might indicate that a fraud has been committed. The signs are referred to as 'red flags'. With intellectual property fraud, there are numerous warning signs such as loss of sales, adverse media coverage due to poor quality, customer complaints and or discovery of adverts for identical products protected by trademarks or copyright.

- Trademark infringement: A complaint about the quality of a product which carries the business's registered trademark (logo) and it transpires the product was not manufactured by the business. Given the business uses the trademark as a badge or origin and an indication of quality this is likely to unjustly erode the business's reputation.
- The emergence of a copy of a registered design produced by the business, where the origin is falsely and intentionally attributed to a third party.
- Discovery of the online sale of counterfeit products such as CDs or DVDs.
- Discovery of the online sale of copyrighted books.
- Discovery of the unauthorised copying, importing, possessing, distributing, advertising and selling of copyright protected computer software, video games, films or recordings.
- Sudden and unexplained adverse press about the quality of the business's products and or a fall in sales.
- Notification by customs officials of the discovery of large quantities of counterfeit goods.
- Difficulty in selling products in a certain geographical region as a consequence of copied products.

Step 4B: Risk identification

Any business should look for potential weaknesses that may undermine its security and provide opportunities for fraudulent activity. The description of the pattern and mechanics of an attack provides a high-level vehicle for examining any vulnerabilities in the business. What information has been shared on the website about the organisational structure and key personnel. What information is included in annual reports in terms of personnel, reporting and financial management? Have the staff been made aware of what and what not to include on social media? Detailed out-of-office messages can unwittingly give valuable information about absence from the office, second in commands and who deals with what subject together with their respective email addresses. What is the culture of the organisation? Are the staff routinely pressurised to hit deadlines and complete assignments on time? How out of the ordinary would it be for an employee to be called upon to make an urgent payment? How readily would a member of staff respond to an email (from a spoofed email account) to make immediate payment to a supplier? Is there a process for updating or amending suppliers' bank details? If a member of staff suddenly realised they had been tricked into making a payment to a fraudster would they know what to do and how quickly to act?

A risk is broken into several components, how these components are articulated is critical to how that risk is viewed, understood and managed. 'Because of a [cause], a [threat] may occur, which would lead to [impact].' The common 'cause' is the motivation of individuals to secure financial gain from a business activity, contract or project. It is a common phenomenon in the business environment and perpetually gives rise to uncertainty. The common causes are included in Table 7.1. Fraudsters are constantly changing their approach to overcome defences that are put in place, build on the experiences of other fraudsters or move to methods that yield the best results.

Table 7.1 Causes of risk threat exposure

Intellectual property fraud threats (Cause → Threat → Impact)	
The **causes** or triggers behind fraudulent activity	
Policy	Cyber security policy is not prepared or prepared and signed off but not disseminated whereby mandated obligations in terms of cyber security are not known and acted upon.
Induction processes	Cyber security is not an integral part of induction processes relying on the training programme where training is only provided very periodically.
Cloud computing	Cyber espionage attack on the Managed IT Service Provider (MSP), engaged to provide cloud services (such as the campaign suspected to be the work of a China-based group widely referred to in the security community as 'APT10').
Cloud service	Temporary loss of the cloud service.
Data loss	Compromise of the cloud providers network resulting in loss of data.
Integration	Difficulties in integrating cloud-based systems with on-premises systems.
SLA	Inadequate service contract (service-level agreement) due to inexperience in commissioning cloud-based services.
RDP	Remote Desktop Protocol (RDP) remains the most common attack vector used by threat actors to gain access to networks. RDP is one of the main protocols used for remote desktop sessions, enabling employees to access their office desktop computers or servers from another device over the internet. Insecure RDP configurations are frequently used by cyber criminals and attackers to gain initial access to victims' devices.

(Continues)

Intellectual property fraud threats (Cause → Threat → Impact)	
VPN	VPN vulnerabilities: Since 2019, multiple vulnerabilities have been disclosed in a number of VPN appliances (for example, Citrix, Fortinet, Pulse Secure and Palo Alto). Cyber criminals exploit these vulnerabilities to gain initial access to targeted networks.
Access	Lack of restricted access to intellectual property across the organisation.
Circulation	No restrictions placed on the circulation of IP outside of the organisation.
Removable storage	Installation and use of removable storage such as the attachment of flash drives and detachable hard drives to computers not blocked.
Mixed peripherals	The storage of documents on printers, copiers and scanners which process documents (and are all typically networked and connected to remote management systems) is not adequately controlled.
Shredders	Shredders are not made available for shredding superseded documents.
Paper management	Uncollected printouts are not removed from printers after a fixed duration, there is no clean desk policy and photocopier access cards are not adopted.
Physical security	Physical security is not established to control access to and circulation within the business's premises such identity verification, use of swipe card entry, lanyard colour coding and visitor escort arrangements (including maintenance and contractor 'gangs'). No control of the movement of laptops and desktops from the premises. No searching of bags of departing staff. No control of lifts which discharge into underground car parks. No control of the use of mobile phones which can be used to take pictures of documents or computer screens.
Partnerships	Partner businesses engaged within the joint development of IP do not embed the same levels of security to protect IP.

The threat exposure may be increased if cyber security hygiene is not undertaken, addressing simple but important subjects like those addressed in Table 7.2.

The impact descriptions below are generic in nature and need to be tailored to the business, its context (market conditions and the prevalence of the theft of intellectual property) and ongoing operations (Table 7.3).

Table 7.2 Primary intellectual property fraud threats

Threats (uncertain events)	
Theft	Theft of intellectual property: malware is unwittingly uploaded onto the business's server (through clicking on a link, opening an attachment, downloading infected software or visiting a spoofed web address); the physical removal of papers, files, computers, computer attachments, and paper waste; and the taking of photographs of documents or computer screens using, say, a mobile phone.
Computer files	Deletion, corruption, movement, alteration or encryption of documents.

Table 7.3 Intellectual property fraud impact descriptions

Impact descriptions (if the threats were to materialise)	
Sales	Fall in sales due to circulation of counterfeit goods or copied products (which have been reverse engineered).
Profitability	Fall in profitability as market share lost due to theft of intellectual property and production of replica products.
Sustainability	Potential for the reduced viability of the business due to the progressive erosion of market share in turn due to the sale of copied products produced more cheaply overseas.
Staff retention	Inability to maintain the same staffing levels arising from a fall in market share, sales and profitability.
Reputation	Tarnished reputation as the replica products (which carry the business's logo and or designs) are of lower quality and are prone to faults.

Step 4C: Risk analysis

When examining the characteristics of a potential threat it commonly involves estimating the likelihood, the impact (in cost and time together with other parameters when appropriate) and the proximity (when is the threat likely to materialise). Included in Table 7.4 is a descriptive analysis of the likelihood, impact and proximity; however, businesses need to capture actual figures for the different categories where possible to highlight the significance and scale of potential disruption. When considering the damage of IP breaches there are the well-understood impacts such as the costs associated with conducting an IT investigation and improving cyber security based on the findings. However, many of the impacts are either not immediately apparent or surface over time, such as loss of market share, contracts, sales, customers and profit.

Table 7.4 Intellectual property risk analysis

Analysis of intellectual property fraud	
Likelihood	As these risks have already been encountered by numerous other firms, the likelihood of their occurrence (in the absence of any mitigation actions being implemented) is very high.
Financial impact	The financial impact, should the risk materialise, will reflect the scale of the theft of intellectual property and how it is deployed.
Time impact	The time impact can be considerable. For the translation of copied designs into the manufacture and distribution of goods may take many months.
Proximity	Out of the cause assessment of 'short', 'medium' and 'long' terms, all of these risks relate to the short term and need to be addressed at the earliest opportunity.

Discernible and less discernible costs

When conducting a risk assessment of the potential impact of the loss of IP there are subjects which immediately spring to mind such as the *discernible costs* associated with a technical IT investigation into how the IP theft occurred during a cyberattack and the increased cyber security measures that have to be put in place to remedy the identified shortfalls. However, there are a myriad of other *less discernible 'costs'* arising from a loss of IP which are not so readily quantified as they commonly emerge over time. They are labelled costs however they commonly relate to a loss of revenue due to a loss of market share followed by a fall in sales reducing the funds available for reinvestment in research and development. This reduced reinvestment is the start of a vicious cycle whereby the business's ability to differentiate its products from its competitors is reduced leading to a fall in market share. Some of the *discernible* and less *discernible costs* of the theft of intellectual property are described in Figure 7.5.

Loss of sales revenue and impact on business spending

According to the joint Detica and Cabinet Office report previously referred to,[9] the reduction in revenue arising from the theft of IP may reduce the funds available for businesses to:

- invest in research and development;
- design new products, services, or processes;
- undertake marketing and sales;
- develop their distribution network; and
- invest in customer service.

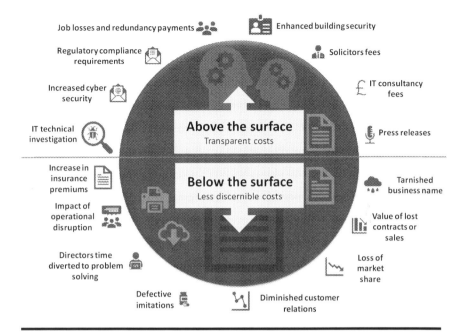

Figure 7.5 Ramifications of an IP breach

Step 5: Response actions

Forms of intellectual property protection

SMEs can protect their intellectual property to a degree by legal means, such as patents, trade marks and non-disclosure agreements. A brief introduction to the forms of protection is provided here with a fuller description provided in Appendix 4.

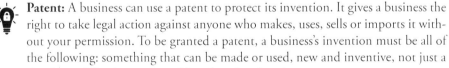

Patent: A business can use a patent to protect its invention. It gives a business the right to take legal action against anyone who makes, uses, sells or imports it without your permission. To be granted a patent, a business's invention must be all of the following: something that can be made or used, new and inventive, not just a simple modification to something that already exists.

Trademark: A business can register a trademark to protect its brand, for example, the name of its product or service. A trademark must be unique. A trademark can be something that allows consumers to distinguish a business's goods or services from those of another.

Copyright: Copyright protects a company's work and stops others from using it without a business's permission. Copyright protection is obtained automatically, it does not require an application or the payment of a fee. A business automatically obtains copyright protection when it creates: original literary, dramatic, musical and artistic work, including illustration and photography; original non-literary written work, such as software, web content and databases; sound and music recordings; film and television recordings; broadcasts; or the layout of published editions of written, dramatic and musical works. A business can mark its work with the copyright symbol (©), the company name and the year of creation.

 Design: A business can register the look of a product it has designed to stop other business's copying or stealing it. The look of a design includes the: appearance; physical shape; configuration (or how different parts of a design are arranged together); and decoration.

Specific response actions: people, systems, connectivity and data

Included in the table below are specific response actions that should be implemented with regard to personnel, systems, connectivity and data (Figure 7.6).

Step 6: Implementation of actions

Considerations need to be given to the prioritisation of planned response actions in terms of what information is critical to the survival of the business, what losses would harm customer relations and impact market share and what needs to be protected for operational reasons (i.e. loss of data would be disruptive but can be replaced from backup files).

Immediate response

The response to an IP breach is typically carried out in three identifiable steps as described below.

Rapid assessment and prioritisation look at what has been accessed, copied, taken or amended. It looks for whether, for instance, designs have been amended to include errors or flaws which when they emerge, would tarnish the business's reputation and cause a reduction in market share, sales and profitability. It looks at how the incident occurred (what defences had proved ineffective) and what immediate steps need to be taken to 'plug' the gap.

Damage control: looks at what legal action should be taken if any, what organisations should be notified of the theft, what improvements in policies, plans and procedures should be made, how the content of regular staff training should be changed or augmented and what long term changes to be made to the IT infrastructure.

Business continuity planning: looks at how the business responded to the breach and the lessons learned from both the breach itself and the response to it. It examines what countermeasures can be adopted and put in place to reduce the benefits being sought by the competitors who stole information.

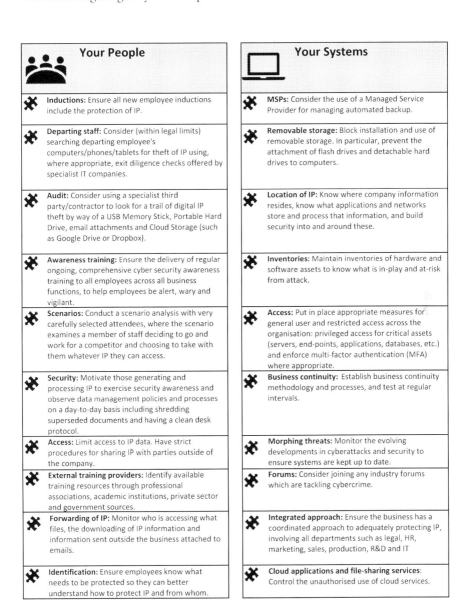

Your People	Your Systems
Inductions: Ensure all new employee inductions include the protection of IP.	**MSPs:** Consider the use of a Managed Service Provider for managing automated backup.
Departing staff: Consider (within legal limits) searching departing employee's computers/phones/tablets for theft of IP using, where appropriate, exit diligence checks offered by specialist IT companies.	**Removable storage:** Block installation and use of removable storage. In particular, prevent the attachment of flash drives and detachable hard drives to computers.
Audit: Consider using a specialist third party/contractor to look for a trail of digital IP theft by way of a USB Memory Stick, Portable Hard Drive, email attachments and Cloud Storage (such as Google Drive or Dropbox).	**Location of IP:** Know where company information resides, know what applications and networks store and process that information, and build security into and around these.
Awareness training: Ensure the delivery of regular ongoing, comprehensive cyber security awareness training to all employees across all business functions, to help employees be alert, wary and vigilant.	**Inventories:** Maintain inventories of hardware and software assets to know what is in-play and at-risk from attack.
Scenarios: Conduct a scenario analysis with very carefully selected attendees, where the scenario examines a member of staff deciding to go and work for a competitor and choosing to take with them whatever IP they can access.	**Access:** Put in place appropriate measures for general user and restricted access across the organisation: privileged access for critical assets (servers, end-points, applications, databases, etc.) and enforce multi-factor authentication (MFA) where appropriate.
Security: Motivate those generating and processing IP to exercise security awareness and observe data management policies and processes on a day-to-day basis including shredding superseded documents and having a clean desk protocol.	**Business continuity:** Establish business continuity methodology and processes, and test at regular intervals.
Access: Limit access to IP data. Have strict procedures for sharing IP with parties outside of the company.	**Morphing threats:** Monitor the evolving developments in cyberattacks and security to ensure systems are kept up to date.
External training providers: Identify available training resources through professional associations, academic institutions, private sector and government sources.	**Forums:** Consider joining any industry forums which are tackling cybercrime.
Forwarding of IP: Monitor who is accessing what files, the downloading of IP information and information sent outside the business attached to emails.	**Integrated approach:** Ensure the business has a coordinated approach to adequately protecting IP, involving all departments such as legal, HR, marketing, sales, production, R&D and IT
Identification: Ensure employees know what needs to be protected so they can better understand how to protect IP and from whom.	**Cloud applications and file-sharing services:** Control the unauthorised use of cloud services.

Figure 7.6 Threat response actions

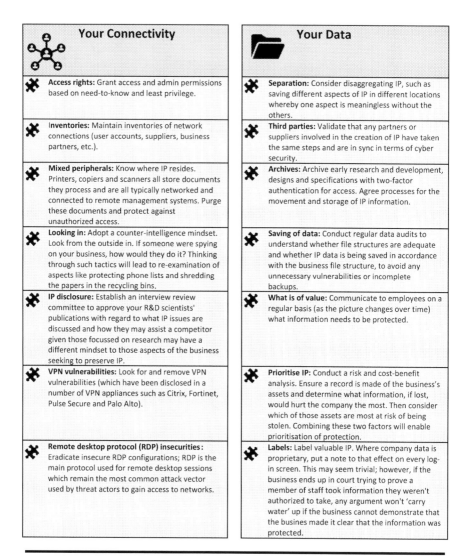

Your Connectivity	Your Data
Access rights: Grant access and admin permissions based on need-to-know and least privilege.	**Separation:** Consider disaggregating IP, such as saving different aspects of IP in different locations whereby one aspect is meaningless without the others.
Inventories: Maintain inventories of network connections (user accounts, suppliers, business partners, etc.).	**Third parties:** Validate that any partners or suppliers involved in the creation of IP have taken the same steps and are in sync in terms of cyber security.
Mixed peripherals: Know where IP resides. Printers, copiers and scanners all store documents they process and are all typically networked and connected to remote management systems. Purge these documents and protect against unauthorized access.	**Archives:** Archive early research and development, designs and specifications with two-factor authentication for access. Agree processes for the movement and storage of IP information.
Looking in: Adopt a counter-intelligence mindset. Look from the outside in. If someone were spying on your business, how would they do it? Thinking through such tactics will lead to re-examination of aspects like protecting phone lists and shredding the papers in the recycling bins.	**Saving of data:** Conduct regular data audits to understand whether file structures are adequate and whether IP data is being saved in accordance with the business file structure, to avoid any unnecessary vulnerabilities or incomplete backups.
IP disclosure: Establish an interview review committee to approve your R&D scientists' publications with regard to what IP issues are discussed and how they may assist a competitor given those focussed on research may have a different mindset to those aspects of the business seeking to preserve IP.	**What is of value:** Communicate to employees on a regular basis (as the picture changes over time) what information needs to be protected.
VPN vulnerabilities: Look for and remove VPN vulnerabilities (which have been disclosed in a number of VPN appliances such as Citrix, Fortinet, Pulse Secure and Palo Alto).	**Prioritise IP:** Conduct a risk and cost-benefit analysis. Ensure a record is made of the business's assets and determine what information, if lost, would hurt the company the most. Then consider which of those assets are most at risk of being stolen. Combining these two factors will enable prioritisation of protection.
Remote desktop protocol (RDP) insecurities: Eradicate insecure RDP configurations; RDP is the main protocol used for remote desktop sessions which remain the most common attack vector used by threat actors to gain access to networks.	**Labels:** Label valuable IP. Where company data is proprietary, put a note to that effect on every log-in screen. This may seem trivial; however, if the business ends up in court trying to prove a member of staff took information they weren't authorized to take, any argument won't 'carry water' up if the business cannot demonstrate that the busines made it clear that the information was protected.

Figure 7.6 (*Continued*)

Summary

Common targets for IP theft are current research and development, designs, innovative technology, development in new materials, novel production and assembly processes, customer contact lists, pricing information, or other valuable documentation. Theft of IP can be from within a business by employees or executed by external actors as demonstrated by the case studies. Even when the IP can be patented or registered, the investment required to maintain the protections may be prohibitive and the protections themselves may force unwanted disclosure. For example, patent applications, which are available in the public domain, can reveal not only elements of the IP that the company would have preferred to keep secret but also their market intentions. The majority of digital IP theft leaves behind a series of hidden artefacts or 'tracks' on the computer or device used to store IP data. Specialist IT companies now offer the service of 'exit diligence checks' locating, preserving and presenting these tracks which they claim are often left by departing employees who are seeking financial gain, favour with a new employer or both. They collect records leaving the suspected employees with no room for manoeuvre in the face of overwhelming evidence. The employer then has the opportunity to retrieve the stolen IP, find out if the employee was induced to obtain the information or acting on their own initiative, discover the business weaknesses and take corrective action.

Notes

1 UK's Innovation Office (2019) "Innovation and Growth Report 2018–19", Crown Copyright.
2 EUROPOL (2020) "EU IPO report on IP crime and its links to other serious crimes", 10 June 2020, News Article. https://www.europol.europa.eu/newsroom/news/europol-%E2%80%93-eu-ipo-report-ip-crime-and-its-links-to-other-serious-crimes.
3 CSO (2019) "Intellectual property protection: 10 tips to keep IP safe". Alyson Behr and Derek Slater. 28 February 2019. https://www.csoonline.com/article/2138380/intellectual-property-protection-10-tips-to-keep-ip-safe.html.
4 BBC (2021) "UK public at risk from hostile state threats – MI5", by Gordon Corera, 14 July 2021. https://www.bbc.co.uk/news/uk-57829261.
5 https://www.legislation.gov.uk/ukpga/2006/35/notes/division/5/5.
6 Reuters (2019) "Apple has 'deep concerns' that ex-employees accused of theft will flee to China". Stephen Nellis. 9 December 2019. https://www.reuters.com/article/us-apple-trade-secrets-idUSKBN1YD2IT. (Prosecutors at a hearing in the U.S. District Court for the Northern District of California alleged Xiaolang Zhang, a Chinese national and a former employee of Apple who had left the company to start work for Gaungzhou-based Xiaopeng Motors (China), took from Apple more than 2,000 files containing 'manuals, schematics, diagrams and photographs of computer screens showing pages in Apple's secure databases' with intent to share them. Agents arrested him in transit to San Francisco International Airport where he was planning to depart for China]. CNN Business (2019) Sherisse Pham. https://edition.cnn.com/2019/03/22/tech/tesla-xiaopeng-motors-lawsuit/index.html. 'Tesla is accusing a former employee of stealing self-driving tech and giving it to a Chinese rival'. (The electric car maker Telsa filed a lawsuit in the US in March 2019, alleging that engineer Guangzhi Cao stole key details from their self-driving car project and took them to Xiaopeng Motors, a Chinese electric vehicle startup. Tesla says Cao uploaded a complete copy of the company's self-driving source code to his personal Apple iCloud account amounting to more than 300,000 files and directories.)

7 CNBC (2019) "1 in 5 corporations say China has stolen their IP within the last year: CNBC CFO survey", Published 1 March 2019, Eric Rosenbaum. https://www.cnbc.com/2019/02/28/1-in-5-companies-say-china-stole-their-ip-within-the-last-year-cnbc.html.

8 Cabinet Office & Detica (2011) "The cost of cybercrime". A Detica report in partnership with the office of cyber security and information assurance in the Cabinet Office 2011.

9 Ibid.

Chapter 8

Business Email Compromise (BEC) fraud

Structure of Chapter 8

Chapter 8 is subdivided into four sections, as illustrated in Figure 8.1. An overview of the fraud type is provided followed by an assessment of the threat posed by the fraud, suggested response actions and the timing of implementation.

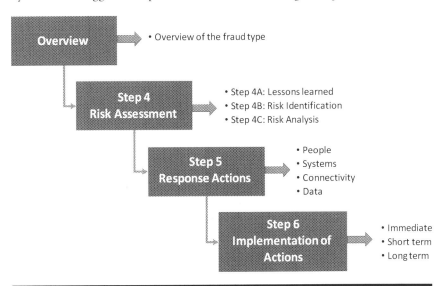

Figure 8.1 Structure of Chapter 8

Overview

In summary, Business Email Compromise (BEC) is a form of phishing attack where a criminal attempts to trick a company employee into transferring funds or revealing sensitive information. It is also sometimes referred to as 'CEO fraud', 'cyber-enabled financial fraud' or 'email account compromise' (EAC). UK Finance (the not-for-profit industry body for the banking and financial services sector), refers to BEC as a type of authorised push payment fraud (APP). It is described by the National Cyber Security Centre, Microsoft, Interpol, Europol, the US's Department of Justice and others as a sophisticated scam perpetrated by criminals who attempt to deceive a company employee into processing a payment request (that they would not have done otherwise) or reveal sensitive company information, by impersonating a high-ranking employee such as a manager, department head, the CEO or CFO. Typically, the criminal (pretending to be the CEO, an executive or senior manager) sends an email to an employee in (say) the finance department requesting them to make an urgent payment or forward sensitive information. They may have gained access to a company's devices or systems through malware, other security vulnerabilities or the spoofed email address of a director having learnt enough about the company's inner workings to convincingly impersonate an executive or manager.

Europol advises that BEC fraud was first detected in Europe in 2012/2013, particularly in France, Belgium and Luxemburg, where most fraud cases were committed in the French language.[1] It is now recognised as one of the fastest-growing threats, especially for small businesses.[2] It exploits the fact that so many organisations rely on email to conduct business. As described by Ryan Kalember,[3] executive vice-president of cyber-security strategy at Proofpoint,[4] 'one of the reasons why this is a particularly difficult problem to stamp out is that it relies on the systemic risk of all of us trusting email as a means of communication'.[5] The Federal Bureau of Investigation (FBI) refers to it as one of the most financially damaging online crimes.[6] This is echoed by Kalember, who states it is 'the most expensive problem in all of cyber-security. There is [no] other form of cyber-crime that has the same degree of scope in terms of money lost'.

Many BEC scams originate in countries that turn a blind eye to such activities. The fraudsters are often members of transnational criminal organisations, which originated in Nigeria but have spread throughout the world.[7] Money mules may be witting or unwitting accomplices who receive ill-gotten funds from the victims and then transfer the funds as directed by the fraudsters. The money is transferred or sent by cheque to the money mule who then deposits it in his or her own bank account. Usually, the mules keep a fraction for their role and then wire the money as directed by the fraudster.

A specific variant of BEC is the BEC Payroll Diversion Scams. These are similar to other BEC attacks by relying on impersonation and social engineering to convince the target victim to send money to the fraudsters. In this case, the fraudsters target the payroll process of a company and attempt to redirect legitimate payroll payments from their intended bank accounts to accounts under the fraudster's control. BEC payroll diversion scams are by necessity focused on specific targets. To succeed, these scams must correctly identify someone in the payroll or human resources department to make changes to an employee's bank details. This threat is on the rise. In the US for instance the FBI has identified that the dollars lost as a result of payroll diversion scams have increased more than 815% between 1 January 2018 and 30 June 2019.

Step 4: Risk assessment

Risk assessment consists of a sequence of activities which answer the questions: what are the possible problems my business may face? how likely are they? what impact will they have? and how soon will they impact? Key questions might be is a single member of staff responsible for making payments, adding new suppliers to company records or amending bank details of suppliers and contractors-all without management oversight? How well these questions can be answered depends on familiarity with the business and the research undertaken. A starting point is undertaking lessons learned. For large businesses operating over a number of years, they may have developed a schedule or database of events, recording how they were managed and what degree of success was achieved. However, for SMEs, they typically have to look outside of their business for lessons learned.

Step 4A: Lessons learned

As with other forms of fraud, recording and revisiting lessons learned provides both a permanent reference point and a reminder of where fraudsters have sought personal gain and found opportunities to deceive the business. Near misses need to be recorded too. LinkedIn is proving to be an excellent resource for attackers looking to map out an organisation's internal structure. The lessons need to be captured on a database or spreadsheet so that they can be readily reviewed and retrieved to inform business protocols. They need to be used to update policies, processes and awareness training. Fraud is evolving quickly and hence as a minimum, awareness training needs to be revisited and updated on a regular basis.

To appreciate the vulnerabilities of a business to BEC requires an appreciation of the sequence or pattern of these fraud events, the tools and techniques employed (described here as the mechanics), historical events (captured in case studies) together with 'red flags' or the 'alarm bells' over potential exposure, as illustrated in Figure 8.2. These activities contribute to Lessons Learned which in turn assist in deciding on the actions to be implemented, to thwart BEC fraud.

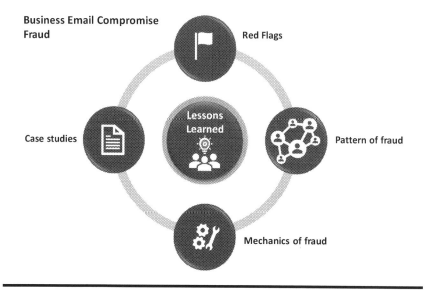

Figure 8.2 The lessons learned from prior events

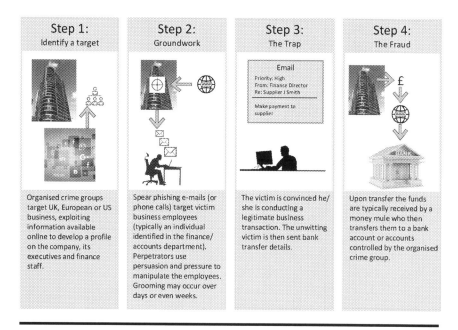

Figure 8.3 The four steps of a BEC fraud

 Understanding the pattern of Business Email Compromise fraud: There are usually four steps to a sophisticated BEC attack as described below and illustrated in Figure 8.3.

Identify a target: Unlike mass, blanket attacks, BEC attackers usually take the time to identify specific individuals within an organisation. Information is gathered from a range of sources to create believable communications once the target's email account is compromised.

The groundwork: BEC attackers often attempt to build relationships with those who have financial decision-making authority. Usually through spoofed (similar) or compromised email accounts. The FBI advises this interaction can take place over days, weeks or even months to build trust and familiarity.[8]

The trap: Once the attacker has compromised an email account, or accounts, and is satisfied that the target employee believes them to be genuine, they make their move. In most cases, the target is asked to initiate a bank transfer or to alter the payment details on an existing pending payment, to a supplier or other third party.

The fraud: Believing the request to be genuine, the victim sends funds to a money mule or direct to the fraudster's bank account. These funds are usually moved on quickly from one bank account to another (possibly overseas), making them harder to recover once the fraud has been discovered.

Understanding the mechanics of BEC fraud: BEC scams are generally accomplished by spearfishing, spoofing and malware.

Use of malware. Malicious software also called malware is often installed via links or attachments in an unsolicited email. It can infiltrate company networks and gain access to legitimate email threads about billing and invoices.

Europol announced in a press release on 27 January 2021 that as the result of an international effort involving eight countries, one of the long-lasting cybercrime services known as EMOTET had been disrupted. While in operation the service had used several hundreds of servers located across the world. EMOTET malware was delivered to the victims' computers via infected e-mail attachments. A variety of different lures were used to trick unsuspecting users into opening these malicious attachments. EMOTET email campaigns have also been presented as invoices, shipping notices and information about COVID-19. All these emails contained malicious Microsoft Word documents, either attached to the email itself or downloadable by clicking on a link within the email itself. Once a user opened one of these documents, they could be prompted to 'enable macros' so that the malicious code hidden in the Word file could run and install EMOTET malware on a victim's computer.

Spear phishing emails. These messages look like they are from a trusted sender such as the CEO or finance manager to trick victims into revealing confidential information. Perpetrators may start the subject lines of their emails with 'Re:' or 'Fwd:' to make it look like their message is part of a previous conversation. The information obtained lets criminals access company accounts, calendars, and data that gives them the details they need to carry out the BEC schemes.

Spoof an email account. Spoof email accounts contain slight variations on legitimate addresses such as david.glancy@finestcompany.co.uk as opposed to david.glancy@fimestcompany.co.uk to fool victims into thinking fake accounts are legitimate.

Timing. The information obtained is used for time requests or to send messages so that accountants or financial managers do not question payment requests. Malware also lets criminals gain undetected access to a victim's data, including passwords and financial account information.

Fake supply chain emails enabling recurring bank transfers. This entails the attacker compromising the email accounts of an employee of a business and that of a regular contact in a legitimate supplier organisation, with whom the business regularly trades, with the attacker controlling both sides of an email exchange. The goal of the attack is for the business to order goods from the supplier then transfer payment by internet banking.

The attacker uses the compromised business email account to place orders with the compromised supplier, attempt to approve their own invoices, and settle the transaction. At the same time, the compromised account on the supplier side is used to ensure the supplier never sees any inquiries regarding those orders. In some cases, the fraudster attempts to gain regular access to company finances, in order to arrange multiple regular, ongoing payments. It creates a regular income until the business finally notices the supplies never arrive and becomes suspicious.

 Case studies of Business Email Compromise: Case studies provide a contemporary window into Business Email Compromise and its debilitating effects. The four common observations that can be drawn from Case studies 8.1 to 8.4 that follow are that the fraudster will:

- most likely be located outside of the UK;
- most probably, but not always, be part of an organised crime group (OGC);
- use deception (sometimes a mixture of charm and vulnerability) together with knowledge gained about a company to acquire specific information relying on human nature and the desire to be 'helpful';

- occasionally use sophisticated malware programs, spyware, remote access tools and spoofed email accounts; and
- move money quickly and any syphoning of funds will be crippling.

 Case Study 8.1 focuses on the hijacking of bank transfers that occurred in the US. The term 'wire transfer' is now used to cover any electronic transfer of money from one person to another or one business to another. Hence 'Operation Wire' derived its name from the criminals' interception and hijack of bank transfers.

Case Study 8.1: Business Email Compromise

'Operation Wire Wire'

'Operation Wire Wire' was carried out in January 2018. It was a coordinated US law enforcement effort aimed at disrupting Business Email Compromise (BEC) schemes designed to intercept and hijack bank transfers from businesses and individuals. The action of the US Department of Justice and three other agencies resulted in a total of 74 arrests including 29 in Nigeria, and three in Canada, Mauritius and Poland, and the remainder in the US. The operation also resulted in the seizure of nearly $2.4 million and the disruption and recovery of approximately $14 million in fraudulent bank transfers. Local and state law enforcement partners on FBI task forces across the country, with the assistance of multiple District Attorney's Offices, charged 15 alleged money mules for their role in defrauding victims. These money mules were employed by the fraudsters to launder their ill-gotten gains by forwarding the funds into other accounts that were difficult to trace. A number of cases involved international criminal organisations that defrauded small to large-sized businesses, while others involved individual victims. Attorney General Sessions commenting on the BEC schemes said: 'These are malicious and morally repugnant crimes'. Since the Internet Crime Complaint Centre (IC3) began keeping track of BEC as a complaint category, there has been a loss of over $3.7 billion reported to the IC3.

Source: US Attorney's Office, Department of Justice: "74 arrested in coordinated International Enforcement Operation targeting hundreds of individuals in business email compromise schemes", Monday, 11 June 2018. https://www.justice.gov/usao-sdfl/pr/74-arrested-coordinated-international-enforcement-operation-targeting-hundreds.

Case Study 8.2 describes extensive BEC scams targeting over 50,000 victims across 150 countries carried out by Nigerian nationals thought to be part of a wider organised crime group.

Case Study 8.2: Business Email Compromise

'Operation Falcon'

In November 2020, Interpol reported that three suspects had been arrested in Lagos, Nigeria following a joint INTERPOL, Group-iB and Nigeria Police Force cybercrime investigation codenamed 'Operation Falcon'. Craig Jones, INTERPOL's Cybercrime Director, highlighted the outstanding cooperation between all three organisations and underlined the importance of public-private relationships in disrupting virtual crimes. Interpol considers the Nigerian nationals were members of a wider organised crime group responsible for distributing malware, carrying out phishing campaigns and extensive BEC scams. The suspects were alleged to have developed phishing links, domains and mass mailing campaigns in which they impersonated representatives of organisations. They then used these campaigns to disseminate 26 malware programs, spyware and remote access tools, including AgentTesla, Loki, Azorult, Spartan and the Nanocore and Remcos Remote Access Trojans. These programs were used to infiltrate and monitor the systems of victim organisations and individuals, before launching scams and syphoning funds. According to Group-iB, the gang is believed to have compromised government and private sector companies in more than *150 countries* since 2017. Group-iB was also able to establish that the gang was divided into subgroups with a number of individuals still at large. At the time of the investigation, some *50,000 targeted victims* had been identified to date. The year-long investigation saw INTERPOL's Cybercrime and Financial Crime units work closely with Group-iB to identify and locate threats, and ultimately, assist the Nigerian Police Force, via the INTERPOL National Central Bureau in Abuja, Nigeria, in taking swift action. Group-iB's participation in the operation came under Project Gateway, a framework which enables INTERPOL to cooperate with private partners and receive threat data directly.

Source: Interpol. Subject to Interpol copyright. Interpol has advised businesses to protect themselves from online scams by following the advice featured in INTERPOL's #WashYourCyberHands, #OnlineCrimeIsRealCrime and #BECareful campaigns, 25 November 2020. https://www.interpol.int/News-and-Events.

The next case study is an example of the use of spear-phishing used in connection with targeted email addresses to gain a back door entry into an employee's computer to gain administrative control.

Case Study 8.3: Business Email Compromise

Installation of a Remote Access Trojan

A system administrator within a high-profile UK organisation was successfully spear-phished and unknowingly installed a Remote Access Trojan (RAT) – a malware program that includes a back door entry for administrative control over the targeted computer. Taking advantage of the user's privileged permissions, the attackers were able to extract information about the network and details for multiple business-critical systems. Fortunately, the compromise was restricted to one computer, and it was detected and effectively investigated as appropriate security monitoring and logging were in place. Identifying and mitigating the lost information impacted the availability of the system to the business and required extensive support from external forensic and technical architecture specialists. The attackers had identified the system administrator and their personal subjects of interest. They crafted and delivered a socially engineered email to the administrator's personal email address. Accessing personal webmail from the admin computer, the administrator read the phishing email and downloaded a Trojanised document from a file sharing service containing the first stage malware. When the Trojanised file was opened, the user was prompted to run an executable which then breached the defences and installed the first stage malware onto the system. The attacker exploited poor security awareness by repeatedly requesting approval to run until the administrator finally clicked 'OK'. Unpacking itself silently into a temporary folder, this first stage malware hid itself as a legitimate file and changed the system to ensure it continued to run between reboots of the computer. Once installed, it started communicating with attacker-controlled domains. After a number of days, the initial malware downloaded a second stage executable (the RAT) and a configuration file. To discover more about the victim organisation, the attackers configured the malware to exfiltrate captured screenshots. Data was covertly delivered for nearly a week until the transfers were detected. The domains were then blocked and the machine was disconnected from the network for forensic analysis. The compromise was detected before any significant damage could be done. However, the investigation and clean-up operation required the assistance of industry experts and disrupted the day-to-day operation of the organisation.

Source: NCSC: "Common Cyberattacks: Reducing the Impact". Cyberattacks White Paper, January 2016.

The following Case Study is an example of the use of 'spoof' email addresses to deceive employees into thinking that the instructions they had received (by email) were from legitimate business colleagues. The behaviour of employees in their response to emails received is always critical to the commencement of BEC incidents.

Case Study 8.4: Business Email Compromise

Spoof email addresses

In November 2020, the FBI reported the prosecution of a Washington man who was sentenced to prison, following what was described as 'a complex email fraud scheme'. He was given a 108-month sentence to be immediately followed by three years of supervised release. He was further ordered to pay compensation of $745,540.70. At the hearing, the court heard additional testimony from witnesses describing the harm the man's actions had caused them. One described not only the harm caused to his company financially but also the toll on his employees, relationships with other victims and the effects on his and his workers' personal lives. 'Business Email Compromise (BEC) is a pervasive threat and one of the most financially damaging online crimes', said FBI Special Agent in Charge, Perrye K. Turner. 'It exploits the fact that so many of us rely on email to conduct business – both personal and professional. In this case, one of the victim companies notified law enforcement and the FBI was able to unmask Kim and put an end to his years-long theft and fraud'. Kim engaged in a Business Email Compromise scheme using 'spoof' email addresses which have similar names to legitimate email accounts he had hacked. He would then use the addresses to create fictitious transactions or to hijack legitimate transactions to convince a victim company or individual to send funds to a bank account Kim actually controlled. For example, Kim created a spoof email account for a Pinehurst-based construction company. He then used that account to convince another company, based in Huntsville, to send over $200,000 to them. In reality, the account where they sent the funds was actually an account Kim controlled. He then took that money and moved it through several different bank accounts before placing it in an offshore account.

Source: FBI, https://www.fbi.gov/investigate/cyber/news. (All information the Bureau provides on its websites [that is not otherwise attributed] is considered public information and may be distributed or copied, subject to Sections 701 and 709 of Title 18, United States Code.)

Red flags: Sometimes the way people or organisations behave might suggest they are committing a fraud. The signs are referred to as 'red flags'. With BEC fraud the four main areas are changes to: bank details; bank transfer arrangements; email accounts; and timings.

The FBI advises businesses and their personnel to be on the lookout for the following 'red flags':

- Unexplained urgency.
- Last-minute changes in bank transfer instructions or recipient bank account information.
- Last-minute changes in established communication methods or email account addresses.
- Requests to communicate only by email and refusal to communicate via telephone or online voice or video platforms.
- Requests for advanced payment for services such as tariffs, import duties or additional transport costs when not previously notified.
- Requests from employees to change direct deposit information.

Step 4B: Risk identification

Any business should look for potential weaknesses that may undermine its security and provide opportunities for fraudulent activity. The 'four steps in an attack' provides a high-level vehicle for examining any vulnerabilities in the business. What information has been shared on the website about the organisational structure and key personnel. What information is included in annual reports in terms of personnel, reporting and financial management? Have the staff been made aware of what and what not to include on social media? The sharing of who is on leave at a particular time can create opportunities for BEC. Detailed out-of-office messages can unwittingly give valuable information about absence from the office, second in commands and who deals with what subject together with their respective email addresses. What is the culture of the organisation? Are staff routinely pressurised to hit deadlines and complete assignments on time? How out of the ordinary would it be for an employee to be called upon to make an urgent payment? How readily would a member of staff respond to an email (from a spoofed email account) to make an immediate payment to a supplier? Is there a process for updating or amending suppliers' bank details? If a member of staff suddenly realised they had been tricked into making a payment to a fraudster would they know what to do and how quickly to act?

The actual vulnerabilities of any business will be dependent on the actual nature of its business, its maturity, its day-to-day processes, its policies and the awareness training provided to staff. Included below are a number of high-level watchpoints for consideration.

■ Lack of recognition of employees being the weakest link in the armoury against BEC.
■ Lack of processes in place to support staff from a BEC attack.
■ New employees not fully inducted in the methods adopted to tackle fraud.
■ There is a culture within the organisation whereby employees are expected to follow instructions without question, in other words, a culture of: 'do as you are told', 'just do your job', 'don't ask questions' or 'do not challenge instructions'.
■ Lack of fraud awareness training and subsequent updates. Any attachment that an employee wants to view should first be saved into a dedicated folder (called say 'scan first') and then scanned with an up-to-date antivirus program before it is opened. Consideration also needs to be given to an attachment being 'clean' but an innocuous macro may then download an actual malicious payload from a remote website.
■ Inadequate vigilance in detecting spoofed email accounts.
■ Lack of immediate praise for employees that spot a fraudulent email.
■ Not all employees are aware of the payment protocols and penalties for breach.
■ Lack of development and dissemination of 'red flag' events.
■ Second authentication of payments not implemented.
■ Lack of scrutiny as to how funds could be transferred out of the business.

The larger the number of employees a business has the greater the ability it will have to enact essential anti-fraud mechanisms. In addition, the larger organisations will have a greater ability to separate duties among staff members to help prevent fraud. BEC fraud can occur at any time but the motivation will always be the same, to secure the transfer of funds to bank accounts managed by criminals or their mules. The focus of the fraudsters will always be those that are thought to control the sanction of payments or undertake bank transfers.

A risk is broken into several components, how these components are articulated is critical to how that risk is viewed, understood and managed. 'Because of [cause], a [threat] may materialise, which would lead to [impact]'. The common 'cause' is the motivation of individuals to secure financial gain from a business activity, contract or project. It is a common phenomenon in the business environment and perpetually gives rise to uncertainty. The list of causes included in Table 8.1 is not exhaustive. Fraudsters are constantly changing their approach to overcome defences that have been put in place, build on the experiences of other fraudsters or move to methods that regularly provide good returns (Tables 8.2 and 8.3).

Table 8.1 Business Email Compromise causes

Business Email Compromise (Cause → Threat → Impact)	
The causes or triggers behind fraudulent activity	
Malware	Malware is unwittingly uploaded onto the business's server through clicking on a link, opening an attachment, downloading infected software or visiting a spoofed web address.
Supply chain infiltration	A criminal manages to infiltrate the email account of a member of the accounts team and a representative of a supplier with whom the business regularly places orders and sets up false payments, crediting an account held by a criminal.
Support	The business is lulled into a false sense of security as it has engaged an IT security firm, without recognising that staff remain ill-prepared to protect their company.
Second authentication	Second authentication is not established for payments.
Red flag list	Red flag list of events is not prepared and circulated to forewarn employees of the watchpoints to be observed for detecting criminal attempts to infiltrate email accounts and/or plant malware.
Training	Staff are not provided with training specific to combatting Business Email Compromise (BEC), and the induction of new staff does not include guidance on how to combat BEC fraud. Staff are not alerted to scams moving to text messaging. It is common to see an attacker ask for someone's phone number but claim to be unable to take a call because they are in a 'meeting'. The attacker may claim that the phone they are dialling from is a personal phone as their work phone is out of battery power.
Payment protocols	Payment protocols are not prepared, disseminated and explained, or the ramifications of non-compliance not clearly spelt out.
Audits	Audits are not undertaken to establish that the procedures established to control payments are being rigorously followed.

Table 8.2 Primary Business Email Compromise threat

Threat (uncertain event)	
Deception by an external actor	Financial losses incurred through an employee or director being deceived by an external actor and unwittingly transferring business funds (generally by bank transfer) into a fraudster's bank account or into the account of a money mule used by the external actor.

Table 8.3 Business Email Compromise impact descriptions

Impact descriptions *(if the threats were to materialise)*	
Profitability	Potential cash flow problems leading to a fall in profitability.
Loss of reputation	The business suffers reputational damage arising from late payments and tarnished customer, supplier, bank and/or partner relationships.
Time	The director's and/or manager's time is diverted away from normal operational activities to understand the extent and damage of a BEC fraud, how it occurred and how such events are to be prevented in the future.
Cost	Monies are transferred to bank accounts controlled by criminals which are not recoverable.
Employee stress	Stress arising from a loss of money to fraudsters due to an employee's direct actions, their anxiety over the inadequacy of the security of business systems, their tense relationships with other employees and concern over the ease with which they had been deceived.
Relationships	Relationships have to be rebuilt after a BEC event.

Table 8.4 Business Email Compromise risk analysis

Analysis of BEC risks	
Likelihood	As these risks have already been encountered by numerous other firms, the likelihood of their occurrence (in the absence of any mitigation actions being implemented) is very high.
Financial impact	The financial impact, should the risks materialise, will depend on how often the business is likely to suffer a BEC incident and the size of bank transfers.
Time impact	The time impact, should the risks materialise, may relate to when the fraud occurs. If supplier payments have been 'lost' to fraudsters when purchasing long-lead items critical to manufacturing, it can lead to deadlines being missed.
Proximity	Out of the cause assessment of 'short', 'medium' and 'long' terms, all of these risks relate to the short term and need to be addressed at the earliest opportunity.

Step 4C: Risk analysis

When examining the characteristics of a potential threat it commonly involves estimating the likelihood, the impact (in cost and time together with other parameters when appropriate) and the proximity (when is the threat likely to materialise). Included in Table 8.4 is a descriptive analysis of the likelihood, impact and proximity; however, businesses need to capture actual figures for the different categories.

Step 5: Response actions

As cyber criminals employ multiple tactics and combinations of impersonation and account compromise, defending against one or two of these tactics is insufficient to address the threat as a whole. Hence a series of actions need to be completed as outlined below. The guidance below is aimed at both small enterprises with a very small number of personnel (below 10) and medium enterprises with between 10 and 49 personnel (Figure 8.4).

Step 6: Implementation of actions

Immediate actions

If a member of staff considers that they have clicked on a suspicious link or attachment they should contact the IT department immediately or for smaller SMEs who have outsourced their IT support, contact the external IT consultancy straight away. In the case where funds have been sent to a new bank account which was subsequently found to be suspicious or clearly wrong, the firm should immediately contact their bank to request a recall of funds.

Medium-term actions

Medium actions are those that do not need to be implemented immediately, may necissitate staged investment or require the appointment of a specialist consultant.

Summary

Business Email Compromise (or BEC) is a form of phishing attack where a criminal attempts to trick a senior executive (or budget holder) into transferring funds, or revealing sensitive information. Employees need to be provided with awareness training (and subsequent refreshers) so that they are constantly vigilant to the threat of criminals seeking financial gain through changes to payment details channelled through false invoices, amended invoices, spoofed email accounts or urgent requests supposedly from senior executives. The recommended actions need to be implemented and regularly assessed for their adequacy to establish if they need to be expanded upon.

Your People

 Training: As BEC/EAC attacks target people rather than hardware, businesses must ensure they are delivering ongoing, comprehensive cyber security awareness training to all employees, across all business functions, to help their employees be alert, wary and vigilant. To identify emails and attachments that if responded to may seriously harm the business, recognising that fraudsters use spoof email accounts and have taken time to understand the inner workings of the business.

 Deception: Train your employees to carefully examine the email addresses, URLs, and spelling used in any email correspondence. Scammers use slight differences to trick your eye and gain your trust. (Note: A URL [Uniform Resource Locator] is the unique address of a web page.)

 Account information: Train your employees not to click on anything in an unsolicited email or text message asking for an update to or verification of account information. Look up the company's phone number on their own (and not to use the one a potential scammer is providing), and call the company to ask if the request is legitimate.

 Social media: Advise personnel to be careful what they post to social media as information may be harvested as part of social engineering. By openly sharing things like pet names, schools attended, links to family members and birthdays, employees can give a scammer all the information they need to guess an employee's password or answer security questions. Put a social media policy in place.

 Security awareness: Provide advanced security awareness training (SAT) for users in your organisation who have the highest risk for business email compromise (i.e., Finance, C-Suite, Executive Assistants).

 Web addresses: Employees should not copy and paste web addresses from messages into a browser. Hyperlinks: Advise employees to be alert to hyperlinks that may contain misspellings of the actual domain name. (A domain name is the address by which Internet users can access your website.)

Links and attachments: Advise employees to avoid clicking on links or attachments from unknown senders. Doing so could download malware onto your company's computers, making you vulnerable to a hack. Any attachment that an employee wants to view should first be saved into a dedicated folder (called, say, 'scan first') and then scanned with an up-to-date antivirus program before it is opened.

Your Systems

 Forwarding of emails: Where web-based accounts are used, periodically check the "rules" setting on the account (or accounts) to ensure that no one has set up auto-forwarding for your emails. For Microsoft Outlook, follow the thread: on the 'Home' tab, in the 'Move' group, click 'Rules', and then select 'Manage Rules & Alerts'. Check for rules created by others.

 Disclosure: Be careful what you post to your company website, especially information about who has which specific job duties. Also be cautious about using out-of-office replies that give too much detail about when your executives are out of the office or the chain of command.

 Anti-fraud policies: Ensure employees are aware of the anti-fraud policies in place and the obligations that they are required to adhere to.

 Two-factor verification: Require two-factor verification for money transfers, particularly big ones. For example, you could require a telephone call to confirm significant bank transfers. Be sure to set up this protocol early in the business relationship and outside the email environment. When the fraudster hacks your email account, you don't want him to be able to see how to evade your security protocols.

 Email accounts: Consider requiring employees to use two-factor authentication to access business email accounts. They would need two pieces of information to log-in, something they know (such as a password) and something they have (such as a dynamic PIN that changes constantly).

 Reporting phishing: Set up a phishing reporting protocol where users can send suspicious emails (as attachments) to the IT security team for further investigation.

Access and privileges: Ensure the business has an identity management system in place that prevents the combinations of access and privileges that BEC attempts prey upon.

Figure 8.4 Business Email Compromise response actions

Your Connectivity	Your Data
✖ **Free accounts:** Avoid free web-based email accounts such as Gmail, Hotmail and Yahoo. These personal accounts exist outside of the IT department's control. They look unprofessional. They are not subject to backup, archiving, security or governance. As they are not saved on company servers, any legal action may be difficult to defend if historical emails are not readily available. If an employee leaves the company, their emails leave with them together with any relevant information, making future searches very challenging (if not impossible). Personal email compromises intellectual property and potentially exposes company correspondence to uncontrolled mining and searching. Establish a company domain name and use it to create formal email addresses for your employees.	✖ **Suspicious requests:** Train your employees to watch for suspicious requests, such as a change in a supplier's bank details or payment procedures. Verify payment and purchase requests in person by calling the person/company to make sure it is legitimate.
✖ **Use of mobile phones:** Advise employees that when responding to emails using a mobile phone, they should first verify that the sender's email address precisely matches the one held for them in the office.	✖ **Personal information:** If a request for personal information is received in an email message, employees should be wary. Most legitimate businesses have a policy that they do not ask for your personal information through email. Employees should be advised to be very suspicious of a message that asks for personal information even if it might look legitimate.
✖ **Email security:** Consider investing in an email security solution that detects and stops impersonation, account compromise, credential phishing and social engineering.	✖ **Bank transfers:** When confirming bank transfer requests, do not rely on phone numbers or email addresses embedded in the request. Look up the number from an external source when calling. Train personnel to be cautious about any unexpected emails or letters which request urgent bank transfers, even if the message appears to have originated from a senior manager or director from the business.

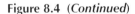

Figure 8.4 (*Continued*)

Notes

1 Europol (2019) Focus on CEO fraud. News Article 22 July 2019. https://www.europol.europa.eu/newsroom/news/focus-ceo-fraud.
2 National Crime Agency (2020) National Strategic Assessment of serious and organised crime.
3 BBC (2019) "Spoofing emails: The trickery costing businesses billions" By Joe Tidy Cyber-security reporter, Published, 27 September 2019.
4 Headquartered in Sunnyvale, California, Proofpoint describes itself as: 'A next-generation cybersecurity company protecting people, data, and brands from advanced threats and compliance risks'.
5 BBC (2019) "Spoofing emails: The trickery costing businesses billions" By Joe Tidy Cyber-security reporter, Published, 27 September 2019.

6 https://www.fbi.gov/scams-and-safety/common-scams-and-crimes/business-email-compromise.
7 US Attorney's office, Department of Justice, Monday, 11 June 2018.
8 https://www.fbi.gov/contact-us/field-offices/sacramento/news/press-releases/sacramento-fbi-encourages-business-community-to-guard-against-and-report-business-email-compromise.

Chapter 9

Identity theft fraud

Structure of Chapter 9

Chapter 9 is subdivided into the following four sections. An overview of the fraud type is provided followed by an assessment of the threat posed by the fraud, suggested response actions and timing of implementation (Figure 9.1).

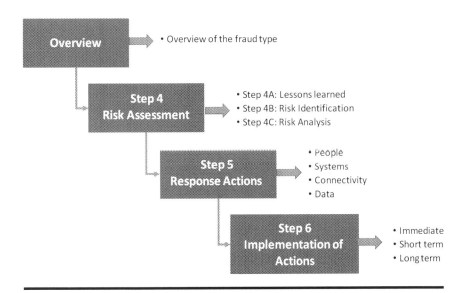

Figure 9.1 Structure of Chapter 9

DOI: 10.4324/9781003200383-11   **139**

Overview

It is important for SMEs to recognise that identity theft is something that threatens businesses of all sizes across all industries. The fact that a business has escaped identity theft to date is no guarantee it will not be targeted in the future. While businesses are preoccupied with growth and sustainability, creating an effective plan to combat identity theft is a prerequisite to ensuring that their entrepreneurial endeavours are not derailed. The National Fraud Investigation Bureau emphasises that the impact of business fraud on small or medium-sized enterprises (SMEs) can be dramatic, where the losses can ruin them.[1] Identity fraud (often abbreviated to ID fraud) is also known as 'corporate identity theft', 'company hijack fraud' and 'corporate impersonation fraud'. Identity fraud can be described as the use of a stolen identity, obtained by criminal elements, to obtain goods or services by deception.[2] As with other forms of fraud, the internet is the highway for cyber criminals. The London Digital Security Centre (LDSC),[3] England's first specialist centre is dedicated to assist SMEs protect themselves from cyber criminals. A former CEO of the LDSC, John Unsworth, considered that CEO's or MD's are responsible for the culture, reputation, expenditure and the bottom-line performance of their business and without implementing the management of impersonation fraud, are effectively undermining all of those business drivers. The UK government guidance 'Crime and fraud prevention for businesses in international trade'[4] reports 'organised criminals attempt to steal the identity of honest businesses so that they can commit credit card and online banking fraud. ID scams are getting more sophisticated and harder to detect'. The UK government has been reporting for a number of years that Companies House deals with around 50 to 100 cases of corporate identity theft every month.[5] Identity theft is a specific type of fraud that requires access to personal data in order for someone to then use that data for financial gain. SME directors need to understand that for someone to impersonate them the fraudster will need their name, address, date of birth and some form of identity such as a utility bill and possibly a passport. In 2018 HM Passport Office reported that 400,000 passports are lost or stolen each year.[6] The *Daily Mail* reported that 600 passports simply vanish in the post each year.[7] Passports are critical identity documents in that they contain valuable information for fraudsters such as a person's name, date and place of birth. Also, according to the Driver and Vehicle Licensing Agency (DVLA), almost a million driving licences were lost by British drivers in 2017. A similar number has been lost in subsequent years. While cards lost or stolen can be replaced, the new card will have the same driver number as before. That means the old licence remains valid until it expires. If it falls into the wrong hands, together with other stolen or forged documents, a lost or stolen driving licence can be used to open bank accounts, obtain credit cards, take out mobile phone contracts or even buy a car on finance. It is clear criminals have no moral compass or compunction about financial theft which can result in businesses struggling to survive or even collapsing, resulting in financial ruin, job losses and hardship.

Identity theft from individuals

Identity theft from individuals is important for businesses for three reasons: job applications by individuals who have stolen someone else's identity, impersonation of a member of staff of a supplier organisation or identity theft of an existing employee putting them in a serious position of debt. The scale of this form of fraud for individuals is enormous. The Crime Survey for England and Wales (CSEW) estimated that there were 3,863,000 fraud offences (of all categories) against adults in England and Wales in the year ending June 2019.[8] In recent years identity fraud in particular has seen a significant rise, as reported in 2020 by Cifas.[9] In 2021 the UK government stated that identity fraud is growing year on year.[10] High street banks warn their personal account customers that the motive of fraudsters to steal personal data is to open a bank account, take control of and manage an existing bank account, apply for a credit card or obtain a loan using another person's identity. The first time a person learns of ID fraud could be when they receive a bill or invoice for something they hadn't ordered, or when they receive letters from debt collectors for debts that are not theirs. A person's identity is defined by a combination of 'attributes' or characteristics that belong to that person. Identity theft happens when fraudsters access enough information about an individuals' identity (such as their name, date of birth, current or previous addresses). As advised by the National Crime Agency,[11] criminals use various techniques to steal personal details, from outright theft and social engineering to harvesting data through cybercrime. Criminals have been known to take documents from rubbish bins or make contact with individuals pretending to be from a legitimate organisation. They may obtain genuine documents such as passports and driving licences in the name of another person. Identity theft from employees of a company can be used to support ransom demands, theft of intellectual property, Business Email Compromise and non-delivery fraud.

Metropolitan and Greater Manchester Police forces

In guarding against identity theft, the Metropolitan and Greater Manchester Police forces provide the following advice for individuals, much of which is relevant to businesses.[12]

Protect your address: If you start getting post for someone you don't know, try to find out why.

Protect your bank accounts: Be extremely wary of unsolicited phone calls, letters or emails from your bank or other financial institution asking you to confirm your: personal details, passwords and or security numbers. Regularly check your bank accounts and chase up any statements that you don't get when you expect them. Dispose of anything containing your personal or banking details by using a cross-cut shredder or tearing into small pieces.

Protect your phone: Never reply to unsolicited text messages, even to get them stopped. Simply delete them. Install antivirus software on your phone.

Protect your computer: Keep your computer security programs, such as antivirus and firewall, up to date. Make sure your web browser and operating system are the latest versions. If you're not sure how to do this, ask a computer specialist or someone you trust. Be wary of clicking on links in unsolicited emails. They may contain viruses or other programs that can harm your computer.

Protect your property: Property fraud is when a person pretends to be you and uses your stolen identity details to mortgage or even sell your land, house or business premises. Properties most at risk are those that are rented out, empty or mortgage-free. You should register your land or property with the Land Registry and keep your contact details up to date. Sign up to receive alerts if someone applies to change the register of your property and put a restriction on your property so no activity will be allowed until a solicitor or conveyancer confirms it's been made by you.

Step 4: Risk assessment

Risk assessment consists of a sequence of activities which answer the questions: what are the possible problems my business may face? how likely are they? what impact will they have? and how soon will they impact? How well these questions can be answered depends on the research undertaken. A starting point is undertaking lessons learned. For large businesses operating over a number of years, they may have developed a schedule or database of events, recording how they were managed and what degree of success was achieved. However, for SMEs, they typically have to look outside of their business for lessons learned. In addition, as technology is moving so rapidly and cyber criminals are constantly evolving their approach and developing new malware, monitoring external sources of information has assumed even greater importance.

Step 4A: Lessons learned

Recording and revisiting lessons learned provides both a permanent reference point and a reminder of where fraudsters have sought personal gain and found opportunities to deceive the business. The lessons need to be captured on a database or spreadsheet so that they can be readily reviewed and retrieved to inform business protocols. They need to be used to update policies, processes and awareness training. Fraud is evolving quickly and hence as a minimum awareness training needs to be revisited and updated on a regular basis.

To appreciate the vulnerabilities of a business to identity fraud requires an appreciation of the sequence or pattern of these fraud events, the tools and techniques employed (described here as the mechanics), historical events (captured in case studies) together with 'red flags' or the 'alarm bells' over potential exposure, as illustrated in Figure 9.2. These activities contribute to Lessons Learned which in turn assist in deciding on the actions to be implemented, to thwart identity theft fraud.

 Understanding the pattern of identity theft fraud: The goal of identity theft fraud as with all other types of fraud is financial gain. The pattern of events can follow the sequence described below, but this is just one scenario.

The fraudster:

- Obtains details about a company and its directors through websites, the media, the internet, social media sites, LinkedIn profiles and or Companies House.
- Impersonates a business through fraudulent submissions to Companies House. Sending in new filings to Companies House and in particular changing the details held such as adding an additional director.
- Determines the business's bank details through smishing, phishing and or searching through rubbish at the business's premises for bank statements to obtain banking details.

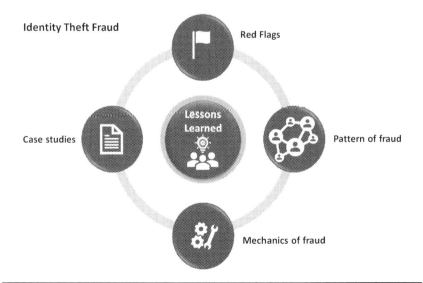

Figure 9.2 The lessons learned from prior events

■ Approaches the business's bank (as one of the directors) and makes a withdrawal, takes out a loan or mortgage or applies for a business credit card (Figure 9.3).

8/ **Understanding the mechanics of identity theft fraud:** Company identity fraud is often accomplished by the following.

Creating false (clone) websites

■ A business may be impersonated with a bogus website that appears to be legitimate. It involves criminals setting up a similar or identical-looking website using the business's logo and information but with a slightly different domain name (web address), perhaps.com instead of.co.uk. A fraudster can then use the domain to send e-mails with fake invoices, at the same time notifying recipients of a change of address and change of bank account details. In addition, bank websites may be cloned which occurred with *ING bank, Shawbrook Bank Ltd.,* and *Marcus by Goldman Sachs.* With regards to the latter, the fraudsters had been using the web address www.marcus-uk.co.uk, very similar to the real website www.marcus.co.uk and had provided a fake email contact and phone number which linked to the fraudsters.

Figure 9.3 Identity theft begins with a fraudster researching a company and its directors on the internet

Smishing

- One of the common types of 'smishing' scam is when criminals send a director a message pretending to be from their bank regarding credit card payments. *ALERT: have you authorised a payment of £320 to 'company abc'. If this was not you cancel via 'website address xyz'.*

Once scammers have got a business's credit card information, they get to work, making purchases on the internet, over the phone or by mail order, all without your card being present.

Phishing

- Many attacks may come through a business's IT system. Thieves may try to access usernames, passwords and credit card details through 'malware' such as computer viruses, worms, Trojans, spyware or adware. Fraudsters may masquerade as Companies House and request a company to visit a website and reset a password for its online filing service. If the link does not contain '.gov.uk' within the address it is not a Companies House page. Companies House will never contact a company by email or telephone to find out where a company's officers are, or to ask for secure information such as authentication codes. If your business receives a suspicious email with an attachment asking for business information to be supplied such as an authorisation code, forward it to phishing@companieshouse.gov.uk and then delete it. For those businesses that have made the transition to a digital workplace, resulting in no paper statements and files existing in the office, the focus of ID theft will be entirely online. Fraudsters may also masquerade as the business's bank. When criminals create their bogus email addresses, they often have the choice of selecting a display name which doesn't have to relate to the email address. They can, therefore, use a bogus email address that will turn up in an employee's inbox with the display name of the company's bank. The three most common ways a fraudster will seek to get an employee to respond are:
- 'We noticed a suspicious transaction on your account. To make sure your account hasn't been compromised, please click the link below to verify your identity.'
- 'During a review of our accounts, we couldn't confirm your information. Click here to review and confirm your information.'
- 'Your account has been overcharged. Please call within seven days for a refund.'

Unsecured Wi-Fi

- Planting an unsecured Wi-Fi hotspot in or around an office with the expectation that an employee will connect to it by mistake. This leaves their system vulnerable and makes proprietary information visible.

Case studies of identity fraud: Regrettably there is a dearth of case studies providing an insight into business identity theft and its consequences.

Case Study 9.1 describes a case where the fraudster engaged in research, forgery, deception and theft. This is a typical combination of activities with the ultimate goal of financial gain at the expense of an entrepreneurial company striving to gain a sustainable foothold in a competitive market.

Case Study 9.1: Identity Theft

Theft of the identity of the director of an SME

In 2017, the deputy director of a UK SME said his identity had been stolen by fraudsters. They used his details to add him as a director to the SME's records at Companies House. In addition, they obtained a fake driver's licence made out in his name and the SME's bank account details from a company cheque. The fraudsters (armed with the driving licence, record from Companies House and the bank account details) persuaded a major high street bank to add his name to the SME bank account and subsequently transferred nearly £20,000 from the business account to the fraudsters own bank account.

Source: Adapted from multiple media accounts of the fraud published in June 2017.

 Case Study 9.2: Identity theft may be in the form of job applicants adopting another person's name or a totally fictitious name. Within its 2020 Global Employment Screening Benchmark Report,[13] UK candidate screening firm HireRight makes four important observations. The first is that the appetite for employment background screening varies widely around the world, for instance in the US, around 95% of employees are screened before the appointment, whereas in Australia, it's 25% and in the UK it's as little 15%. The second is that SMEs are 30% less likely to carry out pre-employment screening than larger organisations, possibly due to the work involved, and hence have a higher exposure to risk. The third is that globally only half of employers screen temporary staff. The fourth is that the most common deliberate misrepresentations in CVs relate to false claims of previous employment and education credentials and the concealment of criminal history. Considering what a CV does not contain is just as important as reviewing what is included. Case Study 9.2 describes a job applicant's concealment of false identity papers.

 Red flags: Sometimes the way people or organisations behave might suggest they are committing a fraud. The signs are referred to as 'red flags'. There are a number

Case Study 9.2: Identity Theft

Job applicant's use of fake documents together with false statements within her CV

In 2016, a 32-year-old woman from Bristol, who had provided false identity documents to secure work as an NHS Student Nurse, was jailed for 16 months. Following a joint investigation by NHS Protect (formerly the NHS Counter Fraud and Security Management Service) and the Home Office Immigration Service,[14] the woman was found guilty of fraud at Bristol Crown Court. Specifically, she was found guilty of four offences under the Fraud Act 2006 and Identity Documents Act 2010. The woman, originally from Nigeria, secured employment at the NHS for eight years using forged and stolen identity documents, false employment references and fake EU documentation. The woman was also awarded a £13,000 NHS student bursary to fund her nursing training. In addition to the 16 months in jail, Judge Harington ordered a victim surcharge and recommended deportation. He said: 'the defendant devised a sophisticated method of remaining in the UK … the use of false identity documents is taken extremely seriously by court'. During the investigation conducted jointly by NHS Protect and the Home Office Immigration Service, passports and other identity documents were tested and found to be false (forged) and improperly obtained. Ian Gilpin, anti-fraud specialist at NHS Protect said:

> Through effective joint working with Home Office Immigration, NHS Protect was able to uncover the full extent of the woman's deception. As a result of adopting these false identities, she was able to deceive the NHS and several other government departments.

Source: Adapted from NHS Protect, *Nursing Times*: "Overseas Student Nurse Jailed for False Identity Fraud", www.nursingtimes.net/news/workforce/overseas-student-nurse-jailed-for-false-identity-fraud-15-08-2016/, *Nursing in Practice*: "NHS Student Nurse Jailed for Identity Fraud", www.nursinginpractice.com/latest-news/nhs-student-nurse-jailed-for-identity-fraud/.

of situations or events which should sound alarm bells within a business, including for instance:

- Surprising questions from the bank about loans applied for, a mortgage application, cheque book request, credit card renewal or change of address.
- Job application details that cannot be verified.

- Invoices for goods that were not ordered.
- Complaints from suppliers regarding non-payment.
- A sudden deterioration in credit ratings.
- Car lease statements for cars not leased by the business.
- Unrecognised bank transfers on bank statements.
- Questions received about the website with reference to content not posted.
- Credit card charges not relating to the activities of the business.
- Notifications from Companies House regarding a change of details not instigated by the business.
- Receipt of notification of the request for new identity documents or queries regarding a recent application for a document.
- Rejected insurance claim not instigated by the business.
- Receipt of letters addressed to the business for the attention of a director who is not known to the business.
- Correspondence regarding land registry and property ownership relating to letters not sent by the business.

Step 4B: Risk identification

Any business should look for potential weaknesses that may undermine its security and provide opportunities for fraudulent activity. The 'four steps in an attack' provides a high-level vehicle for examining any vulnerabilities in the business. In particular, consideration should be given to what information a fraudster would need to say convince the business's bank to add a new director, make a withdrawal from the account or obtain a credit card. Similarly, consideration should be given to what information a fraudster would need to lease a car, a boat or an aeroplane in the name of the business.

A risk is broken into several components, and how these components are articulated is critical to how that threat is viewed, understood and managed. 'Because of [cause], a [threat] may occur, which would lead to an [impact] on the business objectives'. The common 'cause' is the motivation of individuals to secure financial gain from a business activity, contract or project. It is a common phenomenon in the business environment and perpetually gives rise to uncertainty. The list of causes included in Table 9.1 and the list of threats recorded in Table 9.2 are not exhaustive. Fraudsters are constantly changing their approach to overcome defences that are put in place, build on the experiences of other fraudsters or move to methods that yield the best results (Table 9.3).

Table 9.1 Business identity theft causes

Business identity theft (Cause → Threat → Impact)	
The **causes** or triggers behind fraudulent activity	
Malware	Criminals send emails to employees pretending to be a known supplier or customer staff member that they regularly deal with, which has attachments infected with malware. Malware is unwittingly uploaded onto the business's server through clicking on a link, opening an attachment, downloading infected software or visiting a spoofed web address.
Property fraud	Criminals obtain details of a company's property, where there is no mortgage or it is rented together with details of the owners and the company directors and obtain a mortgage or a loan against property by impersonating one of the directors.
Support	Staff do not remain vigilant to the threat of malicious emails or links to corrupted websites. The business is lulled into a false sense of security as it has engaged an IT security firm, without recognising that staff remain the weakest link.
Sensitive information	Criminals search through rubbish bags to obtain details about the business or its banking arrangements. Sensitive information such as letters from Company House, the business accountant or solicitors' letters or invoices as well as financial records and bank statements are not shredded but placed in recycling or waste bins.
Clear desk policy	Employees leave invoices, bank records or copies of financial information on desks overnight. The business does not have a clear desk policy, so documents are clearly visible to cleaners or maintenance staff.
Clear printer policy	Prints of organisational charts, personnel records, contact lists, emails, bank records, financial information or business cases are left uncollected on printers. The business does not have a clear printer policy, so printed documents left on printers are not collected by a security person and shredded.
Red flag list	Red flag list of events is not prepared and circulated to forewarn employees of the watchpoints to be observed for detecting criminal attempts to infiltrate email accounts and/or plant malware.
Training	Staff are not provided with training specific to combatting identity theft and the induction of new staff does not include guidance on how to combat identity theft.
Audits	Audits do not undertake to establish that policies are being rigorously followed.
Checking new employees	A person's identity should never be taken at face value, particularly during the recruitment process, as once a fraudster has been admitted to an organisation, they can gain valuable information by accessing companies' systems for either their own illicit use or the benefit of others.

Table 9.2 Primary business identity theft threat

Threat (uncertain event)	
Deception by an external actor or OGC	An external actor or an organised crime group (OGC) seek financial gain through implementation of a series of activities to lay a foundation for criminal activity (such as amending Companies House records, creating a false identity and obtaining business records), to ultimately deceive the business's bank to permit a bank transfer withdrawal, allow a cash withdrawal, provide a loan, provide a business credit card or provide a mortgage.

Table 9.3 Business identity theft impact descriptions

Impact descriptions (if the threats were to materialise)	
Cash flow, operational finance and profitability	Potential cash flow problems lead to operational difficulties such as payment to employees and fixed known costs such as utility bills, vehicle tax, fuel, insurance and maintenance and council tax.
Loss of reputation	The business suffers reputational damage arising from a perceived lack of security in the wake of identity theft where, for instance, a director's identity is stolen or additional directors are added to company details held at Companies House.
Time	The director's and/or manager's time is diverted away from normal operational activities to (1) understand when and how the identity theft occurred and to reach out to the business's bank, Companies House, suppliers, contractors, partners and any other organisations that may have been contacted by the fraudster or fraudsters, and (2) the time needed to be invested in preventing a similar occurrence.
Cost	Monies are transferred to bank accounts controlled by criminals which are not recoverable.
Employee stress	Employee stress arising from the ease with which fraudsters carried out the identity theft, the loss of business finance to fraudsters and what this means for the survival of the business, uncertainty over whether it can happen again and employment uncertainty.
Relationships	Any relationships that have to be rebuilt with suppliers, contractors and joint venture partners.

Step 4C: Risk analysis

When examining the characteristics of a potential threat, it commonly involves estimating the likelihood, the impact (in cost and time together with other parameters when appropriate) and the proximity (when is the threat likely to materialise). Included in Table 9.4 is a descriptive analysis of the likelihood, impact and proximity; however, businesses need to capture actual figures for the different categories.

Step 5: Response actions

As cyber criminals employ multiple tactics and combinations of impersonation and account compromise, defending against one or two of these tactics is insufficient to address the threat as a whole. Hence a series of actions need to be completed as outlined below. The guidance below is aimed at both small enterprises with a very small number of personnel (below 10) and medium enterprises with between 10 and 49 personnel (Figure 9.4).

Table 9.4 Business identity theft risk analysis

Analysis of identity theft risks	
Likelihood	Identity theft and associated financial fraud are on the rise, and hence, there is a heightened risk of a business being targeted by criminals seeking information to dupe others or to deceive business employees into paying money into a fraudulent bank account.
Financial impact	The financial impact can be considerable if mortgages or loans are taken out in the name of one or more directors, if criminals take over the business's bank account, if land registry details of property owned by the business are altered and the property sold, if supplier representatives are impersonated and bank details changed, if staff are impersonated and if customers are erroneously informed of new bank details for the business.
Time impact	The time impact of a single identity theft incident is difficult to assess and will depend on how the theft manifested itself and the approach adopted to prevent it from happening again.
Proximity	Identity theft and its use for financial gain are on the rise, and current trends show year-on year-increase. Out of the cause assessment of 'short', 'medium' and 'long' terms, all of these risks relate to the short term and need to be addressed at the earliest opportunity.

Your People

Social media: Advise personnel to be careful what they post to social media as information may be harvested to support identity theft.

Reporting phishing: Set up a phishing reporting protocol where employee can send suspicious emails (as attachments) to the IT security team for further investigation clearly annotating them with a warning.

Training: The business must ensure that it is delivering ongoing, comprehensive cyber security and identity theft awareness training to all employees, across all business functions, to help employees to be alert, wary and vigilant. To identify emails and attachments that if responded to may seriously harm the business, recognising that fraudsters use spoof email accounts and have taken time to understand the inner workings of the business.

Bank details: If the business receives an unsolicited email or phone call from what appears to be the company's bank asking for the business's security details, the full password, login details or account numbers should never be revealed. Be aware that a bank will never ask for the business's PIN or for a whole security number or password.

Pre-employment screening techniques: Depending on the nature of the post and the level of exposure to risk, a thorough employee screening should include the following to eliminate candidates that have adopted the identity of another person (dead or alive) or have created a fictitious identity:

- Verify personal details such as addresses and telephone numbers.
- Confirm authenticity of references including the status of the referee.
- Investigate any gaps in employment.
- Exercise caution with persons giving mobile telephone numbers as contact points or temporary addresses where mail can be left.

Your Systems

Anti-fraud policies: Ensure employees are aware of the anti-fraud policies in place and the obligations/processes that they are required to adhere to avoid identity theft.

Financial details: Never permit employees to disclose or email financial details unless they are absolutely sure they know who they are speaking to or that the website they are using is secure. Fraudsters may be looking for information to support what they already know before they attempt to impersonate a director or claim to be a new director.

PROOF scheme: Sign up to the Companies House Protected Online Filing (PROOF) service, a free, secure online-filing scheme to help protect the business from unauthorised changes to your records by preventing the filing of certain paper forms. These include:

- changes to your registered office address
- changes to your officers (appointments, resignations or personal details)
- your confirmation statement.

Any forms covered by PROOF can only be filed online. Companies House will reject any paper versions of the forms and send them back to the registered office address.

Alerts: Use the free "Follow Service" provided by Companies House which sends an email alert of company transactions. The alert informs a business instantly what's been filed with Companies House as soon as it's been accepted. The email will contain a link to the filing history of the company where it can download a copy of the document for free. Alerts are also sent when a transaction is removed.

Banking: Take the following good practice steps:

- Employees to always access internet banking by typing the bank's address into your web browser.
- If emails arrive supposedly from the business's bank asking for an employee or the business to make contact, check to see if it's genuine by making contact with the bank direct.
- Never visit a website from an email link to enter personal details – if in doubt, contact the bank separately on an advertised number.
- Check the business's bank's website for safety tips.
- Check the business's bank statements thoroughly as soon as they arrive.

Figure 9.4 Risk management response actions

- Carry out qualification checks by gaining confirmation directly from the relevant institution or professional body.
- Check for judgements and bankruptcies.
- Check for parallel interests by conducting directorship searches particularly for procurement functions.
- Consider using the services of a vetting agency for more sensitive information.

In the case of agency staff, ensure that recruitment agencies employ procedures at the least the same as your own company and seek proof that investigations have been carried out.

- Employees must not leave their computer unattended when logged on to internet banking.
- Check your bank's online banking security options. Some offer free antivirus and browser security software.
- Direct employees not to leave bank statements or invoices on desks unattended for others to look at.

Shredding: Ensure employees carefully dispose of waste paper, particularly blank headed paper and financial correspondence. Ensure employees tear up or shred statements, invoices to suppliers and signed correspondence that are no longer required. Recycling all paper including bank statements, utility bills, invoices, council tax statements and credit notes while public spirited, plays into the hands of fraudsters.

Equipment: The business should establish measures to control the use and movement of equipment. Ensure staff take care of mobiles, iPads and laptop computers when using them away from business premises. Employees must keep in the back of their minds what information would be useful to a fraudster to enable them to convince their business bank to release funds.

Disclosure: Be careful what the business posts to the company website that may be used to aid identity theft.

Alerts: Use the free "Follow Service" provided by Companies House which sends an email alert of company transactions. The alert informs a business instantly what's been filed with Companies House as soon as it's been accepted. The email will contain a link to the filing history of the company where it can download a copy of the document for free. Alerts are also sent when a transaction is removed.

Credit cards: If an employee's business credit card is lost or stolen, cancel them immediately. Ensure a note is made of the emergency numbers to call.

Statements: If the business is expecting a bank or credit card statement and it doesn't arrive, inform the bank or credit card company.

Your Connectivity

Security: Visit 'Cyber Aware' offered by the National Cyber Security Centre for step-by-step instructions on keeping the business's devices up to date with the latest security updates, and for other online security advice. You can also see the Cybercrime page on the National Cyber Security Centre's web site.

Email security: Consider investing in an email security solution that detects and stops impersonation, account compromise, credential phishing and social engineering.

Your Data

Business property: Consider identity theft in relation to the business's assets where fraudsters seek to mortgage or even sell the business's land or business premises. Properties most at risk are those that are rented out, empty or mortgage-free. The business should register its land or property with the Land Registry, keep the business's contact details up to date, sign up to receive alerts if someone applies to change the register of the business's property and put a restriction on the property so no activity is allowed until a solicitor confirms it has been made by the business.

Personal information: If a request for personal information is received in an email message, employees should be wary in relation to identity theft. Most legitimate businesses have a policy that they do not ask for your personal information through email. Employees to be very suspicious of a message that asks for personal information even if it might look legitimate.

Figure 9.4 (*Continued*)

Step 6: Implementation of actions

Immediate response

If a fraud is suspected, a company must contact its bank and the police straight away. Detection will be triggered by unrecognised entries within company bank statements or unexpected letters from Companies House, the Bank or creditors. The business should sign up to the Companies House Protected Online Filing (PROOF) service as well as the free 'Follow Service', if it has not already done so.

Programme of implementation

Once anti-fraud measures have been decided upon for identity theft (as with other types of fraud), they need to be implemented as part of a project, understanding: the activities required, who will undertake them and the time frame for implementation. A rolling timetable needs to be established for the review of the suitability of the threat response measures to determine any amendments required or if any new measures are required.

Identity document validation technology

Companies that are involved in hiring significant numbers of staff may wish to consider using identity document validation technologies (IDVT)[15] which are forms of technology that can quickly and easily assist businesses to establish the authenticity of documents presented for identity verification purposes, including passports, driving licences and identity cards. IDVTs can play an important role in preventing the use of fraudulent documentation. Whilst they do not replace forgery experts, they provide higher levels of accuracy and assurance than the manual checking of documents by staff not used to checking different forms of identity documents. The forms of technology include a device to scan the identity documents – these include specialised passport and ID card readers, smartphones, webcams and flatbed scanners to capture an image of the document (some of which can also read chipped documents) and software combined with a template library of identity documents – the software checks the security features contained on the document and compares the image of the document against a template stored in the library. Algorithms are used to draw together the results of the checks and score them to indicate whether an identity document is authentic.

Personal identity theft

Credit reference agencies provide a free 'victims of fraud' service for anyone who has had their personal details used fraudulently. Importantly the credit reference agencies liaise with each other, and the banks, to restore compromised personal credit records. The service can be accessed by contacting, for example, Experian, Equifax or ClearScore by using the contact details below:

Experian: Phone: 0844 481 8000, Email: consumer.helpservice@uk.experian. com

Equifax: Phone: 0800 121 4752, Web: www.equifax.co.uk/ask

ClearScore: Web: www.clearscore.com

Summary

Identity fraud (often abbreviated to ID fraud) is also known as corporate identity theft or 'corporate impersonations'. Identity fraud can be described as the use of a stolen identity, obtained by criminal elements, to obtain goods, services or money by deception. Responsibility for identity fraud has been put firmly at the door of business leaders such as CEOs and MDs. SME directors need to understand that for someone to impersonate them the fraudster will need their name, address, date of birth, photograph and some form of identity such as a utility bill and possibly a passport. The fewer the places (such as LinkedIn, social media sites and CVs) where details are shared the lower the likelihood of ID fraud taking place. Key responses include adopting the Companies House 'PROOF' and 'Follow Service' schemes, adopting the good practice steps in relation to the business bank account, pre-employment screening, shredding waste documents and regularly checking bank and business credit card statements. Given the interest criminals have in driving licences and passports they should always be kept secure. As with all types of fraud, businesses need to remain vigilant and take steps to reduce the threat.

Notes

1 National Fraud Intelligence Bureau. https://www.cityoflondon.police.uk/advice/ advice-and-information/fa2/fraud/business-fraud/.

2 Action Fraud. "Identity fraud and identity theft". https://www.actionfraud.police. uk/a-z-of-fraud/identity-fraud-and-identity-theft. Accessed 12 June 2021.

3 The LDSC provides a suite of core subsidised digital services to SME sized businesses through working with the private sector in collaboration with UK Universities (who are providing ethical hacking and digital forensic students to support the initiative). In summary, the LDSC provides small and medium size businesses across London with confidence in trading successfully in a digital environment and ensuring that they safe in managing customer information and data to better protect their business. The services available include Security Assessments to help secure business's digital infrastructure against attacks from cyber criminals and Digital Footprint Reports to help business's understand information which could potentially be used by fraudsters. The LDSC model is unique in that it is the first time that the digital interests of the Metropolitan Police Service (through Project

FALCON), NCA and the City of London Police will work together as one Board, with MOPAC overseeing each annual programme of activity including a campaign of awareness raising and roadshows across London. PDSC regularly runs a series of programmes and events across the UK visiting local businesses with the aim of sharing detailed advice about cybercrime.

4 https://www.gov.uk/guidance/crime-and-fraud-prevention-for-businesses-in-international-trade.

5 UK Government (2021) "Guidance, Protect your company from corporate identity theft". Published 21 November 2014. https://www.gov.uk/guidance/protect-your-company-from-corporate-identity-theft. Last updated 6 May 2021.

6 https://www.gov.uk/government/news/report-your-lost-or-stolen-passport.

7 *Daily Mail* (2016) "Revealed: How almost 600 passports vanish in the post in just a year".

8 Office of National Statistics (2019) "Fraud". https://www.ons.gov.uk/aboutus/transparencyandgovernance/freedomofinformationfoi/fraud.

9 Cifas (2020) "Cifas reveals highest ever number of cases recorded to the national fraud database in 2019". https://www.cifas.org.uk/newsroom/highest-numbers-2019. Cifas is a not-for-profit fraud prevention membership organisation which it claims is the UK's leading fraud prevention service, managing the largest database of instances of fraudulent conduct in the country.

10 Guidance, "How to prove and verify someone's identity", Updated 11 February 2021. https://www.gov.uk/government/publications/identity-proofing-and-verification-of-an-individual/how-to-prove-and-verify-someones-identity.

11 National Crime Agency "Fraud". https://nationalcrimeagency.gov.uk/what-we-do/crime-threats/fraud-and-economic-crime. Accessed 12 June 2021.

12 https://www.met.police.uk/advice/advice-and-information/fa/fraud/personal-fraud/identity-fraud/, https://www.gmp.police.uk/advice/advice-and-information/fa/fraud/personal-fraud/identity-fraud/.

13 https://www.hireright.com/PDFs/2020_Benchmark_Global_Report_FINAL.pdf.

14 IDVT (identity document validation technology). https://www.gov.uk/government/publications/identity-document-validation-technology/identification-document-validation-technology.

15 https://www.gov.uk/government/publications/identity-document-validation-technology/identification-document-validation-technology.

Chapter 10

Social engineering fraud

Structure of Chapter 10

Chapter 10 is subdivided into the following four sections. An overview of the fraud type is provided followed by an assessment of the threat posed by the fraud, suggested response actions and the timing of implementation (Figure 10.1).

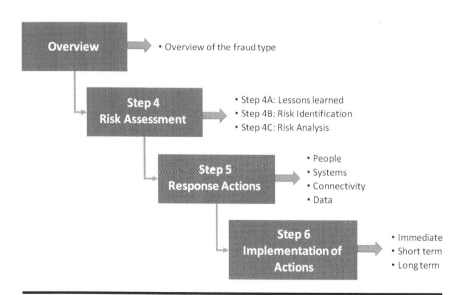

Figure 10.1 Structure of Chapter 10

DOI: 10.4324/9781003200383-12

Overview

Social engineering fraud is a manipulation technique that seeks to deceive and exploit individuals' trust in order for them to voluntarily provide confidential information, spread malware infections or give access to restricted systems. Attacks can happen online, in person and over the phone. Fraudsters aim to piece together information from various sources such as social media platforms, disreputable websites and intercepted email traffic in order to appear convincing and trustworthy while perpetrating a fraud. Social media can unwittingly be a significant aid to social engineering fraud. Social media platforms have grown in number and popularity since the year 2000. Among the commonly recognised platforms are Facebook, Instagram, YouTube, WhatsApp, WeChat, TikTok, Snapchat, and Twitter. Comprehension of their scale, presence and significance starts to dawn when it is understood that Facebook alone has nearly 3 billion active users worldwide with offices in over 80 countries. While social media sites may have been conceived as a way for friends and family to communicate, they are now important for a business to advertise its presence. Facebook declares that over 10 million companies, the majority of which are small and medium-sized businesses, use its advertising tools to connect to new customers. However, these platforms, as their collective name suggests, are used predominantly for individuals to socialise. As far back as 2011, according to a Europol press release,[1] the majority of organisations have come to accept the use of social networking sites in the workplace. Regrettably, these social networking sites have proved to be a rich source of information for fraudsters seeking to exploit employees' trust. The National Cyber Security Centre has confirmed that there was a data breach at LinkedIn, a popular professional networking site, on 5 June 2012, when user names and passwords from 6.5 million user accounts were stolen. LinkedIn has been described by an IT specialist as 'Facebook in a smart suit and tie'. News of the LinkedIn attack resurfaced in the media for many years after 2012, with speculation a much larger breach occurred in terms of the number of accounts affected and that email addresses had also been downloaded. One of the disreputable websites used by hackers was found to contain information secured from the data breach of Facebook in 2019 whereby the phone numbers, full names, locations, birthdates and email addresses of 11 million UK users had been retrieved.[2] From their research, fraudsters may be aware of regular payments that are due or of the structure of a company's organisation, enabling them to impersonate company employees. The regular complex nature of these fraudulent schemes makes it extremely difficult for individuals to spot the fraud before it is too late. Victims range across the whole spectrum from small businesses to large organisations, across numerous industries and geographies. Techniques vary and can include emails purporting to come from employees, suppliers, customers, or trade organisations; it may also include phone calls, text messages, or even leaving a malware-infected universal serial bus (USB) stick lying around in a business's reception or car park.

It should be noted that social media on its own, when accessed by employees at work, has the potential to infect business networks with spyware and other means to harvest large amounts of personal, corporate and accounting records for financial gain. In the same press release, Europol recorded that when questioned, 33% of small and medium businesses in the US said they had been infected with malicious software distributed through social networking sites. Of those infected, 35% suffered financial loss, and more than a third of these lost more than $5,000 as a result of the infection.

Step 4: Risk assessment

Risk assessment consists of a sequence of activities which answer the questions: what are the possible problems my business may face? How likely are they? What impact will they have? And how soon will they impact? How well these questions can be answered depends on the research undertaken. A starting point is undertaking lessons learned. For SMEs, they typically have to look outside of their business for lessons learned. In addition, as technology is moving so rapidly and cyber criminals are constantly evolving their approach and developing new malware, monitoring external sources of information has assumed greater importance.

Step 4A: Lessons learned

To appreciate the vulnerabilities of a business to social engineering fraud requires an appreciation of the pattern of these fraud events, the tools and techniques employed (described here as the mechanics), historical events (captured in case studies) together with 'red flags' or the 'alarm bells' over potential exposure, as illustrated in Figure 10.2. These activities contribute to lessons learned which in turn assist in deciding on the actions to be implemented, to thwart social engineering-based fraud.

 Understanding the pattern of social engineering fraud: There are usually four steps to social engineering fraud which commonly entail direct communication between the attacker and the victim. The goal of the attacker is to motivate the victim to reveal information about their employer's business, its staff or systems with the ultimate objective of persuading a member of staff to transfer funds to a fraudster's bank account.

Steps in a social engineering attack are usually as follows:

1. **Prepare** by gathering background information on the business and a specific target individual or 'victim' within the business to whom an approach will be made.

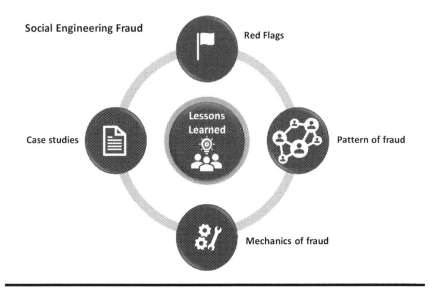

Figure 10.2 The lessons learned from prior events

2. **Infiltrate** a business by initiating an interaction with an employee; establishing a relationship with an employee and striving to gain their trust. The employee has to believe that the person contacting them is genuine and truthful. Successfully masking any lies being told is fundamental to a social engineering attack. The attacker will have undertaken what they believe is sufficient research to create a convincing story (or narrative as it is sometimes referred to), which is unlikely to arouse suspicion.

3. **Exploit the victim** once trust has been established and a weakness (way in) has been identified, methods are adopted to advance the attack. A tried and tested tool in an attacker's arsenal is creating the impression that urgent action is required to either address a serious problem that needs immediate attention or to capitalise on an opportunity which will only be available for a short time. The attacker wants the victim to act quickly rather than ponder whether there is something suspicious.

4. **Disengage** or break off contact once the victim has taken the desired action.

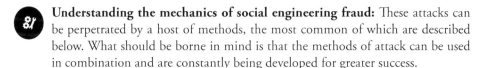

Understanding the mechanics of social engineering fraud: These attacks can be perpetrated by a host of methods, the most common of which are described below. What should be borne in mind is that the methods of attack can be used in combination and are constantly being developed for greater success.

Phishing attacks

Phishing attackers pretend to be a trusted institution or individual in an attempt to persuade employees to share confidential information including bank details.

Attacks using phishing are targeted in one of two ways:

- Spam phishing, or mass phishing which is a widespread attack aimed at many computer users. These attacks are non-personalised and try to catch any unsuspecting individual.
- Spear phishing uses personalised information to target particular computer users. Spear phishing is strongly associated with social engineering fraud where information is gleaned from other sources. The email exchange may develop a relationship based on something wholly none work-related such as sharing a picture from a wedding attended by the victim or claiming to share a mutual friend and mention up-and-coming sporting events or the sale of equipment. The wedding and sporting interests will have been picked up from Facebook or a mixture of Twitter, YouTube and Facebook. Whaling attacks specifically aim at high-value targets like upper management.

Methods used in phishing each have a unique mode of delivery. They include but are not limited to:

- Email phishing which is the most common and well-known means of phishing, using an email urging the victim to reply or follow-up by other means. Web links, phone numbers, or malware attachments can be used.
- Search engine phishing attempts to place links to fake websites at the top of search engine results. The placing of the links may be accomplished by paid ads or the use of legitimate marketing optimisation methods to manipulate search rankings.
- URL phishing links aim to tempt their victim to travel to phishing websites. These links are commonly delivered in emails, texts, social media messages or online ads, Attacks hide links in hyperlinked text or buttons, using link-shortening tools, or deceptively spelled URLs.
- In-session phishing appears as an interruption to an employee's normal web browsing. These may occur as fake login pop-ups for pages an employee is currently visiting. They may be fake antivirus alerts and offering totally useless antivirus products.
- Angler phishing takes place on social media, where an attacker imitates a trusted company's customer service team. They intercept business communications with a brand to hijack and divert a conversation into private messages, where they then advance the attack.

- Voice phishing (vishing) phone calls may be automated message systems recording all your inputs. Sometimes, a live person might speak with you to increase trust and urgency. A good example is a fake call from Microsoft Support claiming that the business has a virus on its system and they can assist to remove it. Or a caller masquerading as a telephone company may offer a new promotion which reduces costs if the existing contract is extended that day.
- SMS phishing (smishing) texts or mobile app messages might include a web link or a prompt to follow-up by way of a fraudulent email or phone number.

Baiting attacks

Baiting attacks abuse individuals' natural curiosity by enticing employees into exposing the business to an attacker. Typically, the possibility of obtaining something for free or exclusive is the manipulation adopted to exploit a victim. The attack usually involves infecting an employee's computer with malware.

Popular methods of baiting can include:

- USB drives left in car parks, outside office reception areas or in office entrance areas; and
- email attachments including details of a free offer, or fraudulent free software.

Physical breach attacks

Physical breaches involve attackers appearing in-person posing as someone legitimate to gain access to otherwise unauthorised areas or information. Attackers may pretend to be a representative of a known, regularly used and trusted supplier. They make their identity obscure but are believable enough to avoid questions. This requires a degree of research on the attacker's part and involves the risk of detection and apprehension. So, if someone is attempting this method, they have weighed up the risks and identified a clear potential for a highly valuable reward, if successful.

- Pretexting uses a deceptive identity as the 'pretext' for establishing trust, such as directly impersonating a vendor or a facility employee. This approach requires the attacker to interact with employees more proactively. The exploit follows once they've convinced the business they are legitimate. A good example is fraudsters dressed as workmen claiming they have come to test smoke alarms and fire extinguishers. A high visibility jacket, clipboard and fake identity badge may be all that is required to persuade reception to permit access particularly if they know the name of the facilities manager, discovered from LinkedIn or the company's own website. If challenged they simply say their company has sent them to the wrong address.

■ Tailgating or piggybacking refers to an attacker attempting to pass through an entrance 'gate' within an office's reception area immediately after an employee that has a 'one at a time' rule, or where ID authentication is required to enter.

Scareware attacks

Scareware is a form of malware which uses social engineering to cause shock, anxiety, or the perception of a threat in order to manipulate users into buying unwanted software. Scareware is part of a class of malicious software that includes rogue security software, ransomware and other scam software that tricks users into believing their computer is infected with a virus, then suggests that they download and pay for antivirus software to remove it. Usually, the virus isn't real and the software is non-functional or malware itself.

As a result, scareware pressures businesses to buy fraudulent cybersecurity software, or divulge private details like business account credentials.

DNS spoofing (also known as DNS cache poisoning)

DNS is an abbreviation for Domain Name System. DNS spoofing manipulates a target's browser and web servers to instead display a malicious website when a legitimate URL is entered. Once infected with this exploit, the redirect will continue unless the inaccurate routing data is cleared from the systems involved. A DNS cache becomes 'poisoned' or polluted when unauthorised domain names or IP addresses are inserted into it. The corruption of the DNS cache can be achieved either by computer malware, or network attacks that insert invalid DNS entries into the cache. There are numerous examples of DNS spoofing including the 2018 attack that affected Amazon's DNS servers, redirecting users to malicious websites.

Watering hole attacks

Watering hole attacks infect popular web pages with malware to impact many users at a time. It requires careful planning on the attacker's part to find weaknesses in specific sites. The term 'watering hole attack' takes its name from predators in nature that loiter near watering holes in the hope of attacking an unsuspecting prey. In the cyber world, these predators monitor websites which are frequently visited by their targets. They pose a high risk as they cannot be easily detected and usually target connected businesses, suppliers or employees with low-security systems. The attacker finds out vulnerabilities in those websites and plants malicious code which redirects target users to a different website hosting malware. The attacker then waits for the user to visit the new website and upon access, the visitor's computer is infected by malware. Good examples include compromised conference and academic journal websites as well as forums used for specific supplier networks.

Man-in-the-middle attacks

Where a business's network is not encrypted, an unknown third party may intercept communications that are being sent. In a 'Man-in-the-middle attack', the attacker penetrates the network and watches the exchanges between two parties. The attacker is then able to steal sensitive information, such as account passwords, banking details, or customer data. A common example of a Man-in-the-Middle attack is 'active eavesdropping'. This is when the attacker makes independent connections with the victims and relays messages between them to make them believe they are 'talking' directly to each other by email, when in fact the entire conversation is controlled by the attacker. For this attack type to yield results, the attacker must be able to intercept all relevant messages passing between the two victims and inject new ones.

 Case studies of social engineering fraud: Case studies provide a contemporary window into social engineering fraud and its debilitating effects. Case Study 10.1 is an example of a Man-in-the-Middle attack.

Case Study 10.1: Social Engineering Fraud

Unsanctioned bank withdrawal

Social engineering is not an end in itself but a way of obtaining information to secure the trust of individuals they are communicating with. Social engineering is used in preparation for say a Business Email Compromise attack. Invoice fraud involves a fraudster notifying an individual within a company that a particular supplier's payment details (that it regularly trades with) have changed and providing alternative bank details in order to carry out fraud. Following patient social engineering, invoice fraudsters are often aware of the relationships between companies and their suppliers and will know the details of when regular payments are due.

The fraud may only be discovered when the legitimate supplier follows up on a non-payment. Fraudulent emails sent to companies are often tailored and well considered, meaning the fraud is difficult to spot without strong operating processes and controls in place. Criminals can access genuine email addresses through malware infected computers. In one instance a company in the property sector was required to pay their supplier in the order of £100,000 at the end of the month. Not long before the payment was due, they received a message advising them of changes to the account details. The payment was duly made to the new account as instructed. A week later, the genuine supplier called to ask why they had not received their funds. As a week had passed, there was now only £300 left in the account penetrated by the fraudsters, the rest had been withdrawn and spent. Consequently, the company's bank was unable to recover the funds.

Source: A national bank.

Red flags: Sometimes the way people or organisations behave might suggest they are committing a fraud. The signs are referred to as 'red flags'. Defending against social engineering fraud requires employees to be *constantly* wary and vigilant. Regardless of whether they receive over 100 emails a day, they must slow down and think before responding, opening attachments or clicking on links. Attackers expect staff, particularly those under time pressure, to take action before considering the risks. Consequently, employees need to do the opposite.

Here are some social engineering red flags employees need to be aware of:

- The sender or the sender's organisation on an email is not recognised.
- A spelling mistake in an email address.
- Unexpected contact from a person claiming to be representing a recruitment organisation.
- Receipt of an email from a known person from within the company who has not made contact before and would be highly unlikely to send an email (such as a director).
- Contact from an unknown person on a faked LinkedIn account seeking to discuss a new opportunity. These are very difficult to detect. LinkedIn is a social network for professionals.
- A job recommendation from a known or unknown LinkedIn account.
- The subject line in an email received is not pertinent to the business, does not match the content, tries to create a sense of urgency, or attempts to create anxiety.

- If an email contains a reference to a request that wasn't actually made by the recipient.
- If an email refers to a conversation that cannot be recalled.
- If an email is received where it has been copied to one or more people who are not personally known, or are known but the grouping does not make sense.
- If an email (rather than the email address) contains spelling mistakes, unusual phrases or bad grammar.
- Receipt of a recommendation to install antivirus software not researched or heard of before.
- An attachment to an email received from a supplier who would not normally send these types of attachments. For instance, if the email claims to have an invoice attached but the attachment is a zipped file, then it's probably best not to open it.
- An email received was timed early in the morning (such as 3 am) when it would be extremely unlikely colleagues would be working that late.
- An email or text message is received on a Sunday evening which calls for urgent attention to avoid data loss, knowing that it would be difficult to raise IT support.
- A direction on an email to click on a hyperlink, particularly if it relates to an offer.
- If an email is received where the sender uses the salutation 'Employee', 'Dear friend', 'Valued customer', it is likely to be a phishing email.
- If an email is received from a person claiming to be working with or for a director of the company whose name and role are unknown.
- The top-level domain looks suspicious. The incorrect domain (companyname.co) might look plausible and be missed if not studied properly, when the real domain is companyname.com. These will be completely different websites and may be owned by fraudsters.
- A phone call from someone seeking information that could have been obtained elsewhere. One of the simplest yet most powerful social engineering techniques is making a deliberate 'mistake'. Most people will go out of their way to be helpful or save someone from embarrassment. This could include providing a director's schedule to someone who 'has a meeting scheduled but must have the wrong day'.
- A simple request from a visitor claiming to be a job candidate attending an interview, to plug in a USB drive to print a resume, as he had spilled coffee on his and doesn't have the time or facility to print another.
- A request made at reception to speak to an employee without an appointment and on being declined admittance asks for the email address or phone number of the member of staff.

Step 4B: Risk identification

Any business should look for potential weaknesses that may undermine its security and provide opportunities for fraudulent activity. The 'four steps in an attack' described above provide a high-level vehicle for examining any vulnerabilities in the business. Social engineering fraud is typically not an end in itself and is used to facilitate other forms of attack such as identity theft, Business Email Compromise and non-delivery fraud. Thinking through why is information collected, where will it be obtained from and how it might be used is a good starting point. Similar to other forms of attack, consideration should be given to the sources of information criminals will turn to, to learn about the organisation. For a Business Email Compromise attack, the perpetrators will want to understand the organisational hierarchy, who works in the finance department, the duties of staff and email addresses. Unwittingly websites can be a mine of information for criminals where they can understand the organisational structure, key personnel, roles and in some cases email addresses. What information is included in annual reports in terms of personnel, reporting and financial management? Have the staff been made aware of what and what not to include on social media? Pictures of office parties or office social events can offer topics of conversation to convince an employee they are exchanging an email with someone who was at one of the events. The sharing of who is on leave at a particular time can create opportunities for fraud. Detailed out-of-office messages can unwittingly give valuable information about absence from the office, second in commands and who deals with what subject together with their respective email addresses. The actual vulnerabilities of any business will be dependent on the actual nature of its business, its maturity, its day-to-day processes, its policies and the awareness training provided to staff. Included below are a number of high-level watchpoints for consideration.

- Lack of recognition of the need to provide employees with the necessary training and tools to defend the organisation against social engineering fraud in the same way they must protect exposure to BEC.
- Lack of a social media policy and the prohibition of the use of social media during office hours.
- Staff email addresses added to the website instead of using a common business email address with 'contact us' forms.
- New employees not fully inducted into the methods adopted to tackle fraud.
- Lack of fraud awareness training and subsequent updates.
- Inadequate vigilance in detecting spoofed email accounts.
- Lack of development and dissemination of 'red flag' events.

A risk is broken into several components, how these components are articulated is critical to how that risk is viewed, understood and managed. 'Because of a [cause], a [threat] may occur, which should it materialise would lead to an [impact] on the business's objectives'. The common 'cause' is the motivation of individuals to secure financial gain from a business activity, contract or project. It is a common phenomenon in the business environment and perpetually gives rise to uncertainty. The list of causes included in Table 10.1 is not exhaustive. As social engineering is a precursor to several fraud types there is overlap between this chapter and others. As it is assumed that this chapter may be read before others, risks and responses are the same or similar to those described in other chapters (Tables 10.2 and 10.3).

Table 10.1 Social engineering causes

Social engineering fraud (Cause → Threat → Impact)	
The **causes** or triggers behind fraudulent activity	
Email	
SMS phishing	A member of staff receives a text or mobile app message which includes a web link or a prompt to follow up via a fraudulent email resulting in malware being downloaded onto a business computer.
Email phishing	An employee receives an email urging them to reply or follow up by other means resulting in malware being downloaded onto a business computer.
Malware link delivery channels	The employee clicks on a link within an email containing interesting or eye-catching words permitting malware to bypass the mail server's antivirus filters.
Phone calls	
Impersonation	As with BEC, an employee in the finance department is duped by a phone call from a fraudster – claiming to be a representative of the business's bank – advising of suspicious activity on the business account and requesting the firm's password and pin to implement a freeze. The employee provides the information requested only to find on contacting the bank that they have no record of the previous conversation, the accounts have been emptied and (as the transactions had been authorised) the funds cannot be recovered.
Voice phishing	Voice phishing (vishing) phone calls may be automated message systems recording all your inputs. Sometimes, an actual person might speak to an employee to increase trust and urgency.
Pretexting	An attacker engages with an employee with the goal of obtaining information using a deceptive identity as the 'pretext' for establishing trust such as impersonating a supplier.

Websites	
Search engine phishing	Links to fake websites are placed at the top of search results. These may be paid ads, or the criminals use legitimate optimisation methods to manipulate search rankings.
URL phishing links	Employees are tempted to open phishing websites. The links are delivered in emails, texts, social media messages or online ads. Attacks hide links in hyperlinked text or buttons, using link-shortening tools, or deceptively spelled URLs.
In-session phishing	An employee's web browsing is interrupted by fake login pop-ups for pages currently being visited.
Scareware	A remote working employee falls foul of a malicious computer program designed to trick computer users into believing their computer is infected with a serious virus, suggesting that they download and pay for fake antivirus software to remove it.
Information disposal	The business does not dispose of company information securely to avoid it being read or readily reconstructed.
Social media	
Drive by download	An employee receives a post on a social media site during work hours. It is masked to look as though it was sent from friends or work associates (sources trusted by the employee). The post is used to entice the employee to click and open. Once the website is open, the drive-by download installs itself on the company computer.
Corporate identity social footprint	The business does not research publicly on social media sites to discover vulnerabilities, and the ease with which names, titles, email addresses of employees and business information can be used by social engineers.
Angler phishing	An attacker imitates a trusted company's customer service team on a social media platform. They intercept the employee's communications with the service team to hijack and divert the employee's conversation into private messages, where they then advance the attack.
Physical breaches	
Physical breaches	Access points are not regularly checked to ensure that they are secure.
Tailgating or piggybacking	Loss of equipment, sensitive hardware or intellectual property resulting from a fraudster trailing an authorised member of staff into a restricted access area of the office.
Cameras and alarms	Surveillance and alarm systems placed to detect intruders are not regularly checked to ensure that they are working.

(*Continued*)

Social engineering fraud (Cause → Threat → Impact)	
Visitor controls	No system in place to ensure that visitors to the business premises can visibly be distinguished from permanent employees in the business (i.e. no colour-coded lanyards and/or passes).
Entry	Reception is not made secure from the rest of the business premises to prevent intruders from gaining access to the offices and taking laptops, phones or files/papers.
Shadowing	Trials are not conducted to establish if non-employees can gain ready access to the premises, such as men in overalls masquerading as repair men.
Baiting	An employee picks up a dropped USB drive or CD-ROM and places in a computer to see who it belongs to, unwittingly infecting the network with malware.
Shoulder surfing	A hacker frequents the company cafeteria or food court and 'shoulder surfs' users working on their tablets or laptops. The hacker secures a large number of passwords and usernames, without having to send an email or malware.

Table 10.2 Social engineering primary threat

Threat (uncertain event)	
Deception by an external actor or OGC	An external actor or an organised crime group (OGC) seeks financial gain through collecting sufficient background information to subsequently carry out Business Email Compromise, theft of intellectual property, identity theft, theft of property, theft of data to sell or other criminal activity.

Table 10.3 Social engineering impact descriptions

Impact descriptions (if the threats were to materialise)	
Prosecution	The Data Protection Act 2018 controls how personal information is used by organisations, businesses or the government. The Data Protection Act 2018 is the UK's implementation of the General Data Protection Regulation (GDPR). Businesses using personal data have to follow strict rules called 'data protection principles'. They must make sure the information is handled in a way that ensures appropriate security, including protection against unlawful or unauthorised processing, access, loss, destruction or damage. The penalties for failure to uphold the data protection principles are financial and considerable. Depending upon the nature of the breach, there are two tiers of fines imposed upon organisations: up to €10 million or 2% of annual global turnover, whichever is greater, and up to €20 million or 4% of annual global turnover, whichever is greater.

Loss of reputation	The business suffers reputational damage arising from the theft of customer or supplier details, late payments, or tarnished customer, supplier, bank and/or partner relationships.
Time	The director's and/or manager's time is diverted away from normal operational activities to understand the extent and damage of a fraud, how it occurred and how such events are to be prevented in the future. It also involves the time establishing fraud prevention in terms of cybercrime, managing physical entry to buildings and engaging consultants to provide training (e-learning or on-site).
Financial	Monies are transferred to bank accounts controlled by criminals which are not recoverable. This in turn may lead to cash flow problems and reduced profitability.
Employee stress	Loss of monies to fraudsters due to an employee's direct actions, their anxiety over the inadequacy of the security of business systems, their tense relationships with other employees and concern over the ease with which they had been deceived.
Loss of intellectual property	The loss of intellectual property results in loss of market share and customers, and results in reduced profitability and in extreme cases the need to downsize and reduce headcount. The largest impact may be phycological in that ideas developed over years have been lost overnight.

Step 4C: Risk analysis

When examining the characteristics of a potential threat, it commonly involves estimating the likelihood, the impact (in cost and time together with other parameters when appropriate) and the proximity (when is the threat likely to materialise). Included in Table 10.4 is a descriptive analysis of the likelihood, impact and proximity; however, ideally, businesses need to capture actual figures for the different categories.

Step 5: Response actions

As cyber criminals employ multiple tactics and combinations of impersonation and account compromise, defending against one or two of these tactics is insufficient to address the threat as a whole. Hence a series of actions need to be completed as outlined below (Figure 10.3).

Table 10.4 Social engineering risk analysis

Analysis of social engineering risks	
Likelihood	As these risks have already been encountered by numerous other firms, the likelihood of their occurrence (in the absence of any mitigation actions being implemented) is very high.
Financial impact	The financial impact, should the risk materialise, will depend on whether the breach was a physical one or a cybercrime; when it was detected; what parts of the business were affected; whether data was deleted, corrupted or passed onto a third party; whether monies were paid to a bogus bank account (i.e. not one of a genuine supplier) and/or whether customers/clients were lost impacting turnover.
Time impact	The time impact is multi-faceted. It includes the loss of time spent away from core business activities when employees are engaged in anti-fraud training; the preparation of anti-fraud policies, processes and procedures; developing joint practices with partners and responding to fraud events.
Proximity	Out of the cause assessment of 'short', 'medium' and 'long' terms, all of these risks relate to the short term and need to be addressed at the earliest opportunity.

Step 6: Implementation of actions

Immediate response

Time is of the essence. Cybercrime is relentless and constantly evolving. The immediate response is to gain an appreciation of the threats, what is already in place to combat those threats and what further work is required. Once anti-fraud measures have been decided upon, they need to be implemented as part of a project, understanding: the activities required, who will undertake them and the time frame for implementation. Consideration needs to be given as to what can be undertaken by employees and what activities need to be outsourced. While SMEs do not have a bottomless pit of funds to finance external IT consultants, consideration needs to be given to potential losses and disruption if there is a cyber security breach. Taking the decision to shelve implementing response actions may be the last decision a business makes.

Monitoring implementation

A rolling timetable needs to be established for the review of the suitability of the measures adopted to determine any amendments required or if any new measures are necessary. Regular entries should be made in the calendar to review social engineering fraud prevention measures.

Your People

 Training: Deliver ongoing, comprehensive cyber security awareness training to all employees, across all business functions, to help their employees be alert, wary and vigilant. To identify emails and attachments that if responded to may seriously harm the business, recognising that fraudsters use spoof email accounts and have taken time to understand the inner workings of the business.

 Social media: Prepare and issue a social media policy. Advise personnel to be careful what they post to social media including LinkedIn as information may be harvested as part of social engineering. By openly sharing things like pet names, schools attended, links to family members or birthday, employees can give a scammer all the information they need to guess an employee's password or answer security questions. Prohibit employees accessing social media sites (and other at-risk sites) using company computers/laptops to avoid employees clicking on what look like innocent links and inadvertently downloading malware onto company systems.

 Pretexting: Make employees aware of deception by pretexting. An attacker phones an employee with the goal of obtaining information using a deceptive identity such as a supplier. The attacker advises they cannot complete an order or send an invoice as they need some specific missing detail.

 Passwords: Develop a regime of using strong passwords (and a password manager). Employees should use passwords that are unique and complex. Encourage the use of diverse character types, including uppercase, numbers and symbols, and also to opt for longer passwords when possible. Consider a move to 'passphases'.

 Business relationships: Advise employees to be wary of business relationships developed solely on-line. While the internet can be a great way to connect with people worldwide, this is a common method for social engineering attacks. Verify the identity of the individual by separate channels of communication.

 Device security: Ensure employees do not leave business devices unsecured in public. When using devices in public spaces like airports and coffee shops, employees must keep them in their possession at all times. Ensure laptops and mobile devices used in the office are locked away at night.

 Personal information: Encourage employees to avoid sharing names of their schools, pets, place of birth or other personal details on social media sites. Staff could unknowingly be exposing answers to security questions or parts of your password.

 Your Systems

 Email: Where web-based email accounts are used, periodically check the "rules" setting on the account (or accounts) to ensure that no one has set up auto-forwarding for your emails. For Microsoft Outlook, follow the thread: on the 'Home' tab, in the 'Move' group, click 'Rules', and then select 'Manage Rules & Alerts'. Check for rules created by others.

 Website content: Be careful what the business posts on its website, especially information about who has which specific job duties. Also be cautious about using out-of-office replies that give too much detail about when your executives are out of the office or the chain of command.

 Phishing address: Set up a phishing reporting protocol where users can send suspicious emails (as attachments) to the IT security team for further investigation.

 2 Factor authentication: Consider requiring employees to use two-factor authentication to access business email accounts. They would need two pieces of information to log-in, something they know (such as a password) and something they have (such as a dynamic PIN that changes constantly).

 Wi-Fi access: Never let 'visitors' connect to your primary Wi-Fi network. Access to a guest Wi-Fi connection should be made available. This allows your main encrypted, password-secured connection to remain secure and interception-free.

 Internet security: Use comprehensive internet security software. To combat rootkits, Trojans and other bots, it's critical to employ a high-quality internet security solution that can both eliminate infections and help track their source.

 Software updates: Keep all your software updated as soon as available. Immediate updates give your business's software essential security fixes. When updates are delayed, the business is leaving known security holes exposed for hackers to target. Since they know this is a behaviour of many computer users, the business becomes a prime target for socially engineered malware attacks.

Figure 10.3 Social engineering fraud response actions

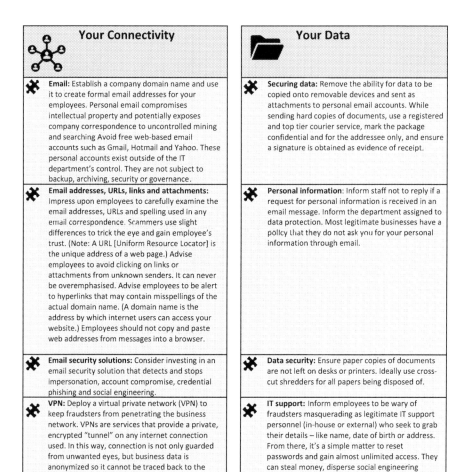

Your Connectivity	Your Data
Email: Establish a company domain name and use it to create formal email addresses for your employees. Personal email compromises intellectual property and potentially exposes company correspondence to uncontrolled mining and searching Avoid free web-based email accounts such as Gmail, Hotmail and Yahoo. These personal accounts exist outside of the IT department's control. They are not subject to backup, archiving, security or governance.	**Securing data:** Remove the ability for data to be copied onto removable devices and sent as attachments to personal email accounts. While sending hard copies of documents, use a registered and top tier courier service, mark the package confidential and for the addressee only, and ensure a signature is obtained as evidence of receipt.
Email addresses, URLs, links and attachments: Impress upon employees to carefully examine the email addresses, URLs and spelling used in any email correspondence. Scammers use slight differences to trick the eye and gain employee's trust. (Note: A URL [Uniform Resource Locator] is the unique address of a web page.) Advise employees to avoid clicking on links or attachments from unknown senders. It can never be overemphasised. Advise employees to be alert to hyperlinks that may contain misspellings of the actual domain name. (A domain name is the address by which internet users can access your website.) Employees should not copy and paste web addresses from messages into a browser.	**Personal information:** Inform staff not to reply if a request for personal information is received in an email message. Inform the department assigned to data protection. Most legitimate businesses have a policy that they do not ask you for your personal information through email.
Email security solutions: Consider investing in an email security solution that detects and stops impersonation, account compromise, credential phishing and social engineering.	**Data security:** Ensure paper copies of documents are not left on desks or printers. Ideally use cross-cut shredders for all papers being disposed of.
VPN: Deploy a virtual private network (VPN) to keep fraudsters from penetrating the business network. VPNs are services that provide a private, encrypted "tunnel" on any internet connection used. In this way, connection is not only guarded from unwanted eyes, but business data is anonymized so it cannot be traced back to the business via cookies or other means.	**IT support:** Inform employees to be wary of fraudsters masquerading as legitimate IT support personnel (in-house or external) who seek to grab their details – like name, date of birth or address. From there, it's a simple matter to reset passwords and gain almost unlimited access. They can steal money, disperse social engineering malware and penetrate the business network.

Figure 10.3 (*Continued*)

Summary

As explained in the introduction, social engineering fraud is a manipulation technique that seeks to deceive and exploit individuals' trust in order for them to voluntarily provide confidential information, spread malware infections or give access to restricted systems. Attacks are known to happen online, in person and over the phone. Attackers are constantly looking for a 'way-in' to steal something of value. There has been an exponential growth in cybercrime as a result of the internet which supports the most common method of communication and the transfer of money. A prime goal of attackers is to plant malware on company networks to gain access to the information they need to support criminal activities. This continues to be achieved by sending emails with attachments or embedded links infected with malware or creating websites similar to popular genuine websites again with the goal of spreading malware. While there are many similarities between Business Email Compromise (BEC) it could be argued that Social Engineering Fraud may include a broad range of attacks and also has a physical element too.

Notes

1　Europol (2011) "The hidden risks of social media". Press release 5 January.
2　Sky News (2021) "Facebook details of more than 500 million users – including 11 million from the UK – found on website for hackers". Sunday 4 April.

Chapter 11

Long and short firm fraud

Structure of Chapter 11

Chapter 11 is subdivided into the following four sections. An overview of the fraud type is provided followed by an assessment of the threat posed by the fraud, suggested response actions and timing of implementation (Figure 11.1).

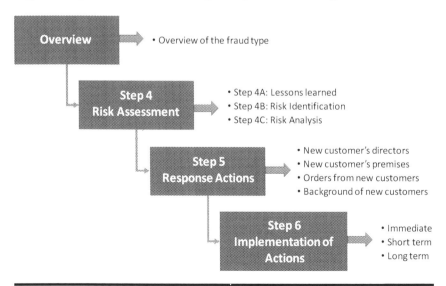

Figure 11.1 Structure of Chapter 11

Overview

Long firm fraud

In simple terms, long firm fraud is a form of deception for financial gain. It starts with criminals establishing a limited company for fraudulent purposes and registering it with Companies House listing fictitious directors and often lodging 'manufactured' accounts. They then place a lot of small orders with wholesalers and manufacturers and pay them promptly. They typically target small and medium-sized enterprises seeking to expand and with less established credit checks. Once the fraudsters have established a good credit history and have won the trust of their suppliers, they then place several larger orders with their suppliers on credit. However, there is no intention to make payment and once they receive the goods, they promptly disappear and sell the goods elsewhere. Their preference is for goods which are both untraceable and easily disposable, such as building materials, computer products and peripherals, printer cartridges, mobile phones, electrical goods, toys, sports goods, wine, spirits and confectionery. The criminals will have researched their market and executed the fraud with a specific shopping list in mind to cater to the demand from predetermined outlets. The creation of the new company requires set-up funds, which may be the proceeds from another crime or a previous long firm fraud. Once a successful fraudulent company has been established the lessons learned may be used to create multiple other companies. The fraud can be prosecuted under the Fraud Act 2006, typically under Section 2 or 11. Section 11 for instance relates to obtaining services dishonestly where the defendant: obtains for himself or another, services dishonestly, knowing the services are made available on the basis that payment has been, is being, or will be made for them and avoids or intends to avoid payment in full or in part.

It has been suggested in the media that the name 'long firm fraud' originates from the activities of organised criminal groups based in the East End of London in the late 1950s and early 1960s, where 'long' is a reference to the fraud being perpetrated over a long period of time and 'firm' being derived from the name given to the criminal organisation led by the Kray twins, thought to be the first to carry out this type of fraud. Ronald 'Ronnie' Kray and Reginald 'Reggie' Kray, were British criminals, the principal perpetrators of organised crime in the East End of London from the late 1950s to 1967. Supported by their gang members, known collectively as the Firm, the Krays were involved in murder, armed robbery, arson, fraud, protection rackets and assaults. Other notable criminals operating in the same era included Eddie Richardson who was considered to be a long firm fraud specialist whose operation included importing goods from Italy.[1]

Short firm fraud

Short firm fraud (sometimes referred to as phoenix fraud), occurs when a firm is established for a short duration for the sole purpose of committing fraud. While similar to long firm fraud, it takes place over a much shorter timescale. Typically the fraudulent business does not try to establish any form of credit history. It may register a limited company with Companies House and file false accounts if merchants or wholesalers will not supply their goods without knowing these details. The fraudulent business has no day-to-day trading activity. The fraud is typically executed by placing several simultaneous small orders on credit from several wholesalers. The fraudsters prefer goods that aren't traceable, turn over quickly and are easily disposable such as computer products and peripherals, printer cartridges, mobile phones, electrical goods, toys, wine and spirits. The fraudulent firm makes a profit by selling the goods immediately, locally or elsewhere. The goods are sold on for cash and the criminals then close the firm down and disappear. Since the fraudulent firm places several small orders with several wholesalers, the total goods received is significant and the fraudulent firm makes a significant profit. The impact for those defrauded is serious financial loss as well as, for instance, low staff morale, adverse publicity, disruption caused by a major investigation, or even further fraud of a similar nature. The SME wholesalers who suffer a loss, while having the option to approach the law courts, may decide not to pursue a claim if they anticipate the legal expenses will exceed the value of the goods taken by the fraudulent firm.

Step 4: Risk assessment

Risk assessment consists of a sequence of activities which answer the questions: what are the possible problems my business may face? How likely are they? What impact will they have? And how soon will they impact? How well these questions can be answered depends on the research undertaken. A starting point is undertaking lessons learned. For large businesses with established enterprise risk management and business continuity planning processes that have been operating over a number of years, they may have developed a schedule or database of events, recording how they were managed and what degree of success was achieved. However, for SMEs, they typically have to look outside of their business for lessons learned.

Step 4A: Lessons learned

Advice and lessons learned can be obtained from the websites of Action Fraud, the Metropolitan Police Force, the Thames Valley Police Force, The Financial Conduct Authority, The Fraud Advisory Panel and The City of London Police. To gain a more in-depth understanding of the vulnerabilities of a business to long and short firm fraud requires an appreciation of the sequence or pattern of these fraud events, the tools and techniques employed (described here as the mechanics), historical events (captured in case studies) together with 'red flags' or the 'alarm bells' over potential exposure, as illustrated in Figure 11.2. These activities

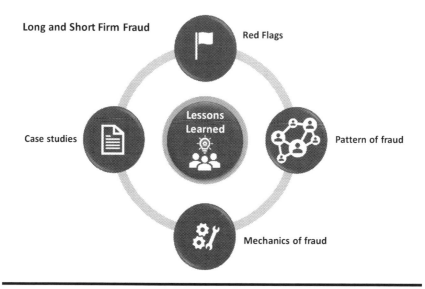

Figure 11.2 The lessons learned from prior events

contribute to Lessons Learned which in turn assist in deciding on the actions to be implemented, to thwart identity theft fraud.

 Understanding the pattern of long firm fraud: The goal of long firm fraud as with all other types of fraud is financial gain, typically to support a lavish lifestyle. The pattern of events typically follows the sequence described below; however, examination of case studies shows that there are variations on a theme.

The criminal group:

- establishes a market for their target goods and in some cases establishes buyers;
- registers a company name with Companies House which typically has been purchased from an online formation agent;
- lists the names of company directors, which are all fictitious;
- registers with Companies House a set of false accounts to give the impression that the business has been operating successfully for at least two years whereas the company may have only been in existence for just a week;
- ensures that the fraudulent accounts record they have either been prepared or audited by a legitimate firm of accountants, although this will have been done without the accountants' knowledge[2];

- prepares fraudulent letters of reference incorporating the logo, web address and telephone number of a legitimate firm of solicitors. Firms are picked which have multiple offices across the UK. Each letter omits the address of the office of origin, a partner's name and a date, to make it very difficult for any of the solicitors, if challenged, to refute or confirm the authenticity of the letter;
- rents business premises on a short-term basis, typically on a multi-occupancy trading estate, in the full knowledge they will vacate at very short notice;
- occupies the rented premises selected for its size and type to suit the size and quantity of the goods to be handled and the length of storage time, which is planned to be as short as possible;
- places a large number of small orders and pays wholesalers and suppliers promptly to establish trust and good credit history;
- trades as a legitimate company for a period of time;
- places a number of very large orders on credit and upon receipt of the goods promptly disappears with the goods and sells them elsewhere; and
- only visits the premises to receive or transfer goods once the large orders have been placed.

Initial success may prompt a criminal group to set up multiple fraudulent companies (Figure 11.3).

Figure 11.3 Prompt movement of goods from the rented accommodation

Understanding the pattern of short firm fraud: The goal of short firm fraud as with long firm fraud is financial gain. The pattern of events is very similar to long firm fraud but with a few distinct differences. The fraudsters:

- do not always register a company with Companies House;
- do not trade as a legitimate company for a period of time to develop a credit history;
- do not place large orders but typically places a very large number of small orders simultaneously;
- place orders with companies a significant distance from where they take receipt of the goods to dissuade companies visiting their premises;
- only obtains goods on credit; and
- create entities that exist for a very short period of time.

Understanding the mechanics of long and short firm fraud: A key activity for the fraudsters is to find suppliers of the goods that they have buyers for and to persuade them to supply goods on credit.

- The fraudsters visit trade shows throughout the UK and Europe with a view to opening accounts and obtaining goods on credit.
- Avoid face-to-face contact with suppliers where possible. Purchases over the phone are popular for the fraudsters as the sales representatives cannot see the buyer or their premises. The fraudsters capitalise on the fact that SMEs typically operate in very competitive markets – and hence are always looking for new clients to increase sales.
- The internet provides even greater benefits. It removes direct contact with the supplier, overcomes any possible language difficulties (dialogue) and removes the traditional benefits for the seller who would normally be able to detect if the buyer was experienced in the industry and in particular whether they were knowledgeable about the product, pricing structures, production times and transportation. For the fraudsters, it also avoids being questioned about the business other than what is included in any fields to be populated on the order forms on seller's the website. Also with internet orders, the sellers are not always able to detect whether the address provided is a business or private address, which in the case of the latter, may relate to a house which has been rented for cash for a fixed short term.

Case studies of long firm fraud: While the threat of long and short firm fraud still exists, as indicated by Action Fraud and the Metropolitan Police, it would appear from historical cases, it is no longer as prevalent as it once was.

Case Study 11.1: Describes a widely reported case involving long firm fraud conducted over nearly ten years involving nine defendants.

Case Study 11.1: Long Firm Fraud

Prosecution of nine defendants for long firm fraud

Operation Barber instigated by the Department of Trade and Industry (DTI) which transitioned into the Department of Business Innovation and Skills (BIS), led to the prosecution of nine individuals who together perpetrated long firm fraud through the creation and operation of nine fraudulent limited liability companies between November 1998 until July 2007. The group traded as construction companies based in the East Midlands. The investigation found that one of the defendants, who was involved with eight of the fraudulent companies, was an insolvency practitioner and used his position to allow the gang leader to defraud creditors, unchecked, for a considerable period of time. The BIS operation led to two trials at Southwark Crown Court, the first led to the conviction of seven defendants, including the ring leader, Demitris Bains, who were sentenced on 28 February 2014 when a total of just over 17 years imprisonment were handed down. His Honour Judge Jeffrey Pegden QC said the case involved: 'A massive fraud of £5 million involving nine companies over a period of seven years which had undermined local business confidence and had caused loss to small traders and businesses which were repeatedly targeted by those involved'. Sentencing, the Judge said:

> You have all been involved in a very significant long firm fraud in the Midlands. You used a number of companies as vehicles for fraudulent trading. Those companies pretended to be legitimate and they persuaded trade suppliers to grant trade facilities in order to obtain goods and material on account. Many, many creditors were left completely unpaid and were often smaller trade creditors, in some cases becoming bankrupt. A serious aggravating feature in this case is that many of the already defrauded trade suppliers were re-targeted by the next company in line.

> These people deliberately set out to defraud local builders and builders' merchants who, in some cases, nearly lost their livelihoods. In January 2007 we worked with three police forces across Derbyshire, Leicestershire and Nottinghamshire with 140 staff executing 31 warrants. It was the biggest operation of its time.

Source: Adapted from www.gov.uk press releases; https://www.gov.uk/government/news/10-year-investigation-ends-as-final-offenders-are-sentenced.

Case Study 11.2: While it is difficult to ascertain with any degree of certainty as to how far records go back for this type of fraud, case studies prepared by the Serious Fraud Office illustrate that long firm fraud has been perpetrated for over 20 years. Case Study 11.2 centred on three long firm frauds carried out by five defendants in the 1990s.

 Case Study 11.3: Represents an example of the deployment of the enforcement tool introduced under the powers enshrined in the 2017 Criminal Finances Act to freeze bank accounts and strip criminals of the proceeds of crime, in this case, a series of long firm frauds.

Case Study 11.2: Long Firm Fraud

Cooperation from US Marshalls leads to bringing a fraudster to justice

An SFO case, accepted for investigation in September 1994, resulted in five defendants being sentenced to a total of nine years and three months. One defendant, Shariq Chughtai (66), former Director of BT Imports Ltd, A&D Supplies (Portsmouth) Ltd and Teamleader Ltd, pleaded guilty on 27 July 1998 to two offences of conspiracy to defraud. He was bailed pending the trial of co-defendants but subsequently failed to appear for sentencing on 9 December 1998. That hearing was adjourned and he again failed to attend court on 19 February 1999 when he was sentenced, in his absence, to four years' imprisonment. The case centred on three long firm frauds. The criminals placed lots of small orders with wholesalers and paid them promptly. Having established good credit history and having won the trust of their suppliers, the fraudsters then placed several larger orders with their suppliers. But once they receive the goods, they promptly disappeared and sold the goods elsewhere.

Mr Chughtai was located in the US and an extradition request was sent in late 2015, by the SFO. Mr Chughtai arrived in the UK on 8 September 2016 and was produced at Portsmouth Crown Court where he was sent to prison to serve his four-year sentence for two counts of conspiracy to defraud. The judge passed a consecutive sentence of three months for a Bail Act offence. The SFO expressed their gratitude for the assistance of the Home Office, Hampshire Constabulary, US Marshals and the United States Department of Justice.

Source: Serious Fraud Office. https://www.sfo.gov.uk/cases/shariq-chughtai/.

Case Study 11.3: Long Firm Fraud

Proceeds from long firm frauds seized

The SFO secured the forfeiture of over £1.5 million from suspected fraudster Nisar Afzal, 61, of Birmingham. The forfeited money came from the sale of two properties in Birmingham, which Afzal originally bought with the funds from a series of long firm frauds. Afzal, who fled Britain for Pakistan in the mid-2000s, was also implicated in a series of mortgage frauds, for which his brother, Saghir Afzal, was convicted and jailed in 2011 for 13 years. The case is believed to represent one of the largest seizures of its kind in the UK and is the SFO's first use of this enforcement tool, brought in under new powers from the 2017 Criminal Finances Act. Mark Thompson, Chief Operating Officer at the Serious Fraud Office said: 'Nisar Afzal decided to become a fugitive from justice instead of remaining in the UK to answer for his activities. Our actions send a clear message to anyone involved in fraud, bribery or corruption – that we will work tirelessly to get back the proceeds of your crimes'. The money recovered will be returned to the Treasury and invested in public projects. Prior to the forfeiture, the money was subject to an account freezing order to prevent Nisar Afzal from withdrawing funds. An arrest warrant for Nisar Afzal remains in force.

Source: Serious Fraud Office, 15 March 2019 (updated 14 June 2021). "SFO Nets £1.52m from Suspected Birmingham Fraudster".

Case Study 11.4: This case is significant in that the fraudsters acquired an existing company to mask their fraudulent activity however they were unmasked by observant and alert credit rating agencies who notified the police. Unfortunately, a significant number of companies suffered substantially in a short space of time.

Red flags: Sometimes the way organisations behave might suggest they are committing a fraud. The signs are referred to as 'red flags'. There are a number of situations or events which should sound alarm bells within a business when reviewing a new customer and its behaviour:

- Large orders received 'out of the blue' when previously the company had only been placing numerous small orders.
- Questions raised by fellow traders on the company's payment history.

Case Study 11.4: Long Firm Fraud

Proceeds from long firm frauds seized

A case led by the West Midlands Police economic crime unit led to the prosecution of five defendants at Birmingham Crown Court for a long firm fraud. All five men were given prison terms, three receiving five years each and the other two both receiving two-and-a-half years each. What sets this case apart from other reported crimes is that the fraudsters used an off-the-shelf business, originally purchased by a Kenyan-born businessman in 1999 which was operated legitimately until 2004, as a front for the fraud. This company, Mercury Distribution Ltd, was in business as a wholesale supplier of electrical goods. When the fraudsters acquired it, the change of ownership and the new director's names were not notified to Companies House as the law requires. In addition, the fraudsters filed false accounts for Mercury Distribution Ltd showing a five-fold growth and assets worth £1 million. These false accounts meant the company was given a high credit rating by reference agencies when suppliers checked their credit status. Over a four-month period from February 2005, the fraudsters ordered goods such as mobile phones, luxury cars, alcohol and steel totalling £1.4 million from well-known firms and small businesses. More than 40 companies supplied the business. Orange was left with a £190,000 debt and Vodafone lost £172,000. A car leasing company lost £200,000 through the lack of recovery of seven luxury cars, including four Mercedes, one worth £75,000 and a Porsche Cayenne valued at £42,000. During credit reference searches Dun & Bradstreet became suspicious of the pronounced change in the company's trading pattern and reported their concerns to the police. Some £300,000 worth of fraudulently obtained goods were recovered by the police. Sentencing the men, His Honour Judge Peter Carr said: 'This case struck at the very heart of the way business operates and it undermines the whole system of trust that must exist between those ordering and those supplying'.

Source: Adapted from West Midland Police economic crime unit; the BusinessLive.co.uk; Birminghammail.co.uk; Motorfinanceonline.com and media reports.

- The accountant named as the auditor on accounts submitted to Companies House denies knowledge of the accounts and the company.
- The solicitors named as references lodged by the company all deny writing a reference.
- The company makes excuses as to why it is not convenient to visit their premises.

- It is difficult to trace the directors listed on the submission to Companies House.
- The years of trading referred to on their accounts do not match the commencement date of the business.
- Neighbouring businesses to the company's premises state that the company has been at its current address for only a short period of time which is inconsistent with details supplied by the company.
- The business is operating in numerous and varied markets which are inconsistent with the Companies House records.
- The business appears to be only trading in untraceable high turnover goods.
- The business has changed from focussing on one sector of one industry like plumbing goods to trading in wine, spirits, electrical goods and cars almost 'overnight'.
- The only way of contacting the business is through webmail-based email addresses and mobile telephone numbers.
- The trade references provided by other companies do not appear authentic and it is suspected criminals have formed companies to fraudulently provide references for each other.
- The trading history is difficult to substantiate.
- One the directors was previously disqualified from acting as a director of a limited company.
- One of the directors is a known associate of a convicted criminal.
- The owner of the domain name of the business's website is inconsistent with the name of the business.

Step 4B: Risk identification

Any business should look for potential weaknesses that may undermine its security and provide opportunities for fraudulent activity. A method for understanding any potential weaknesses is to examine the pattern and mechanics of long and short firm fraud and to keep an eye on the red flags as key indicators of something that may not be right. Case studies are also a guide to potential risks but clearly, those recorded in this chapter only represent a very small sample.

A risk is broken into several components, how these components are articulated is critical to how that risk is viewed, understood and managed. 'Because of a [cause or causes], a [threat or adverse event] may occur, which would lead to [impact]'. The common 'cause' is the motivation of individuals to secure financial gain from a business activity, contract or project. It is a common phenomenon in the business environment and perpetually gives rise to uncertainty. The general risk description is included in Table 11.1. The approach adopted by fraudsters has remained largely unchanged for over 40 years.

Table 11.1 Long firm fraud threat

Long firm fraud (Cause → Threat → Impact)	
Threats (uncertain events)	
New customer places order, does not pay and disappears with the goods	Criminals place an order for and take receipt of goods and subsequently close their business, shut down their premises and disappear with the goods. The directors named on the business records held at Companies House prove to be fictitious as do the lodged accounts and letters of reference, supposedly prepared by legitimate accountants and solicitors, respectively.

Table 11.2 Long firm fraud impact descriptions

Impact descriptions (if the threats were to materialise)	
Cash flow, operational finance and profitability	Potential cash flow problems lead to operational difficulties such as the payment of employees and fixed known costs such as utility bills, vehicle tax, fuel, insurance and maintenance and council tax.
Loss of reputation	The business suffers reputational damage arising from a perceived lack of business maturity, appropriate controls and staff training.
Time	The director's and/or manager's time is diverted away from normal operational activities to review, revise, implement and embed new working and trading practices to prevent a similar occurrence and to understand the impact on their market share if the decision was taken not to issue goods on credit.
Cost	Losses arising from the goods that were never paid for.
Employee stress	Employee stress arising from concerns over the actions of the fraudsters, the potential for it to happen again, the time it takes for fraudsters to be brought to justice, the ability of the business to survive the losses and employment uncertainty.

As with the impact from other fraud types, the impact descriptions below are generic in nature and need to be tailored to the business, its context and ongoing operations (Table 11.2).

Step 4C: Risk analysis

When examining the characteristics of a potential threat it commonly involves estimating the likelihood, the impact (in cost and time together with other

Table 11.3 Long firm fraud risk analysis

Analysis of identity theft risks	
Likelihood	The likelihood of long and short firm fraud is less prevalent than it once was; however, businesses should remain wary and adopt a risk-based approach.
Financial impact	This type of fraud can leave SMEs struggling (such as the ability to pay fixed costs) and in extreme cases bring about their demise.
Time impact	The time impact will depend on the extent of the financial losses and whether it impacts the scale of operations such as the ability to buy raw materials, manufacture, the ability to maintain the current number of employees, the purchase and resale of goods, etc.
Proximity	Out of the cause assessment of 'short', 'medium' and 'long' terms, this type of fraud can occur in any timeframe as it is not limited by technology, traceability or transportation.

parameters when appropriate) and the proximity (when is the threat likely to materialise). Included in Table 11.3 is a descriptive analysis of the likelihood, impact and proximity; however, where possible businesses need to capture actual figures for the different categories.

Step 5: Response actions

There are several steps that a business can take to protect itself from long firm and short firm fraud as included in Figure 11.4. In particular, always treat newly-formed firms with suspicion. In particular, stop and evaluate before accepting a much larger order from a company that your business has been trading with for only a relatively short period of time.

Step 6: Implementation of actions

Implementation of short-, medium- and long-term actions

With most forms of fraud identified, response actions cannot be be implemented all at once due to the typical constraints of cost, time (for fleshing out responses and their implementation), personnel and or know-how. While associations with trade associations can be formed over the medium and long term to understand: current trends; methods adopted; the prevalence of the fraud and recent convictions, key responses need to be carried out in the short term as part of day-to-day operations to take proactive risk management steps to thoroughly assess potential new clients.

New customer's directors

✺ **Checks:** Carry out checks on the directors of limited companies who are potential new customers:

- Identity: Take steps to verify the identity of the directors.
- History: Obtain details of directors' involvement in other businesses, number of years traded, previous references and bankers.
- Director suitability: Check publicly available databases such as the Insolvency Service and Companies House websites to see if the individuals have been bankrupt, or otherwise disqualified from acting as a director of a limited company.
- Credit history: Ask to check the credit histories of the people running the business.

New customer's premises

✺ **Premises:** Carry out checks on the premises:

- Trading duration: How long have they traded from the present and past business addresses?
- Ownership: Are the premises owned or leased?
- Occupation: Are the premises occupied?
- Visit: Cold call on the new customer's premises to carry out first-hand checks on the staff, the main line of the business and the type, range and quality of goods held.
- Occupancy: Check with the landlord of the premises and neighbouring businesses to confirm the length of occupancy.
- Storage: Are the premises large enough for the proposed business?
- Use: Are the premises being used mainly as a delivery point?

Orders from new customers

✺ **Liabilities:** Reduce risk exposure by:

- Payment: Asking for part payment in advance.
- Part orders: Making part deliveries to limit exposure.
- Guarantees: Asking for personal guarantees from the directors.
- Follow on orders: Being very wary of supplying additional orders if a previous payment has not been received.
- Sales and Payment: Ensure the sales and credit control functions speak to each other regularly and particularly on receipt of large orders to be made on credit. Have all previous invoices been settled/paid? Sales should not operate independently of credit control.
- Order size: Stop and consider before accepting a much larger order from a business that the business has only been trading with for a relatively short time.
- Premises: If on visiting a buyer's premises any aspect of their business appears suspect, take advice and supply on a cash-only basis, if at all.

Background of new customers

✺ **New customer details:** Carry out checks on potential new customer's business details:

- Check the trading history: Obtain details of who trades with the business.
- References: Ask the business for trade references. Check the authenticity of the referees/references. If supplied by solicitors, contact the solicitors. Check that references are not provided by other companies owned by the directors.
- Communication: Be wary if the only ways of contacting a business are through webmail-based email addresses and mobile telephone numbers. Check who owns the domain names of any website the business uses.
- Filed accounts: If it's a limited company, find out if it has filed accounts with Companies House; check whether the accounts are credible given the commencement date of the company; and ensure they have been prepared by a genuine accountant.
- Longevity: Establish how long have they been in business?
- Staff changes: Monitor changes in personnel.
- Addresses: Ensure that goods are delivered to identifiable individuals and addresses, and don't allow goods to be cross-loaded to unidentifiable vehicles waiting at the delivery location.

Figure 11.4 Risk management response actions

Summary

Long and short firm fraud are yet more forms of deception perpetrated for financial gain. Both forms of fraud start with criminals establishing a limited company for fraudulent purposes and registering it with Companies House, listing fictitious directors and often lodging false accounts. Long firm fraud is implemented by initially establishing a strong credit rating through prompt payments and then placing large orders on credit where the goods are quickly moved to a secret location and are never paid for. Short firm fraud is similar however a very large number of small orders are placed on credit-only-basis and in the same way, the received goods are quickly moved to a secret location and the suppliers are never paid. The key for the fraudsters is not to leave a trail of any kind. Hence directors' names are false as are any annual accounts or references lodged with Companies House. The fraudsters' preference is for goods which are both untraceable and easily disposable. Typically buyers are established before the fraudsters take receipt of goods. Unfortunately, the same SME may be the target of this type of fraud over and over again as fraudsters establish multiple illegal companies and repeatedly use the same modus operandi. The impact for those defrauded is serious financial loss as well as, for instance, low staff morale, adverse publicity, disruption caused by a major investigation, or even further fraud of a similar nature. A number of responses are proposed relating to checking a new potential customer through examining its directors, premises and trading history. In addition, measures can be taken to reduce potential risk exposure through say limiting the scale of goods offered on credit, insisting on part payment and ensuring sales and credit control functions are coordinated. In addition, lodged accounts and references can be checked as well as determining whether listed directors have ever been disqualified or been declared bankrupt.

Notes

1 The Independent (2012) "Charlie Richardson: Shrewd and ruthless leading figure of London's 1960s criminal scene", Friday 21 September.
2 AccountancyAge (2005) "'Long-firm' scams blight practices". https://www.accountancyage.com/2005/04/25/long-firm-scams-blight-practices/.

Chapter 12

Counterfeit goods fraud

Structure of Chapter 12

Chapter 12 is subdivided into the following four sections. An overview of the fraud type is provided followed by an assessment of the threat posed by the fraud, suggested response actions and timing of implementation (Figure 12.1).

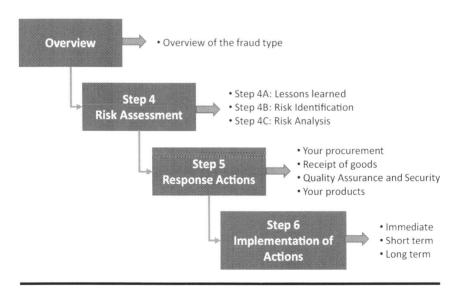

Figure 12.1 Structure of Chapter 12

DOI: 10.4324/9781003200383-14

Overview

Counterfeit products bear the brand or trade name of legitimate goods but violate trademark and intellectual property laws. Product counterfeiting poses a major threat to the public from poor reliability through to illness and death. Regrettably, there is what may be described as a tidal wave of counterfeit goods entering the UK and Europe as a whole. For legitimate businesses within a significant number of industries counterfeiting results in a loss of market share (from a lack of differentiation) together with falling sales and profitability. According to BSI[1] high-end electronics, pharmaceutical, automotive, software and aerospace companies are plagued by counterfeit products due to the short supply and higher profit margin. Europol has highlighted that profits from counterfeiting fund other forms of serious organised crimes like human trafficking, money laundering or labour exploitation, and counterfeiting production factories commonly violate labour and environmental laws as well as basic human rights.[2] During 2019, members of the long-established not-for-profit trade association called the Anti-Counterfeiting Group (ACG),[3] reported increasing numbers of physical products entering the UK by air, sea and road, from countries such as China, Hong Kong, India, Pakistan, Turkey, Singapore, Macedonia, Thailand and Malaysia. The ACG considers these goods to be dangerous to consumers and damaging for businesses. They include electrical products such as chargers and batteries, hair appliances, household goods, toys, luxury goods, fast-moving consumer goods, clothing, footwear and apparel. They are being sold both online and at physical locations such as markets, wholesale and retail shop premises and through social media platforms. The counterfeiters use social media platforms such as Twitter as well as e-commerce sites such as Bonanza, Gumtree, Amazon and Alibaba, due to their worldwide reach to facilitate sales of their fake products. A recent report by the EU Observatory[4] described 25 online business models being adopted by criminals as they bring goods to markets, using legitimate shipping and fast parcel operations, trading platforms and payment facilities. According to research conducted by the Organisation for Economic Co-operation and Development,[5] imports of counterfeit and pirated goods to the UK in 2016 accounted for as much as £13.6 billion – the equivalent of 3% of genuine UK imported goods. Between 2018 and 2019, Government figures show electrical fires were responsible for 1,584 deaths and injuries, or more than four each day. Electrical Safety First,[6] a consumer-focused charity, has run major media campaigns to raise public awareness of the dangers of counterfeits, specifically the online sales of fake electrical goods, which may deliver a fatal shock or catch on fire. According to the 2009 CIMA Fraud risk management guide, in 2006, 14 Siberian towns declared a state of emergency due to mass poisoning caused by fake vodka. Around 900 people were hospitalised with liver failure after drinking industrial solvent that was being sold as vodka. In the same year at least 100 children died after ingesting cough syrup that had been mixed with counterfeit glycerine. The counterfeit compound, actually a dangerous solvent, had been used in place of more expensive glycerine. As highlighted by Electrical Safety First:

> It has never been easier for counterfeit products to enter the UK marketplace, with internet-based sales portals, social media marketplaces and the ability for anyone with a bank account and internet access to import products from anywhere in the world.[7]

In addition, lower sales in the wholesale and retail sector in the UK due to counterfeit and pirated imports results in lower tax revenues for the UK Government from value-added tax (VAT), corporate income tax, personal income tax and social security contributions.

Step 4: Risk assessment

Risk assessment consists of a sequence of activities which answer the questions: what are the possible problems my business may face? How likely are they? What impact will they have? And how soon will they impact? How well these questions can be answered depends on the research undertaken. A starting point is undertaking lessons learned. For large businesses operating over a number of years, they may have developed a database of events, recording how they were managed and what degree of success was achieved. However, for SMEs, they typically have to look outside of their business for lessons learned. There are a number of organisations combatting the sale of counterfeit goods which describe the threat and possible responses. These include the UK government's Intellectual Property Office, the World Health Organization (WHO), Interpol, Europol, the World Customs Organization (WCO), the World Intellectual Property Organization (WIPO), the International Trademark Association (INTA), Electrical Safety First, the National Trading Standards and the Chartered Trading Standards Institute.

Step 4A: Lessons learned

To appreciate the vulnerabilities of a business to counterfeit fraud requires an appreciation of the sequence or pattern of these fraud events, the tools and techniques employed (described here as the mechanics), historical events (captured in case studies) together with 'red flags' or the 'alarm bells' over potential exposure, as illustrated in Figure 12.2. These activities contribute to Lessons Learned which in turn assist in deciding on the actions to be implemented, to counterfeit fraud.

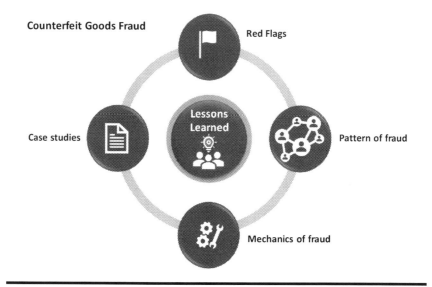

Figure 12.2 The lessons learned from prior events

Understanding the pattern of counterfeit goods fraud: The production, movement, storage and sale of counterfeit goods follows a simple pattern as described in Figure 12.3. The pattern typically (but not exclusively), follows the four steps below. While the potential benefits (in terms of financial income) can be huge, the production, movement and sale of counterfeit goods requires an initial at-risk investment as well as knowledge of recruitment, staff management, acquiring raw materials, production, packaging, branding, storage, distribution, advertising, web design, social media, logistics and sales. If the counterfeit goods are to be sold cheaper than the original products then all these aspects need to be carefully controlled. The pattern of the fraud is best described by the following steps.

Manufacture: Fake goods are manufactured predominantly outside Europe using cheap labour usually flouting local employment and environmental laws. The quality of counterfeit products is improving and they now look like exact copies of the original brand.

Distribution: Counterfeiters use all the regular modes of transport such as air, sea and road. Packaging copies the legitimate manufacturers packaging to avoid detection.

Storage: Once received from road transportation the goods are commonly held in commercial self-storage units for onward sale.

Sale: The sale of fake products occurs predominantly online through illegitimate websites or on social media. Looking at a product on a computer screen and without the ability to touch and feel it; it can be more difficult for buyers to spot the difference between a genuine and a fake product.

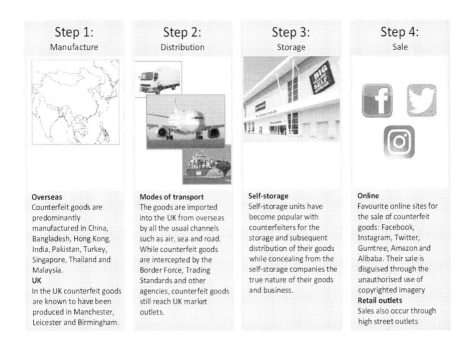

Step 1: Manufacture	Step 2: Distribution	Step 3: Storage	Step 4: Sale
Overseas Counterfeit goods are predominantly manufactured in China, Bangladesh, Hong Kong, India, Pakistan, Turkey, Singapore, Thailand and Malaysia. **UK** In the UK counterfeit goods are known to have been produced in Manchester, Leicester and Birmingham.	**Modes of transport** The goods are imported into the UK from overseas by all the usual channels such as air, sea and road. While counterfeit goods are intercepted by the Border Force, Trading Standards and other agencies, counterfeit goods still reach UK market outlets.	**Self-storage** Self-storage units have become popular with counterfeiters for the storage and subsequent distribution of their goods while concealing from the self-storage companies the true nature of their goods and business.	**Online** Favourite online sites for the sale of counterfeit goods: Facebook, Instagram, Twitter, Gumtree, Amazon and Alibaba. Their sale is disguised through the unauthorised use of copyrighted imagery **Retail outlets** Sales also occur through high street outlets

Figure 12.3 The pattern of the production and distribution of counterfeit goods

Understanding the mechanics of counterfeit goods fraud: Once counterfeiters have produced, distributed and stored their goods they need to advertise them. In the past counterfeiters sold their goods at Sunday markets, informal street markets, or from the back of a car or lorry. In this way, a counterfeiter's audience was limited to the immediate vicinity. In addition, the earliest counterfeiters were cautious and operated in the shadows to avoid detection. However, when eCommerce became commonplace, counterfeiters realised that the Internet could allow them to sell direct to consumers through a global marketplace which was largely unregulated and was not controlled by any one legal jurisdiction. The internet is now used in a number of ways to support both advertising and sales. The Internet affords the counterfeiter an audience of thousands of wholesalers and distributors, and millions of consumers. All the counterfeiter needs to do is get their attention so they visit their website.

Sellers of counterfeit goods use:

- **Legitimate websites** such as eBay, Gumtree, Amazon and Alibaba.
- **Organisations supporting new ecommerce websites** such as Shopify, EKM and BigCommerce.
- **Rogue websites** created specifically for the sale of their fake products. Rogue websites are clones of genuine websites and mirror logos, use copied

pictures, and match font types. Multiple websites are created (sometimes in their hundreds) in case a single website is discovered selling fake goods and is taken down by enforcement agencies. Counterfeiters accept various legitimate payment methods.

- **Advanced marketing techniques** are used such as paid search ads, search engine optimisation, unsolicited emails or the use of branded terms in domain names.
- **Social media is adopted** as a sales platform where pictures and prices of the products are displayed. Social media is favoured as buyers cannot touch and feel the products, and hence, it can be more difficult for buyers to spot the difference between a genuine and a fake product.
- **Legitimate couriers** are used to transport their goods to add to the masquerade of the products to be genuine.

 Case studies of the sale of counterfeit goods: Case studies provide valuable insights into the sale of counterfeit goods. It is not possible here to provide example case studies from all industries and sectors as the volume of material would be prohibitive. Reported case studies addressing counterfeit goods fraud describe very serious implications for both the victim businesses and for the buyers of these goods. An OECD report in 2019 highlighted that, in absolute terms (i.e. when measured by itself), the UK industries that have been especially targeted by counterfeiters over recent years are vehicles and parts, electrical household appliances, electronic and telecommunications equipment, pharmaceutical products, clothing, handbags, footwear and related products.[8] Counterfeit car parts when installed compromise performance, damage the environment and may risk lives. It is not only the drivers that are at risk of injury or worse but also their passengers and other road users. Counterfeit car parts and accessories are seized on a regular basis around the world including in the UK. The UK government has identified that the influx of counterfeit car parts on the market is huge and is on the rise.[9] Industry insiders have highlighted that the most common counterfeit car parts include filters, brake disks and linings, lights, body panels, wheel rims, spark plugs and air bags. While many are essential components, they represent serious safety issues.

Case Study 12.1: following on from the theme of counterfeit car parts introduced in the brief introduction to the case studies, the first case study refers to counterfeit oil and air filters. Apart from the sale of these goods being illegal, cars fitted with these parts would have suffered from performance and maintenance issues.

Case Study 12.2: continuing the theme of counterfeit car parts, the second case study refers to counterfeit spark plugs and fuel injector parts. As with the previous case, apart from the sale of these goods being illegal, cars fitted with these parts would similarly have suffered from performance and maintenance issues. Frequently there is a correlation between price and quality. Hence if a fraudster acquires cheap car parts to sell on at a higher price, in all probability the counterfeits will be of a lower quality than the

---

Case Study 12.1: Counterfeit Goods

A Northumberland trader was prosecuted for selling counterfeit car parts

In August 2021, an independent company based in Northumberland was prosecuted and fined over £15,000 for supplying counterfeit car parts. The case was tried at Newcastle Upon Tyne Magistrates Court where the company was found guilty of six offences under the Trademarks Act 1994. The company, Northumbria Ltd., which traded as '4D' was fined £10,000 and ordered to pay a total of £5,638.70 costs and a £181 victim surcharge. The court also ordered the forfeiture and destruction of the counterfeit parts seized by officers during the investigation. These goods had a street value of around £5,000 putting the overall penalty levied to Northumbria Ltd at over £20,000. The company was taken to court by Northumberland County Council's Trading Standards Service following an investigation in which it was found to be supplying counterfeit oil and air filters. The company was selling counterfeit goods made in Poland and Turkey to garages in the northeast on the basis that they were genuine Citroen and Peugeot parts when this was clearly not the case. Northumberland County Councillor, Colin Horncastle, said:

> This prosecution should serve as a warning to any other traders or individuals considering selling counterfeit goods. This will not be accepted in Northumberland and our Trading Standards team are vigilant in ensuring that this kind of activity is actively monitored and robustly enforced.

Philip Soderquest, the council's head of housing and public protection, said:

> We will not hesitate to investigate and prosecute traders who cause consumers and other businesses to be misled or disadvantaged by the sale or supply of counterfeit goods. The quality of such items is often far inferior to that of the genuine article where significant care is taken during the manufacturing process to ensure it meets relevant safety and quality standards.

Source: Adapted from Northumberland County Council. https://www.northumberland.gov.uk/News/2021/Aug/Firm-prosecuted-for-selling-counterfeit-car-parts.aspx.

legitimate parts, will perform differently and have a shorter life expectancy before replacement is required.

Case Study 12.3: is another case relating to the motor parts industry. This time it relates to the counterfeit bonnet, wheel and grill badges and tyre valve sets. It is assumed the fraudsters had some association with this sector of the motor industry prior to embarking on the sale of counterfeits.

Case Study 12.2: Counterfeit Goods

A Hailsham trader was prosecuted for selling counterfeit car parts

In May 2019, an online trader caught with almost £40,000 worth of counterfeit motor parts for sale was handed a suspended prison sentence. The trader admitted 25 breaches of the Trade Marks Act 1994 and was handed a four-month prison sentence, suspended for 18 months, in a hearing at Hove Crown Court on May 28. In addition, the offender was ordered to carry out 125 hours of unpaid work and a forfeiture and destruction order was made for the counterfeit goods. The 43-year-old had been selling the parts by way of internet auction sites to customers around the country, passing them off as products by well-known, reputable manufacturers. East Sussex Trading Standards officers discovered the parts which included spark plugs and fuel injector parts, in the living room of the trader's home in George Street, Hailsham, UK. The officers found the trader had been laser printing labels bearing registered trademarks of legitimate companies at home and affixing them to cheaper, inferior products. Tests carried out on the items seized, revealed they were of poor quality, and in some cases could have caused damage if fitted to car engines. Cllr Bill Bentley of East Sussex County Council said:

> This unscrupulous individual was caught with counterfeit motor parts with a very high value ... He was knowingly selling these items online to unsuspecting consumers and businesses around the country, to the detriment not just of the buyers, but of the manufacturers whose products he claimed to be offering and to genuine traders trying to make an honest living. This prosecution is a great result and testament to the hard work of our trading standards officers and should send out a strong message to anyone thinking about selling fake goods.

Source: Adapted from East Sussex County Council. https://news.eastsussex.gov. uk/2019/05/30/suspended-jail-term-for-bogus-motor-parts-trader/; the *Journal of Trading Standards*. https://www.journaloftradingstandards.co.uk/automotive/online-motorparts-trader-prosecuted/; Chartered Trading Standards Institute, *Hailsham News*, comunityad.co.uk.

Case Study 12.3: Counterfeit Goods

A Wokingham couple were prosecuted for selling counterfeit car parts

On 17 June 2016, a Wokingham-based car accessory dealer was sentenced to two years imprisonment following an investigation by West Berkshire and Wokingham Trading Standards. The dealer, 31 years of age, formerly of Bellamy House in Ashville Way, Wokingham, was sentenced at Reading Crown Court by Judge Stephen John after pleading guilty to breaching the Trade Marks Act 1994. His partner, 32 years of age, of the same address, pleaded guilty to one count of money laundering and was sentenced to 21 months imprisonment suspended for two years, and 200 hours unpaid work. The dealer's partner was also ordered to pay £38,538 for confiscation costs within three months or have a further nine months added to her sentence. Trading standards officers were first alerted to the case in the summer of 2014 when they were contacted by BMW Group (UK) Ltd about a counterfeit black and white bonnet badge bought on eBay. Further enquiries led to a warrant executed at the couple's address in autumn 2015 when more than 3,600 items were seized along with a number of computers and phones. The fake items included bonnet, wheel and grill badges and tyre valve sets bearing the registered trade mark of major car manufacturers including BMW, Ford, Jaguar Land Rover, Mercedes, Honda, Peugeot and the VW Group. The seized computers and phones contained hundreds of images of counterfeit goods, which helped officers piece together a picture of the pattern of offending. Other evidence also showed the dealer had been contacted by eBay for trade mark violations concerning the BMW products. Investigations into the financial aspects of the case showed items valued at more than £100,000 had been sold in addition to the goods seized valued at £35,000. Furthermore, it was shown the partner had been involved in money laundering in relation to some £38,000 of this amount. According to Wokingham Borough Council Councillor Pauline Jorgensen 'This was another successful complex investigation carried out by the West Berkshire and Wokingham Shared Trading Standards Service'. 'Ultimately it was an investigation that revealed a high level of criminality which was reflected in the sentences passed by the crown court'. Following on, she said: 'Finally I would like to thank Thames Valley Police for their assistance with whom we work on many investigations'.

Source: Adapted from Wokingham Borough Council. https://news.wokingham.gov.uk/news/wokingham-car-accessory-trader-jailed-for-counterfeit-parts/.

Case Study 12.4 focuses on a lawsuit brought by Amazon against 13 individuals for advertising, promoting, and facilitating the sale of counterfeit luxury goods in Amazon's store. Amazon is an American multinational technology company

---

Case Study 12.4: Counterfeit Goods

Sale of counterfeit luxury goods in Amazon's store

On 12 November 2020, Amazon filed a lawsuit against 13 individuals (labelled the defendants) in the United States District Court for the Western District of Washington for advertising, promoting, and facilitating the sale of counterfeit luxury goods in Amazon's store, in violation of Amazon's policies and the law. The lawsuit alleges the defendants operated in concert with each other to sell counterfeit products and engage in false advertising. The suit claims that two named individuals acting as influencers conspired with sellers of products to evade Amazon's anti-counterfeiting protections by promoting counterfeit products on Instagram, Facebook and TikTok as well as their own websites. Cristina Posa, Associate General Counsel and Director, Amazon Counterfeit Crimes Unit, said that the defendants were 'brazen' about promoting counterfeits on social media. Posa has encouraged social media sites to also vet, monitor, and take action on bad actors using their services to facilitate illegal behaviour. Posa called for cross-industry collaboration in order to drive counterfeiters out of business. Amazon has made it clear that it 'strictly prohibits counterfeit products in its stores, and in 2019 alone, invested more than $500 million to protect customers and brands from fraud, abuse, and counterfeit'. In addition, Amazon has stated it undertakes proactive 'investment in preventing the sale of counterfeit goods by way of robust seller vetting, advanced machine-learning-based technologies, and industry-leading brand protection tools like Project Zero, Brand Registry, and Transparency'. In June 2020, Amazon launched its Counterfeit Crimes Unit, a global team with specialists experienced in investigating and bringing legal action against bad actors. Amazon's 'Project Zero' uses automated protections to proactively and continuously scan more than 5 billion attempted product listing updates daily to look for suspicious listings.

Source: Adapted from *CNBC News:* "Amazon Takes Counterfeit Sellers to Court for First Time". https://www.cnbc.com/2016/11/15/amazon-takes-counterfeit-sellers-to-court-for-firsttime. html; *Amazon:* "Amazon Files Lawsuit against Counterfeiters using Social Media to Promote Sales". https://press.aboutamazon.com/news-releases/news-release-details/amazon-files-lawsuit-against-counterfeiters-using-social-media; *Bloomberg:* "Amazon Files Lawsuit against Counterfeiters using Social Media to Promote Sales". https:// www.bloomberg.com/press-releases/2020-11-12/amazon-files-lawsuit-againstcounterfeiters-using-social-media-to-promote-sales

which predominantly focuses on e-commerce as well as cloud computing, digital streaming, and artificial intelligence. It is one of the Big Five companies in the US information technology industry, along with Google, Apple, Microsoft, and Facebook. Amazon is important to UK SMEs through the support it provides to businesses in terms of its 'Fulfilment by Amazon' (FBA) Program and Amazon's worldwide network of distribution centres supporting both inventory and logistics.

Red flags: There are a series of signals that fake businesses are committing a fraud. The signs are referred to as 'red flags'. Defending against counterfeit goods requires businesses producing legitimate original products to be on the lookout for websites that are clones of their own or social media sites that have copied their logos and pictures of their products. Legitimate retailers and resellers need to be wary of the following:

- The price seems too good to be true.
- Websites offering highly discounted prices. Scam websites use low prices to lure shoppers to quickly sell fake or non-existent items.
- Website pages 'About us' and 'Contact us' do not contain full details: name of the company, address, phone number or an official email address.
- Websites that have grammar and/and spelling mistakes or the site looks unfinished.
- The domain name contains the words 'genuine', 'replica' or 'original', or the name of a brand or product, but adding words like 'offer' or 'discount'.
- Domain names which end in.net or.org, as they are rarely used for online shopping.
- Website photos are of bad quality, are resized or difficult to see, or the opposite, are copied from original websites or are stock photos.
- Identical reviews on multiple social media sites. Reviews can be fake. For example, if there is a similarity in the reviews across several websites, or the same users are commenting.
- The website does not offer a return policy, terms and conditions and a privacy policy. A legitimate company should tell you how and where to return a faulty item.
- The website does not describe what they do with your data to comply with GDPR.
- The Websites selling clothes is using stock photos from runway shows rather than pictures of the actual products.
- The website is secure and its URL begins with 'https' instead of 'http'. This means that the site is secured using an SSL Certificate (the s stands for secure). Even if a website shows secured pictures from most known payment institutions it could be fake.

Step 4B: Risk identification

The risks for a manufacturer of legitimate original products or an e-commerce retailer buying goods for sale, all have different risk exposures depending on how they interface with commercial buyers or the general public. All are liable to suffer reputational damage if the goods they are retailing over a digital platform are counterfeit. A risk is broken into several components, how these components are articulated is critical to how that risk is viewed, understood and managed. 'Because of [cause], a [threat] event may occur, which would lead to an [impact] on a business's objectives'. The common 'cause' is the motivation of individuals to secure financial gain from criminal activity. It is a common phenomenon in the business environment and perpetually gives rise to uncertainty. The general causes behind risk exposure are described in Table 12.1. The approach adopted by fraudsters has changed significantly with the arrival of the Internet.

Table 12.1 Counterfeit goods causes

Counterfeit fraud (Cause → Threat → Impact)	
The **causes** or triggers behind fraudulent activity	
Safety checks	Counterfeit electrical goods, for instance, are not put through the same vigorous safety checks as legitimate items and are often very dangerous. Likewise, fake medicines, alcohol and food are not subjected to the same health and safety procedures as legal items and so the damage can potentially be fatal.
Reputation	Poor product performance of fake products falsely branded as those of a legitimate business may adversely affect customer satisfaction threatening future sales, market share and profits. This can result in serious damage to a legitimate business's brand and reputation. In addition, these products can also present potential product liability and litigation risks.
Job redundancies	Lower sales reduce the demand for labour. Job losses in the UK are more pronounced in the retail and wholesale sectors.
Incorporation of counterfeit products	Late-stage detection of the presence of counterfeit components within assembly processes can result in cost overruns and expensive production delays.
Safety-critical systems	Late discovery of the unknowing use of counterfeit products used to replace defective components in safety-critical systems can expose businesses to catastrophic failure and severe reputational damage.
Visual recognition	Many fake and counterfeit products are so identical in look and feel to genuine parts that it is becoming more difficult to distinguish them visually.
Penalties and claims arising from the replacement of faulty products	Discovery of the unwitting inclusion of counterfeit parts in a client's project, such as construction of a new factory, can result in potential contractual claims and penalties. Replacement within a completed or partially completed building can be very expensive.

Counterfeit fraud (Cause → Threat → Impact)	
Unfair competition	For manufacturers of branded products in high demand with a significant market share, counterfeit products sold at heavily discounted prices will compete unfairly with planned sales and unsuspecting buyers may procure and use these fake products.

Table 12.2 describes the risk exposure common to the majority of SMEs seeking to survive in typically highly competitive markets.

Table 12.2 Counterfeit goods threats

Threat (uncertain event)	
Down time (loss of production time)	Down time following unwitting inclusion of counterfeit parts (by a legitimate company) within its manufacturing plant.
Customer complaints	Customer complaints following unwitting inclusion of counterfeit parts (by a legitimate company) within its products.
Component failure	Failure of components included in a plant room within a new construction project.

Table 12.3 Counterfeit fraud impact descriptions

Impact descriptions (if the threats were to materialise)	
Cash flow, operational finance and profitability	Potential cash flow problems leading to operational difficulties such as the payment of employees and fixed known costs such as utility bills, vehicle tax, fuel, insurance and maintenance and council tax.
Loss of reputation	Where counterfeit products are clearly branded as the original legitimate products but are of inferior quality and have a shorter product life or quickly fail, the legitimate company suffers reputational damage. The situation is worse where the counterfeit product causes an injury or fatalities.
Loss of market share	The production, distribution and sale of cheaper counterfeit products using cheap labour and/or inferior materials result in a loss of market share.
Redundancies	Job losses arise from a loss of market share, a fall in revenue and a reduction in finance to pay staff.
Claims and legal action	A business is the subject of claims or legal action arising from faulty goods or where they have brought about production downtime, the halt of construction projects, the recall of serviced vehicles or personal injury claims.

Step 4C: Risk analysis

When examining the characteristics of a potential threat, it commonly involves estimating the likelihood, the impact (in cost and time together with other parameters when appropriate) and the proximity (when is the threat likely to materialise). Included in Table 12.4 is a descriptive analysis of the likelihood, impact and proximity; however, where possible over time businesses need to capture actual figures for the different categories.

Table 12.4 Counterfeit fraud risk analysis

Analysis of counterfeit theft risks	
Likelihood	The likelihood of a particular business being impacted by counterfeit goods depends to a degree on the ease with which the products can be made, distributed and sold. So, the likelihood of bulldozers being cloned is very remote, whereas smaller items such as spark plugs and oil fitters are very high.
Financial impact	This type of fraud can leave SMEs struggling to compete in the marketplace and, as described above, can lead to the need to make redundancies. The scale of losses for a legitimate business depends on an array of factors such as the industry and sector they are working in, their current market share, anticipated new market entrants, years of operation, the profit margin per product, the scale of penetration and sale of counterfeit goods.
Time impact	The time impact is different for this type of fraud. Each business that has suffered from counterfeiting will have to determine the measures to be undertaken to combat the rogue products–such as enabling buyers to more readily discern the fake from the genuine products, supported by changes in marketing, advertising, packaging and labelling. The time required will vary from business to business.
Proximity	The production, distribution and sale of counterfeit goods are constant and are occurring on a vast scale, as described in the overview above.

Step 5: Response actions

Included in Figure 12.4 are specific response actions that should be implemented by manufacturers seeking to buy components to include within their product ranges – with regard to procurement, goods received, quality assurance/security and products.

Your Procurement

Assessment: Establish purchasing processes which assess the risk of receiving counterfeit parts from potential sources of supply. Assessment may be a survey, audit, product review or the review of a suppliers quality data to verify past performance. The goal is to ensure that approved sources of supply are themselves maintaining effective processes for mitigating the risk of passing on/supplying counterfeit parts. Maintain a list of approved suppliers along with their scope of approval in order to minimize the risk associated with the receipt of counterfeit parts. Ask suppliers if they have a returns policy or guarantee. Most rogue traders will not offer this. The Purchase Order must specify to the supplier the applicable requirements of the business's counterfeit part procedures. In order to minimize the risk of procuring counterfeit parts, the Purchase Order will include requirements to ensure conforming, original and authentic parts are provided. The Purchase Order may list requirements for Certification and Traceability, a deliverable record of test and/or inspection results, and quality management system requirements for the supplier.

Product sources: Clearly establish the legitimate source(s) of those products and components critical to the operation of the business. Buying from authorised distributors provides a degree of assurance of product quality and integrity of authentic parts. Buying on the internet or from other alternate sources or importing directly increases the chance of becoming a victim of counterfeit product frauds.

Testing: If the business is forced to procure a critical part from an alternate source (a business not previously traded with) because a part is not available from the usual authorised distributor, the business must increase its own verification efforts to ensure the integrity of parts by additional testing regimes. Sometimes, reconditioned and salvaged parts may be passed off/sold as new and may not meet required specifications.

Price: The business should not buy on the basis of the lowest price alone. While in difficult economic times, there is a temptation to buy at the lowest possible cost; if the price offered is a deeply discounted rock bottom price compared to known price ranges for the products being sought, it should raise suspicion alerting further investigation.

 Receipt of goods

Inspection: Those employees given the responsibility of receiving and inspecting incoming parts/materials/products must examine them to ensure the drawing, specification, part number, type, class, style, manufacturer, Certificate of Conformance or other related information is present, to detect or identify suspect or counterfeit parts.

In addition, inspection should look for:
- Parts not containing the full assembly.
- Used, refurbished or reclaimed parts presented as new products.
- Parts with a different package label, style, type or finish to that ordered.
- The delivery of part orders.
- Parts delivered as refurbished, refinished or updated.
- Parts sold or delivered with modified labelling or markings intended to misrepresent the form, fit, function or grade of the intended product.

Consistency: For products regularly ordered, look for unusual packaging:
- Where there is an inconsistency in the appearance, colour or dimensions of the packages.
- Variations between what should be identical items in a package.
- Repairs to packaging or where goods have obviously been re-packaged.
- Modifications to or what appears to be refinishing or repainting of old/salvaged parts.

Part labelling: Look for incomplete or inconsistent information on name plates, product markings or certification numbers on incoming parts to be included in larger assemblies. Reject parts where the manufacturer's name plate, model or serial numbers have been altered or are worn.

Documentation: Be on the lookout for irregularities in various documentation (such as shipping papers, certificates and technical data) for missing dates, signatures, dispatch addresses and quality checks.

Figure 12.4 Specific responses actions to the problem of counterfeit goods

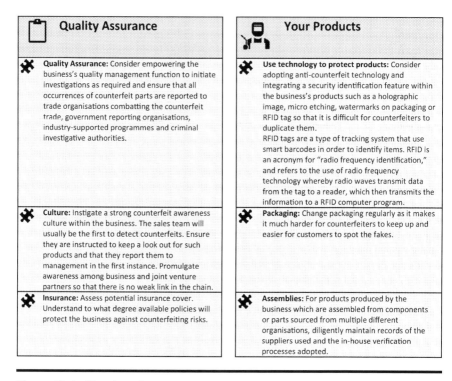

Quality Assurance	Your Products
✳ **Quality Assurance:** Consider empowering the business's quality management function to initiate investigations as required and ensure that all occurrences of counterfeit parts are reported to trade organisations combatting the counterfeit trade, government reporting organisations, industry-supported programmes and criminal investigative authorities.	✳ **Use technology to protect products:** Consider adopting anti-counterfeit technology and integrating a security identification feature within the business's products such as a holographic image, micro etching, watermarks on packaging or RFID tag so that it is difficult for counterfeiters to duplicate them. RFID tags are a type of tracking system that use smart barcodes in order to identify items. RFID is an acronym for "radio frequency identification," and refers to the use of radio frequency technology whereby radio waves transmit data from the tag to a reader, which then transmits the information to a RFID computer program.
✳ **Culture:** Instigate a strong counterfeit awareness culture within the business. The sales team will usually be the first to detect counterfeits. Ensure they are instructed to keep a look out for such products and that they report them to management in the first instance. Promulgate awareness among business and joint venture partners so that there is no weak link in the chain.	✳ **Packaging:** Change packaging regularly as it makes it much harder for counterfeiters to keep up and easier for customers to spot the fakes.
✳ **Insurance:** Assess potential insurance cover. Understand to what degree available policies will protect the business against counterfeiting risks.	✳ **Assemblies:** For products produced by the business which are assembled from components or parts sourced from multiple different organisations, diligently maintain records of the suppliers used and the in-house verification processes adopted.

Figure 12.4 *(Continued)*

Step 6: Implementation of actions

Immediate response

Report suspected counterfeit goods to the local Trading Standards Office and Action Fraud (www.actionfraud.police.uk/a-z-of-fraud/counterfeit-goods-fraud).

Understand the organisations involved in combatting counterfeiting. Visit their websites. Details of the more well-known organisations are included below. These organisations will provide a greater understanding of the problem of counterfeiting and the potential response.

■ The Intellectual Property Office (IPO) is the official UK government body responsible for intellectual property (IP) rights including patents, designs, trademarks and copyright. IPO is an executive agency, sponsored by the Department for Business, Energy & Industrial Strategy. www.gov.uk/ government/organisations/intellectual-property-office.

- National Trading Standards Authority's website: www.nationaltrading-standards.uk (Strives to safeguard businesses through cross-boundary intelligence-led enforcement projects in England and Wales).
- Business Companion website: www.businesscompanion.info (a UK government-backed website aimed at providing guidance only, it does not provide legal advice).
- Chartered Trading Standards Institute website: www.tradingstandards.uk (CTSI represents trading standards professionals working in the UK and overseas, in local authorities, business and consumer sectors and central government).
- BSI Group: www.bsigroup.com. (Its mission is to share knowledge, innovation and best practice to help people and organizations make excellence a habit. This is underpinned by its role as the national standards body. BSI advocates control of the supply chain to thwart counterfeit goods. (BSI states that 'its suite of supply chain intelligence and risk management services and solutions can be used independently to target specific needs or combined together to seamlessly identify, analyse and manage global supply chain operations and risks'.)
- International Anti-Counterfeiting Coalition: www.iacc.org/resources/about/what-is-counterfeiting. (Formed in 1979, the International AntiCounterfeiting Coalition Inc. (IACC) is a Washington, DC-based non-profit organization devoted solely to combating product counterfeiting and piracy.)
- The Chartered Institute of Procurement and Supply whose website is: www.cips.org/who-we-are/what-we-do/. CIPS is a not-for-profit organisation. It describes itself as a 'professional body for the procurement and supply profession, is using its global standard, network, education, expertise and charter for public good'.
- The Anti-Counterfeiting Forum. The Anti-Counterfeiting Forum is wholly owned and managed by Elan Business Support Ltd. www.anticounterfeitingforum.org.uk/default.aspx.

Short-term response

Develop an Implementation Plan which charts a logical sequence of activities to be implemented tailored to the specific needs of your business to protect the business against counterfeit goods and the wave of problems that they bring with them. Consider:

- Mapping and understanding the risks. Categorise them in a structured manner to make the task easier. Say industry, sector, supplier, partner. Develop sub-sets for the primary categories. Understand what is the cause and impact of each threat. Over time develop a risk register.

- Gaining a better understanding of the supply chain.
- Developing the expertise to detect counterfeit goods. Undertake detection and screening of incoming goods before they are used.
- Obtaining support from external specialists.
- Developing and providing awareness training for staff which is regularly updated. Use an experienced training provider.
- Protecting the intellectual property of your own products as necessary.

Long-term response

Main contact with trade organisations, external specialists, other suppliers in your industry and government guidance to develop and maintain an intelligence of both developments in counterfeit goods and how to protect the business.

Summary

Counterfeit products can cause businesses to lose market share resulting in reduced income, falling profitability and job losses. Product counterfeiting poses a major threat to the safety of business employees and the public alike as well as causing maintenance issues. For legitimate businesses within a significant number of industries counterfeiting results in a loss of market share from a lack of differentiation together with falling sales and profitability. According to reports high-end electronics, pharmaceutical, automotive, software and aerospace companies are plagued by counterfeit products due to the short supply and higher profit margin. Europol has highlighted that profits from counterfeiting fund other forms of serious organised crimes like human trafficking, money laundering or labour exploitation. To be attractive counterfeit goods need to be cheaper. As a consequence counterfeiting production factories are known to violate labour and environmental laws as well as basic human rights. Counterfeit products continue to enter the UK by air, sea and road, from countries such as China, Hong Kong, India, Pakistan, Turkey, Singapore, Macedonia, Thailand and Malaysia. The counterfeiters use social media platforms such as Twitter as well as e-commerce sites such as Bonanza, Gumtree, Amazon and Alibaba due to their worldwide reach, to facilitate sales of their fake products. Criminals operating counterfeit businesses use multiple online business models to bring goods to retail outlets, using legitimate shipping and fast parcel operations, trading platforms and payment facilities.

Notes

1 https://www.bsigroup.com/en-GB/about-bsi/.
2 Europol: https://www.europol.europa.eu/dontfakeup.
3 Founded in 1980, the Anti-Counterfeiting Group (ACG) is an international association respected as one of the world's leading specialists in the fight against the growing global trade in counterfeit goods. ACG is a not-for-profit trade association, committed to representing it members, in the UK, EU and around the globe.
4 The European Observatory hosted by EUIPO provides accurate, impartial and verifiable information to help safeguard Europe's knowledge and competitive edge in the global marketplace.
5 The Organisation for Economic Co-operation and Development (OECD) describes itself as an international organisation that works to build better policies for better lives.
6 Electrical Safety First is the UK's leading charity committed to reducing fires, injuries and damage arising from electricity – the cause of over half of all domestic fires in the UK.
7 Electrical Safety First. "A shocking rip off the true cost of counterfeit electrical products".
8 OECD (2019) "Trade in Counterfeit Products and the UK Economy, 2019 update", published by the Organisation for Economic Cooperation and Development in conjunction with the UK's Intellectual Property Office.
9 Guidance: Think before you buy – counterfeit vehicle parts, Published 25 July 2018. https://www.gov.uk/government/publications/counterfeit-vehicle-parts/think-before-you-buy-counterfeit-vehicle-parts.

INTERNAL 'ACTORS'

Introduction to Section 3

As explained in Chapter 1, 'Layout of the book' Section 3 describes the types of fraud committed by employees or internal 'actors' within the business which similarly require a specific action to limit their occurrence. Employees committing fraud want to avoid discovery and hence may well adopt sophisticated methods of concealment. As a consequence, businesses need to both regularly forensically examine the business accounts (calling upon external support as required) and wherever possible, remove opportunities for employees to commit fraud.

Chapters 13 to 16 describe the types of fraud committed by employees and directors of the business which require tailored risk management strategies.

Case studies demonstrate these frauds are frequently carried out by long-standing trusted employees with high levels of responsibility working at the heart of the business whose actions may go unnoticed for considerable lengths of time, in some cases many years, as a consequence of the methods adopted to cover up their fraudulent behaviour – to avoid detection.

Content of the chapters within Section 3

Steps 4, 5 and 6 in the risk management process are adopted to describe the unique characteristics of each fraud type and develop tailored responses to improve the capabilities of a business to combat it. Similar to the chapters in Section 2, each business needs to learn lessons from its own processes together with external case studies. They need to understand the threats that their business is exposed to, how these threats may impact them and then develop tailored proportionate responses. The responses may need to be implemented over time due to the constraints of personnel, in-house expertise and costs. In addition, they should follow government guidelines where appropriate and seek consultancy support as required. Each chapter contains a description of the steps described in Figure S3.1.

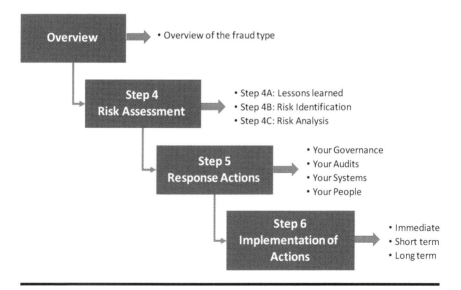

Figure S3.1 Content of Chapters 13–16

Chapter 13

Asset misappropriation fraud

Structure of Chapter 13

Chapter 13 is subdivided into the following four sections. An overview of the fraud type is provided followed by an assessment of the threat posed by the fraud, suggested response actions and timing of implementation (Figure 13.1).

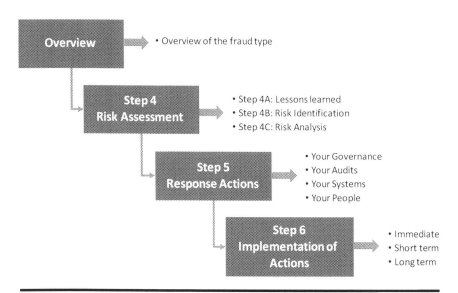

Figure 13.1 Structure of Chapter 13

DOI: 10.4324/9781003200383-16

Overview

As described by Action Fraud, asset misappropriation fraud involves third parties or employees in a business who abuse their position to steal from it through fraudulent activity for personal gain. It is also referred to as insider fraud. This type of fraud can be committed by company directors or its employees, or anyone else entrusted to hold and manage the assets and interests of a business. Typically, the assets stolen are cash or cash equivalents (such as credit notes or vouchers). However, the fraud can extend to include company data or intellectual property. At one end of the scale, asset misappropriation fraud may be limited to isolated cases of fraudulent expense claims or an employee lying about his or her qualifications and experience to get a job. At the other end, it might involve a prolonged and deliberate manipulation of a business's accounts to conceal fraud. The definition of asset misappropriation is not typically associated with the theft of physical assets. Ultimately, it's the cash flow of the business that suffers. Action Fraud highlights that if they are not tackled, opportunistic one-off frauds can become systemic and spread throughout a business, creating a culture of theft and fraud. When this happens, fraudsters think their actions are the norm and as such acceptable. They have no moral compass and fail to make the distinction between company funds and their own finances. At one end of the spectrum, asset misappropriation fraud can erode an organisation's staff morale and reputation and at the other end cause job losses or even business closure.

Step 4: Risk assessment

Risk assessment consists of a sequence of activities which answer the questions: what are the possible problems my business may face? How likely are they? What impact will they have? And how soon will they impact? How well these questions can be answered depends on the research undertaken. A starting point is undertaking lessons learned. For large businesses operating over a number of years, they may have developed a database of events, recording how they were managed and what degree of success was achieved. However, for SMEs, they typically have to look outside of their business for lessons learned. Sources of information may include financial advisers, the business accountant or solicitors specialising in fraud.

Step 4A: Lessons learned

To appreciate the vulnerabilities of a business to misappropriation of assets fraud requires an appreciation of the sequence or pattern of these fraud events, the tools and techniques employed (described here as the mechanics), historical events

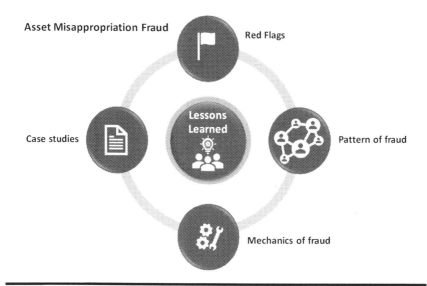

Figure 13.2 The lessons learned from prior events

(captured in case studies) together with 'red flags' or the 'alarm bells' over potential exposure, as illustrated in Figure 13.2. These activities contribute to Lessons Learned which in turn assist in deciding on the actions to be implemented, to thwart this fraud type.

 Understanding the pattern of misappropriation fraud: There are usually three steps to an asset misappropriation fraud as described below. It is uncommon for a finance specialist to join a firm with the intent of committing fraud. Either their circumstances change during the course of their employment (as with gambling or debt) or observation of the business's financial practices leads to the perception that the subversion of funds would not be noticed.

- **Theft:** The theft may commence with just one single amount. Its lack of initial detection may encourage a second theft until it almost becomes routine, while at the same time not wishing to attract attention to the thefts. The size and timing of the theft may be calculated to deflect attention. With growing confidence, the thefts may snowball.
- **Transfer:** In most instances, money is transferred to the employee's own bank account or accounts; however, the theft may involve company assets as opposed to money.
- **Concealment:** The greatest effort will be invested in concealment, to deceive the business's directors (and any accountants or auditors that they

may appoint), that all of the payments made (to suppliers and others) are legitimate and are borne out of the normal day-to-day running of the business.

Understanding the mechanics of asset misappropriation fraud: By considering the methods that may be perpetrated and the financial and reputational damage that they may cause will establish the anti-fraud measures that need to be put in place and the prioritisation of those measures. Included below are the more common mechanics adopted. As mentioned in the 'pattern of misappropriation fraud', the theft of assets is often accompanied by false or misleading records or documents in order to conceal the fact that the assets are missing.

- Skimming by theft of payments received but not recorded.
- The creation of false supplier invoices.
- The inflation of invoices from existing suppliers.
- Fraudulent disbursement/expense claims.
- Fictitious 'ghost' employees have been created on payroll systems.
- Data theft.
- VAT payment irregularities.
- Tax payment irregularities.
- Intellectual property shared with a third party.
- Physical asset theft; however, this is uncommon.

Skimming: skimming is a type of 'off-the-books' theft, as the perpetrator steals cash before it can be recorded in the accounting system. Skimming is often difficult to detect, as there is no direct audit trail obtainable from the business accounts. Employees who are in a position to receive payments can easily skim cash if there are no effective internal controls to mitigate against it. One of the most common skimming schemes is when goods or services are sold to a customer, and an employee is able to collect and keep the customer's payment without the sale being recorded. Loss of gross margin and inventory shortages are indicators that this problem exists.

Fake invoices: Fake invoices may be created for existing or new suppliers, consultants or contractors with purposefully created bank details which relate to a bank account or accounts controlled by the employee.

Inflated invoices: An employee may establish a relationship with a supplier's representative whereby invoices are inflated over and above the actual costs with the difference split between the employee and the supplier's employee.

Fraudulent expenses: Employees may be guilty of inflating or altering acceptable reimbursable expenses, creating fictitious expenses or claiming for non-business expenses. They may also create expenses incurred by 'ghost' employees.

Payroll fraud: The most common type of payroll fraud involves 'ghost' employees, individuals who do not work for the company but are included in the monthly payroll. The non-employee can be either a fictitious person or a real one who's not a bona fide/actual employee. Former employees may be included.

Data theft: Theft of data can occur where the employee has found a market for the information. This may involve an employee colluding with a competitor and disclosing technological data (component assembly or component manufacturing processes) in return for payment.

VAT payment irregularities: VAT payments may be used as a smoke screen to hide payments to the employee and are used as a method to thwart detection.

Tax payment irregularities: Like VAT payments, tax payments may be used as a smoke screen to hide payments to the employee and again used as a method to thwart detection.

Intellectual property theft: Intellectual property that has been digitalised and is online is particularly vulnerable. The theft occurs when an employee copies or removes digitalised designs (for instance) which are the property of and unique to the business.

Physical asset theft: Stealing physical assets such as stealing inventory (regular business supplies) for personal use or for sale. An example might be facilities management supplies such as cleaning products, light bulbs and print paper.

Case studies: Case studies of events that have already occurred within other companies provide a rich source of information when combined with insights and guidance from accountants supporting businesses in the same business sector. Five common observations can be drawn from the case studies included below:

- The role of the fraudster in the business.
- The enormous scale of fraudulent behaviour.
- The length of time the thefts go undetected.
- The hugely debilitating effect theft has on employers.
- How positions of trust can be abused.

Case Study 13.1 is an example of where fraud went undetected for a number of years which is all the more surprising when the trial judge said the firm had been 'left on its knees' as a consequence of the fraud. The apparent motivation for the fraud was the desire for a very significant improvement in lifestyle. Given the sum of money involved, this is one of the more pronounced examples of this type of fraud.

Case Study 13.2 describes the situation where an employee abuses her position of trust in the management of her employer's business accounts. The fraud was motivated by the need to fuel a gambling habit that had spiralled out of control.

Case Study 13.1: Asset misappropriation fraud

Theft by an employee from a firm of solicitors to fund a luxurious lifestyle

A trusted cashier at a firm of solicitors stole £1.7 million in just under seven years to finance a luxurious lifestyle for herself and her husband. She was sentenced at Gloucester Crown Court to five years imprisonment. The court was told she purchased five cars, a house, luxury holidays, jewellery, designer shoes, a public house and a share in a racehorse. She was responsible for managing petty cash, client bank accounts and expenses and was given increasing responsibility throughout the near 20 years she worked at the firm. During the seven-year fraud, she regularly deceived the partners at the firm about the forged cheques presented to them for signing. It was only when the cashier went on holiday that irregularities were discovered and an internal investigation uncovered what she had been doing. During the court hearing, the judge said 'In April 2002 you began to systematically steal from the client account, thereby abusing the great trust they had in you. Over the next seven years, you plundered that account to quite a remarkable degree, which required you to lie and forge. You did this with calmness and a large degree of cunning to an extent that fooled not only your employers but the auditors'. The judge added: 'The impact of your offending has been devastating. I do not exaggerate when I say the firm has been left on its knees through your actions'. The senior partner at the firm said: 'This case shows that the criminal actions of a determined fraudster employed in a position involving a degree of trust can undermine the integrity of well-regulated accounting systems'. He went on to say:

> we had a system of supervision in place and we used specialist accounting software. No accounting irregularities were reported to us prior to our discovery, despite regular checks by our in-house accountant and six-monthly reviews and annual reports from the independent Chartered Accountants. We also had additional external checks, none of which revealed any problem.

Source: Adapted from the *BBC News*: "Solihull Cashier Stole £1.7m from Solicitors'". https://www.bbc.co.uk/news/uk-england-birmingham-11555535; the dailymail.co.uk: "Solicitors' Cashier Who Stole £1.7m to Buy Racehorse, Pub, and Luxury Holidays Is Jailed". https://www.dailymail.co.uk/news/article-1320880/Solicitors-cashier-stole-1-7m-buy-racehorse-pub-luxury-holidays-jailed.html; and *The Independent*. October 2010: "Woman jailed for stealing £1.7 million from employer".

Case Study 13.2: Asset misappropriation fraud

Theft from employer to finance a gambling debt

An accounts manager from North East Lincolnshire was jailed for two years eight months for misappropriating £346,000 from her employer, a logistics company, in just ten months. The money was used to fuel her secret gambling habit. The court heard how the accounts manager who had no previous convictions became trapped in the 'powerful grip' of a gambling addiction. At the height of her gambling, she was losing in excess of £1,000 a day on (thought to be) online betting. The theft of the huge sum caused serious problems for her employer. The manager admitted fraud and false accounting while working for the company as the accounts manager at its head office near Grimsby between February and December 2018. The Manager tried to cover her tracks during the long-running fraud by falsifying records for VAT payments. She turned to using the company's money after initially borrowing cash from family members but losing the trust of friends and relatives because of her gambling. The long-lasting impact on the company has been profound because of the systematic fraud when she had sole access to its business account. In a similar case, a wholesale manager was jailed at Nottingham Crown Court for three years for taking £370,000 from his employer, The Cake Decorating Company, between May 2015 and November 2018. Again, he stole the money to feed his gambling habit. It forced the company to take out high-interest loans to stay afloat.

Source: Based on *GrimsbyLive*: https://www.grimsbytelegraph.co.uk/news/grimsby-news/lives-torn-apart-gambling-addiction-4336197; *Mirror* https://www.mirror.co.uk/news/uk-news/mum-jailed-after-stealing-35000-22373285; *Daily Star*: https://www.dailystar.co.uk/news/latest-news/single-mum-stole-346000-work-22374888.

Case Study 13.3 is a further example of where the fraud went undetected for a significant number of years and the motivation for committing the fraud was an improvement in lifestyle.

Case Study 13.4 is another illustration of a breach of trust. In this instance, the company owner was forced into considering making staff redundant due to the disparity between the running costs and the business income.

Case Study 13.3: Asset misappropriation fraud

Theft from employer to finance a luxurious lifestyle

An accounts manager pleaded guilty to dishonestly appropriating almost £500,000 from an SME in Staffordshire supplying Formula One racing teams between October 2009 and June 2018. She was sentenced to 16 months' imprisonment. Stafford Crown Court heard that the manager was in a position of trust and managed the company's accounts. She used the money to fund a lifestyle well in excess of her legitimate income. She had multiple new cars and a holiday home on the Yorkshire coast. She stole by transferring money from the business into her own bank and credit card accounts. She perpetrated a clever fraud of keeping two sets of books that hid cash taken and that was allocated to unpaid suppliers. She then covered up these payments by way of false accounting. The fraud came to light towards the end of May 2018. In an interview with detectives, she admitted to stealing £478,000. Detective Constable Nicholas Gorman, of Staffordshire Police, said: 'This was a serious and sustained fraud which was perpetrated over several years and caused significant damage to the business. It was an appalling breach of trust'. The managing director of the design company said: '[our accounts manager] worked for me for over 24 years and was trusted with everything I had and I considered her to be a close friend. To find over two years ago she was guilty of stealing between £9k and £12k a month for years was a great shock. Good, hard-working staff lost their jobs through her dishonesty'.

Source: Staffordshire Police: https://www.staffordshire.police.uk/news/staffordshire/news/2020/october/woman-who-stole-half-a-million-from-employers-jailed/; Tamworth Informed, "Woman Who Stole Half a Million from Lichfield Employers Jailed" Thursday, 22nd October 2020.

Red flags: Sometimes the way employees behave might suggest they are committing a fraud. The signs are referred to as 'red flags'. Defending against misappropriation fraud requires employers to be on guard for fraudulent behaviour, even by employees who have been with the business for a long period of time.

Here are some misappropriation frauds red flags employers need to be aware of the following.

Case Study 13.4: Asset misappropriation fraud

Theft from employer ledt Managing Director under serious stress

In 2019 a bookkeeper who stole £47,000 from a Bury firm in Greater Manchester was sentenced to 33 months in prison. In 2017, the bookkeeper, working at the family-run Tottington Motor Company, made 51 separate transactions from the firm's business account into her own personal bank account over a seven-month period. The fraud and financial loss, amounting to £46,851.43, meant that the company had to consider making redundancies, and left the managing director under serious stress, Manchester Crown Court (Minshull Street) heard. Her fraud at the Tottington company was discovered by the firm's managing director after he noticed a discrepancy between invoices that had been received for three training courses and four payments that had been made. He said:

> Her actions have had an impact on my business, and we are currently looking to make people redundant as a result. I am not sleeping due to stress, thinking why did I not notice it early on, as well as the stress of making people redundant as a result of this crime.

Sentencing the bookkeeper, Judge Nield said her offences represented a 'significant breach of trust' which had had repercussions for the Tottington Motor Company, and in particular its owner, his family and their mental health. Judge Nield added:

> There is an assumption that fraud, no matter how much money is involved, is an offence with faceless victims. And where large companies are concerned there can be a mistake in perceiving that the money can simply disappear and not have any impact on any individuals. If that assumption were ever to be proven wrong this is a case where it has been. And looking at the victim impact statement of the owner of Tottington Motor Company it makes that abundantly clear.

Sources: theBoltonNews.co.uk: "REGIONAL: Mother jailed for stealing £47k from Tottington company months after defrauding another firm.REGIONAL: Mother jailed for stealing £47k from Tottington company months after defrauding another firm" https://www.theboltonnews.co.uk/news/17601606.regional-mother-jailed-stealing-47k-tottington-company-months-defrauding-another-firm/; BuryTimes.co.uk: "Mother jailed for stealing £47k from Tottington company months after defrauding another firm" https://www.burytimes.co.uk/news/17601605.mother-jailed-stealing-47k-tottington-company-months-defrauding-another-firm/; the *Daily Mail*: "Mother-of-one, 39, stole £46,000 from car firm to take son on 'memory-making' trips to Rome and the Lake District while under police probe over £122,000 fraud at previous job" https://www.dailymail.co.uk/news/article-6927237/Mother-one-39-stole-46-000-car-firm-son-memory-making-trips-Rome.html; and Thisislancashire.co.uk: "Mother jailed for stealing £47k from Tottington company months after defrauding another firm" https://www.burytimes.co.uk/news/17601605.mother-jailed-stealing-47k-tottington-company-months-defrauding-another-firm/

Employee fraud red flags

A large proportion of fraud affecting organisations comes from within the organisation itself, mainly from employees. Some of the behavioural signs of employee fraud include but are not limited to:

- living beyond their means
- financial difficulties
- unusually close relationship with a supplier
- unwillingness to share duties
- divorce or family problems
- addiction problems (typically but not exclusively gambling)
- frequent complaints about inadequate pay
- history of debts (from a divorce settlement, drugs or life style excesses)
- past employment problems
- refusal to take vacations
- social isolation
- past legal problems and any financial settlement costs.

Clearly, an employee may exhibit more than one behavioural problem such as an addiction which has led to divorce which in turn has led to financial difficulties. As identified by the United States Association of Certified Fraud Examiners, it is very common for people who are engaged in an occupational fraud scheme to display certain behavioural traits or characteristics associated with fraudulent conduct. Understanding how these behavioural clues are linked to fraudulent conduct can help employers improve the chances of detecting misappropriation fraud early and minimising fraud losses.

The most common and clearest indicator of potential fraud is a pronounced change in lifestyle. Some employees may change their lifestyle abruptly by spending more than their salary allows. The purchases can be expensive cars, holidays, luxury goods or even houses. Sometimes, the employee's lifestyle may exceed that of their employer. An employee's explanation that they received inheritance money may be a deception.

Step 4B: Threat identification and impact

Understanding the vulnerabilities of the business from asset misappropriation fraud involves examining every accounting process involved in the receipt of payments and expenditure on goods and services. While theft of money dominates media interest this type of fraud also entails the theft of assets. It involves examining the receipt and storage of all supplies, materials, furniture, IT equipment (hardware and software), plant, machinery, tools and any other asset that can be removed from the business. It also involves the facilitation of theft by others.

A risk is broken into several components, how these components are articulated is critical to how that risk is viewed, understood and managed. 'Because of a [cause or causes], a [threat] may occur, which should it materialise would lead to an [impact] on the business's objectives.' The common 'cause' is the motivation of individuals to secure finances to meet their pressing financial needs or to enjoy a lifestyle beyond their means. Whenever processes and procedures are changed, they need to be viewed in terms of whether they increase vulnerability to fraud. The list of causes included in Table 13.1 is not exhaustive.

Table 13.1 Misappropriation fraud causes

Misappropriation of assets (Cause → Threat → Impact)	
The **causes** or triggers behind fraudulent activity	
Policies and processes	
Governance	Policies and procedures are not developed with the goal of preventing misappropriation of assets.
Policies	Policies do not state that the business has a zero tolerance to fraud committed by employees, suppliers, consultants, contractors or any third party engaged by the business.
Roles and segregation of duties	
Roles	Roles are not segregated to prevent one employee having total control of receipts and payments.
Employee holidays	Employees are not required to take compulsory holidays.
Role rotation	Role rotation is not implemented.
Vetting	
Screening	Social media sites are not examined to learn about the background to job application candidates.
Qualifications	Candidates claim to have qualifications they have not achieved and checks are not made to verify their degrees.
Previous employers	References are not taken up altogether or previous employers are not contacted to verify if a prospective candidate was previously employed there and they were not dismissed.
Criminal record	Candidates for new roles are not asked to obtain proof of no criminal record through DBS* (significant for businesses that deal with client's sensitive information).
Proof of identity and address	Candidates are not asked for proof of identity (passport or birth certificate) and proof of address (recent utility bill, council tax demand or driving licence – card version).

Misappropriation of assets (Cause → Threat → Impact)	
Financial standing	Candidates are not asked if they have ever filed for bankruptcy, they own their own home or subject to county court judgements.
Audits	
Audits	Audits are not commissioned with a remit to look for fraudulent activity.
Surprise audits	Surprise audits are not conducted to limit the opportunity for concealment of wrong doing.

Note: *Candidates can apply for a basic Disclosure and Barring Service (DBS) check to get a copy of their criminal record. This is called 'basic disclosure'. It is available for individuals working in England and Wales. See https://www.gov.uk/request-copy-criminal-record.

The impact descriptions below cannot address all possible scenarios and hence are generic in nature and need to be tailored to the business, its context and ongoing operations (Tables 13.2 and 13.3).

Table 13.2 Misappropriation fraud threats

Threats (uncertain event)	
Transfer of funds	A member of the accounts team transfers funds belonging to the business to a personal account.
Theft of assets	An employee steals company assets (which may include supplies, equipment, materials, furniture, IT equipment [hardware and software], plant, machinery and tools).
Theft of data	An employee steals data to set up a rival company or to sell to a competitor or a criminal organisation.
Theft of intellectual property	An employee steals intellectual property to sell, to take to a new employer or to establish their own business.
Accounting processes	An employee amends accounting practices, processes or procedures to make misappropriation easier and/or to facilitate concealment of one or a series of thefts.
Falsification of documents	A candidate falsifies qualifications and/or experience to secure the role.
Falsification of identity	A candidate falsifies their identity as they have a criminal record or they are taking up the role with the express intent of theft and subsequent evasion of traceability and detention.

Threats (uncertain event)	
Conspiracy	Employees conspire together to steal assets through securing access, security pass codes, transportation, security details, the timing of the receipt or movement of assets, etc.
Down time (loss of production time)	Down time following unwitting inclusion of counterfeit parts (by a legitimate company) within its manufacturing plant.
Customer complaints	Customer complaints following unwitting inclusion of counterfeit parts (by a legitimate company) within its products.
Component failure	Failure of components included in a plant room within a new construction project.

Table 13.3 Misappropriation fraud impact descriptions

Impact descriptions (if the threats were to materialise)	
Prosecution	If the employee has stolen the client's money which is no longer recoverable, the business will need to understand what its liabilities are and any exposure to prosecution.
Loss of reputation	The business suffers reputational damage and may make customers/clients nervous about continuing to provide the firm with business particularly if the firm handles clients' money, such as solicitors, rental estate agents, auctioneers, banks, building societies, investment companies and umbrella companies.
Time	The director's and/or manager's time is diverted away from normal operational activities to understand the extent and damage of a fraud, how it occurred and how such events are to be prevented in the future. It also involves revisiting the degree of success or otherwise of previous audits and their recommended response actions.
Cost	Monies are transferred to bank accounts controlled by employees which may only be recoverable through the courts. This in turn may lead to cash flow problems and reduced turnover and profitability.
Director stress	Directors may have the added stress of considering business longevity, redundancies, securing loans to support the business going forward and redefining roles to split duties.

Step 4C: Risk analysis

When examining the characteristics of a potential threat, it commonly involves estimating the likelihood, the impact (in cost and time together with other parameters when appropriate) and the proximity (when is the threat likely to materialise) (Table 13.4).

Table 13.4 Misappropriation fraud risk analysis

Analysis of identity theft risks	
Likelihood	The likelihood of a particular business being impacted by misappropriation of assets is difficult to discern as not all frauds are reported and it is a consequence of human behaviour. Certain businesses such as banks, solicitors and accountants would not want to publicise if one or more members of staff had been involved in fraud as it may undermine confidence and cause a loss of trade.
Financial impact	This type of fraud can leave SMEs struggling to compete in the market place and can lead to the need to make redundancies. The scale of loss for a legitimate business depends on an array of aspects such as the industry and sector they are working in, their current market share, anticipated new market entrants, years of operation, the profit margin per product, the scale of penetration and sale of counterfeit goods.
Time impact	The time impact will depend on the scale of financial losses, the ability to retrieve any of the stolen funds or property, the scale of any redundancies required, and whether it was possible to conceal the event from customers and the media.
Proximity	It could be argued that proximity will depend on how good the business is at preventing those with the intent to commit fraud from doing so.

Step 5: Risk response actions

The structured risk management process needs to establish the unique characteristics of this fraud and develop tailored responses to improve the capabilities of the business to combat it. It needs to learn lessons from its own processes, external case studies, government guidelines and outsourced consultancy support when appropriate. The constraints relate to say the finances that are available (for say software and consultancy support), current knowledge of the types of business fraud as well as the time that staff can devote to fraud management. The enablers relate to available cyber security software, online guidance including government websites and consultancy support.

Specific response actions: governance, audits, systems and people

There are two commonly recognised response actions:

- Active detection methods involving a deliberate search for misconduct from someone within the organisation or an internal control designed to detect fraud.
- Passive detection methods where a business discovers the fraud by accident or receives a confession, an unsolicited notification from another party or a notification from a government agency.

Included in Figure 13.3 are specific response actions that should be implemented with regard to governance, audits, systems and people (Figure 13.3).

Step 6: Implementation of actions

Immediate response

If a fraud is suspected, a company must contact the police. The suspected employee(s) should be immediately suspended to prevent further losses. An estimate should be made of the direct losses it is believed the firm has suffered. An investigation should be carried out to determine if the same fraud is being conducted independently by other employees elsewhere in the business in case there is a systemic failure. An assessment should be made to determine if the losses can be recovered. Consideration must also be given to reputational damage to prevent or reduce loss of customers and market share. Financial organisations are very vulnerable to reputational damage if internal theft comes to the media's attention. It may be necessary to allay any concerns that the staff have about the long-term prospects and viability of the company if the losses turn out to be substantial. If the scale of the losses is potentially high, it may be prudent to take advice as to whether a statement should be released to the media provided it is not prejudicial to any court proceedings.

Monitoring implementation

Once anti-fraud measures have been decided upon, they need to be implemented as part of a project, understanding: the activities required, who will undertake

Your Governance

 System: Directors should develop a system by which the business can be directed and controlled.

 Accounts: Ensure that accurate, timely and relevant financial information is prepared to inform decision making and enable scrutiny of transactions.

 Risk management: Establish financial risk management practices focussed on preventing fraud.

 Controls: Develop a robust system of anti-fraud controls as a deterrent, as well as a proactive prevention and detection mechanism, in addressing potential fraud.

Your Audits

 External audits: Organise external audits of financial statements on a regular cycle.

Internal audits: Conduct at least six monthly internal audits of sufficient granularity to detect misappropriation of assets.

Surprise audits: Implement surprise internal audits so that employees do not have the opportunity to conceal any wrongdoing.

Audit composition: Ensure that internal audits are adequately prepared in terms of fraud detection practices, particularly when carrying out surprise audits.

Your Systems

 Certification: Arrange for management certification of financial statements. This will provide an 'independent eye' on the accounts.

Fraud function: Where resources permit, create a dedicated fraud function as a department, team or an individual with no links with the management of accounts.

Policy: Prepare, issue, circulate and gain commitment to an anti-fraud policy (as well as drink and drug-taking policies).

Approach: Adopt and rigorously implement a 'zero-tolerance' approach towards employee fraud.

Accounts reconciliation: Conduct regular reconciliation of bank statements against accounts, and assessment of invoices raised against a client list and invoices not paid.

Payments: Use tiered authority and signature levels for payments.

Access: Restrict and closely monitor access to sensitive financial information.

Recovery: Have a clear response plan in place in case fraud is discovered.

Your People

 Vetting: Vet candidates for employment positions thoroughly checking CVs, qualifications, references, identity, proof of address, length of time at their current address and if they have had any previous debt problems or addictions. Those with debts, or say, gambling addictions may be desperate to secure additional finance even if it involves engaging in fraudulent activity. Use the Cifas Enhanced Internal Fraud Database which records individuals suspected of dishonest conduct against their employer.

Check: Ensure recruitment agencies undertake a criminal record check on recruits that have passed the interview stage.

Training: Provide fraud prevention training for employees and management.

Segregation: Impose clear segregation of duties considering job rotation/mandatory vacations/role shadowing.

Whistleblowing: Consider implementing a whistleblowing policy and payment of rewards for whistleblowers. While candidate vetting may screen out unwanted employees, debts or addictions may develop during employment and need addressing.

Code of conduct: Prepare, circulate and gain commitment to a code of conduct for all staff.

Culture: Promote a culture of fraud awareness among staff.

Role rotation: Inform recruits on joining that the business operates a system of role rotation as part of its zero tolerance to fraud. Implement role rotation within the finance and internal control functions.

Figure 13.3 Threat response actions

them and the time frame for implementation. A rolling timetable needs to be established for the review of the suitability of the measures to determine any amendments required or if any new measures are required.

Summary

Misappropriation fraud is one of the most debilitating frauds. Perpetrators can be company directors or employees but are most likely to be from within the accounts department. Positions of trust are abused. If well concealed, theft can occur over many years rather than just months. As soon as fraud is suspected a predetermined response should be put in place commencing with contacting the police. Every effort should be made to recover the losses however depending on when the fraud took place, this may be difficult if not unrealistic.

Chapter 14

Financial statement fraud

Structure of Chapter 14

Chapter 14 is subdivided into the following four sections. An overview of the fraud type is provided followed by an assessment of the threat posed by the fraud, suggested response actions and timing of implementation (Figure 14.1).

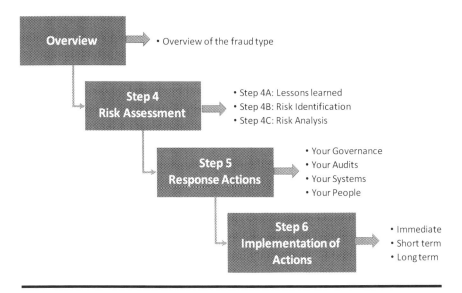

Figure 14.1 Structure of Chapter 14

DOI: 10.4324/9781003200383-17

Overview

Financial statement fraud is the deliberate material alteration of a company's financial statements in order to mislead and deceive the users of financial information to create either a healthier or more fragile picture of the company's financial position than actually exists. It involves the intentional overstatement and or the understatement of balances in the financial statements. Specifically, it may entail the understatement of profits and the overstatement of expenses. Fraud has always existed and given human nature; it is always likely to. As a consequence, businesses must be constantly vigilant and open to the possible occurrence of financial statement fraud. This type of fraud is difficult to detect and the ways of committing it are continually evolving. Individuals may be motivated to commit fraud by internal or external organisational pressures to hit performance targets, attract additional equity or bank financing, reduce tax liabilities, bring about an increase in the business's share price or secure indirect benefits such as avoiding the loss of a bonus payment. Fraud may involve sophisticated and carefully organised schemes designed to conceal it, such as forgery, deliberate failure to record transactions or intentional misrepresentations being made to those with oversight. The higher audit threshold for smaller businesses means that SMEs are not subject to external checks and if a business files its own reports from the internal accounts department rather than using an accountant, fraud may initially go undetected. The ability to detect a fraud depends on factors such as the knowledge and skill of the perpetrator, the time the employee has occupied their role, the frequency and extent of manipulation, the degree of collusion involved between employees, the relative size of individual amounts manipulated, and the seniority of those individuals involved.

Step 4: Risk assessment

Risk assessment involves the identification and analysis of threats as described in Chapter 3 'Approach to Fraud Risk Management'. It entails considering the threats that may materialise and considering their likelihood, proximity and the potential impact they may have. Proximity refers to when a threat may materialise. Identification can be considerably enhanced by looking at lessons learned. While examination of what has occurred in the past is not a foolproof way of predicting what may occur in the future, it forms a foundation to build on. In addition, lessons learned should never be based on static records or notions and beliefs, but reflect the evolving nature of accounting practice and emerging fraudulent practices.

Step 4A: Lessons learned

To understand the vulnerabilities of a business to financial statement fraud requires an appreciation of the sequence or pattern of these fraud events, the tools and techniques employed (described here as the mechanics), historical events (captured in case studies) together with 'red flags' or the 'alarm bells' over potential exposure, as illustrated in Figure 14.2. These activities contribute to Lessons Learned which in turn assist in deciding on the actions to be implemented, to thwart fraud.

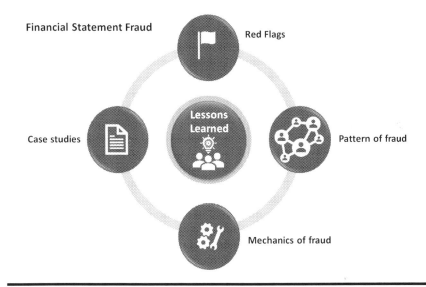

Figure 14.2 The lessons learned from prior events

 Understanding the pattern of financial statement fraud: Financial statement fraud as described here refers to a fraud that is perpetrated within the business rather than by external third parties seeking financial gain at the expense of a business. Managers of businesses engage in fraudulent financial reporting, through the deliberate and material manipulation of financial statements, to reduce the tax burden, keep existing stakeholders on board, attract new investment or maximise performance-based earnings. To retain their position and to maintain or improve their earnings, managers have to cope with both external and internal pressures. There may also be personal pressures due to a manager's personal circumstances.

External pressures

Economic, industry, or market operating conditions, may put pressure on the business and threaten its profitability or its very longevity, such as:

■ high degree of competition or limited growth opportunities due to market saturation from new businesses entering the industry;

- high vulnerability to rapid changes in technology leading to product obsolescence;
- significant decline in customer demand;
- turbulent economic environment arising from micro and macro-economics;
- operating losses leading to the bank rescinding its loan(s);
- recurring negative cash flows from operations or an inability to generate cash flows from operations;
- new accounting, statutory or regulatory requirements;
- a pandemic;
- the prolific theft of intellectual property across the industry by a rogue nation-state; and
- a seismic shift in the county's trade relationship with a major trading partner.

Operating pressures

Excessive pressure to meet the requirements or expectations of third parties are due to the following:

- Profitability expectations created by directors in, for example, overly optimistic statements to shareholders, in press releases or where applicable within introductions to annual reports.
- The need to obtain additional financing to stay competitive – including the financing of capital expenditure on say new buildings, manufacturing plant, major research and development or vehicles.
- Anticipated adverse effect of reporting poor financial results on tender submissions for major contracts that require the submission of the last three years of accounts.

Personal pressures

The personal financial situation of members of management (or those responsible for governance) is threatened by the business's financial performance arising from the following:

- significant portions of their compensation (for example, bonuses, share options, and expense arrangements) being dependent upon achieving aggressive targets for turnover, cash flow or profitability;
- existing mortgage, loans against their property or second home or multiple negative credit card balances.

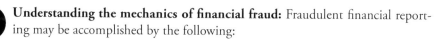 **Understanding the mechanics of financial fraud:** Fraudulent financial reporting may be accomplished by the following:

- **Overstatement of revenue:** Numerous financial statement manipulations are achieved by inflating sales. This can be achieved by recording completely fictitious sales or by recording a sale before the revenue is actually earned.
- **Overstatement of assets:** This could include not writing down assets. Assets with impaired values or items like obsolete inventory may also not be written down or written off.
- **Understatement of expenses:** This usually occurs by holding expenses over to a later period, even when they were incurred in the current period. A company may also wrongly capitalise an item and expense it over several periods, rather than properly expensing it immediately.
- **Understatement of liabilities:** This may involve the failure to record liabilities or their deliberate concealment.
- **Improper use of reserves:** Balance sheet reserves are entered as liabilities on the balance sheet and represent funds that are set aside to pay future obligations. Over-reserving can result in an opportunity cost to a business as there are less funds available for investment. Conversely, under-reserving can falsely boost profitability as more funds are freed up to invest. Commonly abused reserve accounts include reserves for accounts receivable, liabilities, sales returns, and inventory obsolescence.
- **Manipulation:** Manipulation, falsification (including forgery), or alteration of accounting records or supporting documentation from which the financial statements are prepared.
- **Misrepresentation in, or intentional omission of information:** Deliberate misrepresentation in, or intentional omission of information from the financial statements of events, transactions or other significant information.
- **Misapplication of accounting rules:** Intentional misapplication of accounting principles beneficial to the planned fraud, relating to amounts, classification, manner of presentation, or disclosure.
- **Management override:** The overriding of controls that otherwise may appear to be operating effectively. Fraud can be committed by a member of management by overriding controls using such techniques as intentionally:
  - concealing the true value of the business's debts;
  - recording fictitious financial records, particularly close to the end of an accounting period, to manipulate operating results or achieve other objectives;
  - adjusting assumptions and changing judgments used to estimate account balances;
  - omitting, advancing or delaying the recording (in the financial statements) of events and transactions that have occurred during the reporting period;

- omitting, obscuring or misstating disclosures required by the applicable financial reporting framework, or disclosures that are necessary to achieve fair presentation; and
- concealing facts that could affect the amounts recorded in the financial statements.

■ **Concealment:** Concealment of financial reporting irregularities behind overseas operations. The nature of the industry or the entity's operations provides opportunities to engage in fraudulent financial reporting that can arise from the following:

- significant operations located or conducted across international borders in jurisdictions where differing business environments, accounting practices and cultures exist;
- use of business intermediaries for which there appears to be no clear business justification;
- significant bank accounts or subsidiary or branch operations in tax-haven jurisdictions for which there appears to be no clear business justification;
- assets, liabilities, revenues or expenses based on significant estimates that involve subjective judgements or uncertainties that are difficult to corroborate.

■ **Deceitful:** Deliberate manoeuvring to avoid the discovery of financial reporting irregularities. Preconceived methods adopted to avoid the business's accounts being scrutinised to any great depth:

- The regular change of accountants and auditors implemented shortly before the end of a reporting period denying these external parties sufficient time to study both previous accounts and current financial data.

Case Studies: The following case studies focus on highly publicised events involving financial statement fraud. While the cases relate to large companies, SMEs are just as exposed to financial statement fraud, albeit on a smaller scale. The case relating to Patisserie Valerie again highlights that the holder of the position of Finance Director may succumb to human frailties and manipulate financial statements to suit their own goals.

Case Study 14.1 is an example of where a company's debts had been understated, the amount that it was owed overstated and the valuation of the firm's assets had been manipulated.

Case Study 14.2 demonstrates that well-respected household names in the retail sector can have their reputations tarnished by the actions of their employees as well as leaving them exposed to fines and the need to undertake a compliance programme.

Case Study 14.1: Financial Statement Fraud

Overstatement of financial position at Patisserie Valerie

Patisserie Valerie's finance director was arrested and bailed on 11 October 2018 following the discovery of what was described as significant and potentially fraudulent accounting irregularities. Patisserie Valerie collapsed into administration on 22 January 2019 resulting in the loss of 920 jobs and the closure of 70 of its stores and concessions. The café chain was found to have overstated its cash position by £30 million and failed to disclose overdrafts of nearly £10 million. On entering administration, any hope investors had in recovering any value from their shares was lost. Millions of pounds were written off. It was reported at the time that forensic accountants KPMG had uncovered that the company's debts had been understated, the amount that it was owed overstated and there was a discrepancy in the way the firm valued its assets. In fact, the company had overstated its position by approximately £94 million. It was discovered that there had been an extensive misstatement of its accounts and very significant manipulation of the balance sheet and profit and loss accounts. On 18 June 2019, the Serious Fraud Office (SFO) stated as part of a joint operation with the Hertfordshire, Leicestershire and Metropolitan police services, five individuals had been arrested and interviewed in connection with the SFO investigation of individuals associated with the collapse of Patisserie Holdings PLC. The chain's former chairman, on learning of the fraud, said it had been like entering a nightmare parallel universe. Other than the SFO, the collapse attracted the attention of several other organisations including the Financial Reporting Council, the Insolvency Service, the Aim market regulator and the Her Majesty's Revenue and Customs (HMRC) fraud investigation service.

Source: Adapted from reports by the Serious Fraud Office: "Patisserie Holdings PLC". https://www.sfo.gov.uk/cases/patisserie-holdings-plc/; BBC News: "Patisserie Valerie Scandal: Five People Arrested". https://www.bbc.co.uk/news/business-48736447; *The Independent:* "Patisserie Valerie Collapses into Administration Putting 2,800 Jobs at Risk". https://www.independent.co.uk/news/business/news/patisserie-valerie-collapses-into-administrationjobs-at-risk-a8741161.html; *The Guardian:* "Police Arrest Five in Patisserie Valerie Investigation". https://www.theguardian.com/business/2019/jun/23/sfo-arrests-five-inpatisserie-valerie-investigation; *The Daily Mail:* "Fraud Investigators Arrest Five More over Collapse of Patisserie Valerie Chain with Cost of 900 Jobs after £100m Black Hole was Found in Its Accounts". https://www.dailymail.co.uk/news/article-7171993/Patisserie-Valerieinvestigations-sees-five-arrests-according-Fraud-Office.html; *Cityam:* "Patisserie Valerie Enters Administration after Bank Talks Fail". https://www.cityam.com/patisserie-valerie-filesadministration/; and the *Financial Times:* "Five Arrested in Patisserie Valerie Fraud Probe". https://www.ft.com/content/f3de68ba-959d-11e9-9573-ee5cbb98ed36.

Case Study 14.2: Financial Statement Fraud

False accounting at Tesco Stores

The SFO entered into a Deferred Prosecution Agreement (DPA) with Tesco Stores Limited on 10 April 2017. Through the DPA, Tesco Stores Limited accepted responsibility for false accounting practices. Between February and September 2014, instead of working to safeguard the financial interests of the company and its shareholders, a culture existed at Tesco that encouraged illegal practices to meet accounting targets, including adopting improper accounting practices in relation to the UK accounts, by 'pulling forward' income from subsequent reporting periods. Carl Rogberg, John Scouler and Christopher Bush, former Tesco employees who held senior management roles in the Tesco UK business, were charged over allegations of fraud and false accounting on 9 September 2016. Under the terms of the DPA, Tesco agreed to pay a £129m fine and £3m investigation costs. The company also undertook and implemented an ongoing compliance programme during the three-year term of the DPA. On 7 April 2020, the SFO served a Notice of Discontinuance on the Court, confirming that Tesco Stores Ltd had fully complied with the terms of the DPA. The three-year term of the DPA came to end on 10 April 2020.

Source: Serious Fraud Office UK, https://www.sfo.gov.uk/cases/tesco-plc/.

Case Study 14.3 again highlights that the actions of the holder of the position of Finance Director need to be closely monitored for the perpetration of false accounting.

Case Study 14.4 describes the collapse of Worldcom which had hugely overstated its profits for a considerable period. It was one of the most reported business collapses of its time with its demise being featured by the media worldwide.

Red flags: Business owners defending against financial fraud need to look for 'red flags', warning signals of fraudulent activity. However, in the case of financial statement fraud, the deliberate concealment of poor financial performance and associated misreporting means that detection of wrongdoing is not so readily discernible. The motivation for financial statement fraud, like the misappropriation

Case Study 14.3: Financial Statement Fraud

False accounting as Serco plc

Following a six-year investigation, the UK's Serious Fraud Office (SFO) reported in December 2019 that it had charged two former directors of the outsourcing company Serco with fraud and false accounting as part of its investigation into the electronic monitoring contract with the Ministry of Justice. Serco plc is one among the Financial Times Stock Exchange (FTSE) top 250 companies managing over 500 contracts worldwide and employing over 50,000 people. It operates internationally across four geographies, UK and Europe, North America, the Asia Pacific and the Middle East, and across five sectors, namely defence, justice and immigration, transport, health and citizen services. The SFO statement said that the former Finance Director of Serco Home Affairs and the former Operations Director of Field Services (within Serco) had been charged with fraud by false representation and false accounting in relation to the Ministry of Justice contract between 2011 and 2103. In July 2019 Serco had been fined £19.2 million and charged £3.7 million in costs after it had reportedly charged the government for electronically monitoring people who were either dead, in jail or had left the country. The fines formed part of a deferred prosecution agreement with Serco which was approved by Mr. Justice William Davis on 4 July 2019.

Source: Adapted from reports by the Serious Fraud Office: "Serco". https://www.sfo. gov. uk/cases/serco/; the *BBC*: "Two Ex-Serco Bosses Charged with Fraud over Alleged Tagging Scandal". https://www.bbc.co.uk/news/uk-50806919; the *Financial Times:* "Two Former Serco Directors Charged with Fraud". https://www.ft.com/content/66df-f8a2-2012-11ea-b8a1-584213ee7b2b; and *Reuters:* "UK's SFO Charges Two Former Serco Directors with Fraud, False Accounting". https://www.reuters.com/article/serco-groupsfo-idUSL4N28Q32B.

of assets, may also be financial but from a different perspective. This type of fraud may be perpetrated by senior managers or finance directors seeking to maintain their position, level of remuneration and the lifestyle that it supports. In particular, they seek to maintain their level of salary, bonus, pension and expenses. The fraud is carried out by members of the management team who falsify, change or inaccurately report the health of the business through fraudulent financial statements. A list of possible warning signals or fraud alerts is provided below.

Case Study 14.4: Financial Statement Fraud

False accounting and downgrading of pre-tax profits at WorldCom

WorldCom filed for bankruptcy protection in June 2002. It was hard on the heels of the Enron scandal. At the time it was the biggest corporate fraud in history, only to be eclipsed a few years later by the collapse of Lehman Brothers. Its failure was largely due to treating operating expenses as capital expenditure. WorldCom, to become renamed MCI, admitted in March 2004 that the total amount by which it had misled investors over the previous ten years was almost US$75 billion (£42 billion) and reduced its stated pre-tax profits for 2001 and 2002 by that amount. WorldCom stock began falling in late 1999 as businesses slashed spending on telecom services and equipment. A series of debt downgrades raised borrowing costs for the company, struggling with about US$32 billion in debt. WorldCom used accounting tricks to conceal a deteriorating financial condition and to inflate profits. Former WorldCom chief executive Bernie Ebbers resigned in April 2002 amid questions about US$366 million in personal loans from the company and a federal probe of its accounting practices. Ebbers was subsequently charged with conspiracy to commit securities fraud and filing misleading data with the Securities and Exchange Commission (SEC) and was sentenced to 25 years in prison. Scott Sullivan, former Chief Financial Officer, pleaded guilty to three criminal charges and was sentenced to five years in prison. Ultimately, losses to WorldCom shareholders were close to US$180 billion and the fraud also resulted in the loss of 17,000 jobs. The SEC said that WorldCom had committed 'accounting improprieties of unprecedented magnitude' – proof, it said, of the need for reform in the regulation of corporate accounting.

Source: Adapted from *The Guardian:* "WorldCom Accounting Scandal". https://www. theguardian.com/business/2002/aug/09/corporatefraud.worldcom2; *The New York Times:* "Worldcom's Collapse: The Overview; Worldcom Files for Bankruptcy: Largest US Case". https://www.nytimes.com/2002/07/22/us/worldcom-s-collapse-the-overview worldcom-files-for-bankruptcy-largest-us-case.html; *Financial Times:* "Ebbers to Pay $45m in WorldCom Deal". https://www.ft.com/content/54988d86-e98a-11d9-ba15-00000e2511c8; the *BBC:* "Ebbers Guilty of Worldcom Fraud". http://news.bbc.co.uk/1/hi/business/4351975.stm.

This should not be considered an exhaustive list, as alerts will appear in many different guises according to circumstances.

- Management methods and behaviours which undermine appropriate accounting practices, ethical standards and internal controls:
  - recurring attempts by management to justify inappropriate accounting methods;
  - transactions initiated without the appropriate authority;
  - lack of diligence in maintaining approvals or authorisation signatures;
  - inadequate communication, implementation, support, or enforcement of businesses values and ethical standards;
  - evidence of alteration of documents and records;
  - accounting and information systems that are not effective, including situations involving significant deficiencies in internal control;
  - communication of inappropriate practices, values or ethical standards, which conflict with laws and regulations;
  - management failing to remedy known significant deficiencies in internal control on a timely basis;
  - extensive use of 'suspense' accounts;
  - inappropriate or unusual journal entries.
- Deliberate attempts to hinder, misdirect, restrict or influence the work of auditors:
  - frequent disputes with the auditor on accounting, the scope and focus of auditing, or reporting matters.
  - unrealistic time constraints placed on the auditor regarding the completion of the audit or the issue of the auditor's report.
  - restrictions placed on the auditor that inappropriately limits access to people or information;
  - attempts to influence the scope of the auditor's work or the selection or continuation of personnel assigned to or to be consulted during the audit.
- Corporate track record in terms of past investigations by HMRC and claims against the business by suppliers and other third parties over non-payment:
  - known history of claims against the business, its senior management, or those charged with governance alleging fraud or violations of laws and regulations.
- High turnover in senior management which may be an indication of interference in their duties or disquiet over business ethics or management practices:
  - high turnover of senior management, legal counsel, risk management or those charged with governance;

- high turnover rates or employment of staff in accounting, information technology or the internal audit function.
- Employee behaviour:
  - emails sent at unusual times, with unnecessary attachments or to unusual destinations;
  - unusual, irrational, or inconsistent behaviour;
  - use of photocopies of documents in place of originals;
  - systems being accessed outside of normal work hours or from outside the normal work area;
  - lack of escalation of signature or handwriting discrepancies;
  - higher than average number of failed login attempts.
- Indications of tampering such as the deliberate and unauthorised modification of information:
  - unexplained alterations to documents received from third parties;
  - serial numbers used out of sequence or duplicated;
  - addresses and company logos not consistent on a supplier's documents;
  - format changes to one or more documents within a series of documents;
  - information that would be expected to be included in a spreadsheet of accounts is absent;
  - alphanumeric invoice references that differ from others in a series from a third party/regular trading partner;
  - unusual prices or costs for goods on repeat order;
  - information that appears implausible or inconsistent with earlier records;
  - copies of documents presented rather than originals;
  - electronic documents with unexpected 'last edited date'.

Step 4B: Threat identification and impact

A risk is broken into several components, how these components are articulated is critical to how that threat is viewed, understood and managed. 'Because of a [cause], a [risk event] may occur, which should it materialise would lead to an [impact].' The common 'cause' is the motivation of individuals to secure financial gain from a business activity, contract or project. It is a common phenomenon in the business environment and perpetually gives rise to uncertainty. The list of causes included in Table 14.1 is not exhaustive.

While there are multiple causes that can be identified that may trigger a fraud as indicated in Table 14.1, they do not all have to be present and they do not automatically act as a catalyst for wrongdoing. It is the behaviour of an employee or director acting alone or in collusion with others that may lead to fraud. As a consequence of one or more of the causes listed, a business may be exposed to the threat described in Table 14.2.

Table 14.1 Causes or triggers of threat events

Financial statement fraud (Cause → Threat → Impact)	
The **causes** or triggers behind fraudulent activity	
Negative pressure from the business's operating environment	
Competition	High degree of competition or market saturation.
Rapid changes	High vulnerability to rapid changes such as changes in technology resulting in product obsolescence. New accounting, statutory or regulatory requirements.
Falling customer demand	Significant decline in customer demand.
Deteriorating economy	Increasing business failures from a slow-down in the economy, significant increases in interest rates/loan charges and/or declining margins.
Operating losses	Operating losses making the threat of bankruptcy, foreclosure or hostile takeover imminent.
Negative cash flows	Recurring negative cash flows from operations or an inability to generate cash flows from operations.
Negative pressure from third parties	
Profitability	Third parties (investors) have unrealistic profitability expectations due to, say, overly optimistic press releases or annual report messages.
Need for additional financing	Need to obtain financing to stay competitive such as financing research and development or capital expenditure.
Debt	Marginal ability to meet debt repayment.
New contracts	Anxiety over reporting poor financial results on significant pending contract awards.
Pressure due to personal circumstances	
Financial interests	Significant financial interests in the business.
Remuneration	Significant elements of remuneration package being dependent upon achieving performance targets.
Guarantees	Personal guarantees of debts of the business.
Opportunities which may be capitalised on	
Lack of audit	Significant transactions not audited or audited by another firm.
Dominant position	Ability to dominate a certain industry sector that allows the business to dictate terms or conditions to suppliers or customers.
Estimates	Assets, liabilities, revenues or expenses based on significant estimates that involve subjective judgements or uncertainties that are difficult to evaluate.

Financial statement fraud (Cause → Threat → Impact)	
Complex transactions	Significant, unusual or highly complex transactions, especially those close to period end.
Ineffective monitoring by management	Oversight by those charged with overseeing the financial reporting processes and internal control is not effective.
Unclear organisational structure	Difficulty in determining the individuals that have controlling interest in the business.
Deficiencies in internal control	Inadequate processes to monitor the business's financial reporting, high staff turnover in accounting, information technology, internal audit function staff and/or ineffective accounting and information systems.

Table 14.2 The overall threat event

Threat (uncertain event)	
Threat	A member (or members) of the senior management team or a director engages in fraudulent financial reporting as a consequence or one or more of the causes listed in Table 14.1.

The impact descriptions below cannot address all possible scenarios and hence are generic in nature and need to be tailored to the business, its context and ongoing operations (Table 14.3).

Step 4C: Risk analysis

When examining the characteristics of a potential threat, it commonly involves estimating the likelihood, the impact (in cost and time together with other parameters when appropriate) and the proximity (when is the threat likely to materialise). Included in Table 14.3 is a descriptive analysis of the likelihood, impact and proximity; however, businesses need to capture actual figures for the different categories. Table 14.4 describes the risk impact analysis in terms of likelihood, financial impact, time impact and proximity.

Step 5: Response actions

Specific response actions: governance, audits, systems and people

Included in Figure 14.3 are specific response actions that could be implemented with regard to governance, audits, systems and people to address the assessed

Table 14.3 Financial statement fraud impact descriptions

Impact descriptions (if the threat were to materialise)	
Prosecution	Prosecution of individuals. Persons guilty of an offence under the Financial Services Act 2012, on conviction, are liable to imprisonment for a term not exceeding seven years or a fine, or both. Prosecution of company representatives. Section 12 of the Fraud Act 2006: Liability of company officers for offences by a company. This section provides that if a person who has a specified corporate role is a party to the commission of an offence under the Act by their body corporate, they will be liable to be charged for the offence as well as the corporation. This offence applies to directors, managers, secretaries and other similar officers of companies and other bodies corporate. Subsection (3) provides that if the body corporate charged with an offence is managed by its members, the members involved in management can be prosecuted too.
Loss of reputation	If false statement accounting is ever detected particularly by external third parties such as external auditors, forensic accountants, shareholders or HMRC, the business's reputation will be tarnished and business trust will be undermined. Loss of reputation may in turn impact market share, loss of contracts and deterioration of relationships with suppliers and contractors. Loss of reputation may also impact partnerships, joint ventures, planned mergers and recruitment.
Time	The time it takes to recover from the discovery of fraud will, as expected, be dependent on a number of variables such as how widely known the fraud is outside of the business, the scale of the fraud, understanding the true financial position of the business and how quickly the business changes its operating practices.
Cost	Costs arising from fraud detection: Costs associated fines or penalties from HMRC for understatement of revenue and overstatement of running costs/expenses, hiring replacement staff, loss of revenue from reduced market share resulting in reduced profitability and higher interest charges on loans.
Employee stress	Loss of key personnel: Key personnel may leave if they are pressured into hindering, misdirecting, restricting or influencing the work of the auditor, manipulating accounting rules, engaging in unethical practices, inaccurate reporting to HRMC, Companies House or stakeholders or the deliberate over- or understating of revenue, assets or expenses.

Table 14.4 Financial statement fraud risk impact analysis

Analysis of financial statement fraud risks	
Likelihood	While there have been a number of high-profile cases of financial statement fraud among large organisations, most noticeably in the US, there is far less visibility of the frequency of this type of fraud carried out by SMEs in the UK. Despite the lack of visibility, given the seriousness of the fraud, it cannot be overstated and a cautious approach would be to treat this fraud type as likely.
Financial impact	The financial impact, should the risk materialise, will depend on whether the performance of the business has been deliberately over- or understated and the rationale for doing so. A deliberate understatement to deceive HMRC may result in fines and penalties. An overstatement, to raise finance from banks or stakeholders, when detected may result in the cancellation of existing loans and a call for the immediate return of all loans from existing lenders hampering operations and cash flow.
Time impact	The time impact is multi-faceted. It will take directors away from their core duties to take steps to (1) prevent a similar occurrence through, say, anti-fraud training, the preparation of anti-fraud policies, and the preparation of processes and procedures; and (2) call in forensic accounting specialists to unravel exactly what has occurred, what is the actual financial status of the business and what needs to be done to ensure the longevity of the business.
Proximity	Of the assessments of 'short', 'medium' and 'long' terms, this risk relates to the short term and needs to be addressed at the earliest opportunity.

threat of a material misstatement of accounts as part of fraudulent financial reporting. The threat responses included below are only examples and accordingly, they may not be the most appropriate or necessary for every business. Also the order of the responses described is not intended to reflect their relative importance.

Step 6: Implementation of actions

The timing of the implementation of response actions will depend on an assessment of what's already in place, the business's current vulnerabilities, the prioritisation of business needs and the resources available to introduce change.

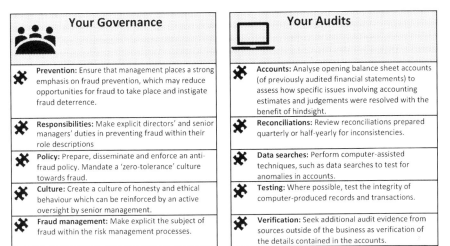

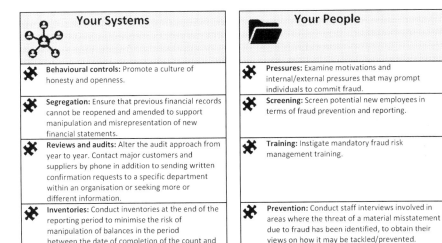

Figure 14.3 Response actions

Intermediate

Consider role rotation of critical roles in the finance department. Discuss with the business's accountant the merit of conducting a forensic review of the accounts based on for instance the number of employees, annual turnover, number of clients and suppliers and whether the accounts function is in one place or split over multiple sites.

Short term

In the short term, identify who within the business is best placed to review the needs of the business, understand its vulnerabilities and develop a plan of specific actions to be implemented.

- Prepare or revisit the anti-fraud policy.
- Make explicit the consequences for those that commit fraud.
- Re-examine the anti-fraud content of induction and periodic employee training and employing e-learning where appropriate.
- Consider contacting the business's bank to gain advice and support in reducing exposure to fraud.
- Regularly reconcile incoming invoices against payments.
- Prevent aggressive accounting practices such as bringing forward anticipated income or delaying the declaration of operational costs and expenses.

Long term

Consider the scope of audits and the merit of conducting surprise audits to halt the concealment of any wrongdoing.

Summary

Financial statement fraud is the deliberate alteration of a company's financial statements in order to mislead and deceive the users of financial information to create either a healthier or more fragile picture of the company's financial position than actually exists. The drivers behind fraudulent behaviour may include external, operational or personal pressures. The four case studies described provide a window into previous fraudulent behaviour, recognising it is the larger organisations and particularly the well-known household names which are considered more 'newsworthy' and hence dominate the media headlines. It is difficult to discern the level of fraud encountered within SMEs due to limited reporting. The list of 'red flags' provide generic indicators that should sound alarm bells if multiple similar events or situations are detected. The existence of fraud will generally be difficult to detect due to measures adopted to conceal it. The damage caused by the discovery of fraudulent accounts can be multi-faceted and include prosecution, loss of reputation, interruption to operations (and the time it takes to recover), costs and or employee stress. It is management's responsibility to put controls in place to limit their exposure to this form of fraud, guided where appropriate by forensic accountants or auditors with specialist training.

Chapter 15

Bribery

Structure of Chapter 15

Chapter 15 is subdivided into the following four sections. An overview of the fraud type is provided followed by an assessment of the threat posed by the fraud, suggested response actions and staged timing of implementation (Figure 15.1).

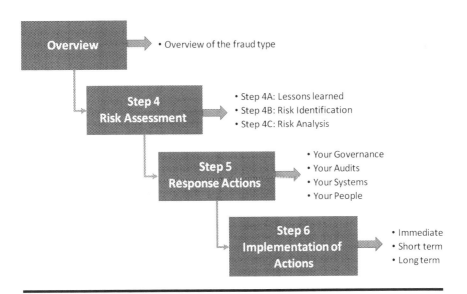

Figure 15.1 Structure of Chapter 15

DOI: 10.4324/9781003200383-18

Overview

All SMEs operating in the UK need to consider their exposure to the risks of bribery and corruption and the measures needed to prevent wrongdoing. While a business may have the best policies, processes and systems in the world, it is the behaviour of its staff that will determine whether it keeps a 'clean sheet' and avoids committing acts of fraud. Employees are the most effective control against bribery and corruption. The government legislation addressing anti-bribery and corruption is the Bribery Act 2010 (the Act). As advised on the government web-page headed 'Bribery Act 2010 guidance',[1] a commercial organisation (a company or partnership) failing to prevent bribery under Section 7 of the Bribery Act, can be criminally liable for failure to prevent bribery, if a person associated with their organisation bribes another person in pursuit of its business objectives. An organisation that can prove it has adequate anti-bribery and corruption procedures in place to constrain persons associated with it from bribing will have a defence to the Section 7 offence. Any business seeking to expand its operations overseas, particularly into high-risk areas where corruption is known to be a problem, needs to know how to protect itself from the perils of bribery and corruption.

National Crime Agency

The National Crime Agency (NCA) leads the UK law enforcement's response to bribery, corruption and sanctions evasion within the UK and works with partners to tackle the threat. The agency provides regular support to partner agencies by developing intelligence and by providing specialist operational capability. The NCA advises companies and partnerships operating in the UK of the need to consider the risks of bribery, corruption and sanctions evasion and the measures needed to prevent wrongdoing. They stress companies need to ensure that they do not negligently or unwittingly facilitate the abuse of legitimate processes and services. The NCA has singled out accounting and legal professionals as well as estate agents who particularly need to ensure they are not criminally exploited as the NCA considers that collectively they can pose a very significant threat: 'they can act as intermediaries and use their skills, knowledge and abilities to draft documentation, disseminate funds, and allow highly complex structures to be created that move and store large amounts of criminal money and conceal ownership effectively'.[2] The Act has a global reach and applies to UK nationals and residents, companies and partnerships operating in the UK, wherever incorporated. This means that strict anti-bribery laws go with employees, agents and anyone working on behalf of the business when they travel anywhere in the world and they will put themselves and their company or partnership at risk of prosecution if during the pursuit of business they adopt bribery practices. The NCA states:

> Bribery of public officials erodes public confidence in the judiciary and government, and undermines the rule of law. Where UK

companies or individuals are involved, it can undermine the UK's ability to promote sustainable growth and to meet our international obligations. Corrupt payments to secure contracts distort markets and endanger fair competition, contributing to economic hardship, social inequality and loss of jobs.[3]

Corruption committed by foreign public figures in developing countries can be very destabilising. The NCA goes on to say:

> The scale of corruption can be vast, with individuals often siphoning billions of pounds from state funds. In many developing nations endemic corruption can be a key factor in civil disturbance and regime changes. Corruption increases poverty and inequality, undermines good business and threatens the integrity of financial markets.

Ministry of Justice

In their joint report published in 2015, the Ministry of Justice (MOJ) and the Department for Business, Innovation and Skills (BIS)[4] described their findings from a survey of 500 SMEs and their awareness of the Bribery Act 2010. Two-thirds (66%) of the SMEs surveyed had either heard of the Act or were aware of their corporate liability for failure to prevent bribery. Awareness was greater among SMEs exporting to regions that are less developed. In addition, SMEs were asked whether their company had ever assessed the risks of being asked for bribes and were given the example that bribes may take the form of cash payments, gifts, donations, or goods offered or given in order to obtain or retain business or an advantage in the conduct of business. A business advantage can include, for example the speeding up of routine official administered procedures. A third of SMEs (33%) said that they had assessed the risk of being asked for bribes, leaving two-thirds that had either not assessed the risk (59%) or did not know if they had assessed the risk (8%). Hence if the survey population was representative of the whole community of SMEs a large proportion of SMEs still need to both understand and address the potential risks of falling foul of the Act, prosecution and significant reputational damage.

Step 4: Risk assessment

Risk assessment consists of a sequence of activities which answer the questions: what are the possible problems my business may face? how likely are they? what impact will they have? and how soon will they impact? How well these questions can be answered depends on the research undertaken. A starting point is undertaking lessons learned. For large businesses operating over a number of years, they may have developed a database of events, recording how they were managed and what degree of success was achieved. However, for SMEs, they typically have to look outside of their business for lessons learned. A starting point is to view the latest government guidance on the Bribery Act and managing risk exposure.

Risk management is commonly recognised as a versatile tool in combating fraud and in particular bribery and corruption. As advised by Transparency International UK, a UK charity which provides global anti-bribery guidance:

> Risk assessment is the foundation for the design of an effective anti-bribery programme. It is a continuing procedure which gives a company a systematic and prioritised view of where the significant inherent bribery risks lie. The results of risk assessments are used to design the controls to mitigate the prioritised bribery risks. The process is critical as the information gained through risk assessment will shape the design of the anti-bribery programme and ensure through repeated risk assessments that the design is always valid and being improved.

Step 4A: Lessons learned

To appreciate the vulnerabilities of bribery and corruption fraud requires an appreciation of the sequence or pattern of these fraud events, the tools and techniques employed (described here as the mechanics), historical events (captured in case studies) together with 'red flags' or the 'alarm bells' over potential exposure, as illustrated in Figure 15.2. These activities contribute to Lessons Learned which in turn assist in deciding on the actions to be implemented, to thwart bribery and corruption.

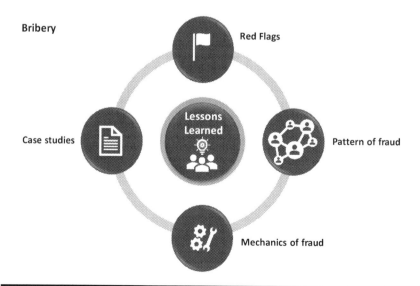

Figure 15.2 The lessons learned from prior events

Understanding the pattern of bribery: Bribery and corruption can be perpetrated in a vast array of methods and as a consequence, there is no single discernible pattern. Plus, bribery can operate in two directions. A company (or its agents or consultants) can strive to influence sales to say foreign governments by offering inducements (bribes), or government officials may insist on receipt of 'facilitation payments' if they are to recommend or arrange for a company to secure a contract. For those companies that follow the route of paying bribes, they introduce uncertainty and delay. No contracts are signed formalising bribes, so any arrangements are never permanently fixed. As a consequence, experienced bribe-takers often identify and create opportunities for leveraging higher payments. Delays may increase as more officials become aware of the bribe and want to be included in the arrangements. The additional bribes introduce delay. It takes time to work out how the bribe is going to be concealed in the accounts. False invoices have to be raised or non-existent contractors, subcontractors or survey companies have to be created. The bribe funds have to be arranged. In addition, as bribery is illegal everywhere, regardless of whether or not the local anti-bribery laws are actively enforced, there is no recourse when the bribe recipient reneges or sells the same deal to a higher bidder. Companies are not in a position to sue for breach of a bribe-orientated contract.

Understanding the mechanics of bribery: Activities involved in bribery may entail one of more of the following. However, while it might appear a long list, unfortunately, there are many more avenues whereby the desire for financial gain may seek to circumnavigate honest legal practices:

- **Sales and marketing:** Bribes made to win orders or to gain insider information such as tender invitation lists, contact details of the tender evaluation team, tender evaluation criteria or submitted tender values.
- **Procurement and contracting:** Contracts awarded to a contractor who then pays a 'reward' to the employee who made the purchase decision.
- **Supply chain management:** Acceptance of bribes from suppliers and intermediaries.
- **Transportation:** Payment of bribes to transport organisations, regulatory approval bodies, and or border controls (air, sea, river or road).
- **Construction management:** On construction projects, for a contractor or supplier to be able to pay an inducement or 'reward' for being appointed, the majority of the funds for the payment will have to be generated through changes to specifications and or substitution of inferior materials-to aid concealment.
- **Human resources:**
  - Bribes paid to outsourcing contractors to influence searches, poaching, advertising space, recruitment and appointments.
  - Bribery of public officials to circumvent regulations related to sponsorship, human resource practices (such as lower grade housing for workers), quotas for local nationals, quotas for foreign temporary workers and visas.

- Bribes received for the employment of customers' relatives.
- Bribery of or by union officials.
- **Corporate affairs:** Donations to government officials, politicians and political parties.
- **Facilities and assets management:**
  - Bribes received by employees for awarding contracts or providing access to facilities and assets.
  - Bribes paid to officials to obtain planning permission, building regulation approval, fire certificates or the prompt connection to utilities.
  - Assets used to influence public officials.
- **Financial functions:** Bribes received for enabling criminality such as data theft, fraud or robbery.
- **Financial trading and services:** Bribes received to steer recommendations for products and suppliers.
- **Mergers and acquisitions:** Bribery to obtain insider information on the financial standing of a business, bad debts, customer base, etc. to gain more favourable terms.
- **Safety and quality management:** Acceptance of bribes to falsify approvals, accept sub-standard processes or overlook non-compliance.
- **Research and development:** Bribery of researchers to falsify results or of officials to obtain regulatory approvals.
- **Security:** Bribery to circumvent a company's security controls, to gain information on say customers, technology or progress made in research and development.
- **Goods inwards:** Bribes to falsify documentation such as falsely certifying goods received.
- **Regulatory licenses:** Bribery of officials to obtain approvals or other services. Examples include research and development (testing and approval of drugs), telecommunications, casinos and lotteries, facilities management (water, power, building and plant planning approvals). A sales agent or consultant pays a bribe specifically to secure business, keep existing business, or gain a business advantage for your organisation.

Case studies

Case studies provide a rich source of information on fraud events that have occurred in the past. While the case studies described here relate to large organisations, the key aspects of the frauds are relevant to any size of organisation. If employees wonder 'off-piste' of their own volition and engage in bribery or are not wary and vigilant of the antics of public officials they may place their employer in a whole world of pain that could have been avoided. Companies can be subject to financial penalties but the reputational damage suffered may take far longer to recover from.

Case Study 15.1: The following case study is an example of the behaviour of a subsidiary which has embroiled its parent company in criminal prosecution and reputational damage. It emphasises that for any business, the prevention of bribery and corruption needs to extend to all corners of a business.

Case Study 15.1: Bribery

Case study concerning the criminal conduct of Rolls Royce spanning three decades

Following a four-year investigation, the Serious Fraud Office (SFO) and Rolls-Royce entered into a Deferred Prosecution Agreement (DPA) which was approved by Sir Brian Leveson, President of the Queen's Bench Division on 17 January 2017. The DPA enabled Rolls-Royce to account to a UK court for criminal conduct spanning three decades in seven jurisdictions and involving three business sectors. The DPA involves payments of £497,252,645 (comprising disgorgement of profits of £258,170,000 and a financial penalty of £239,082,645) plus interest. Rolls-Royce was also required to reimburse the SFO's costs in full (c£13 million). The DPA is related to two entities ultimately owned by Rolls-Royce Holdings plc, namely Rolls-Royce plc ('Rolls-Royce') and its Delaware incorporated subsidiary, RollsRoyce Energy Systems Inc ('RRESI'). It covers the conduct of Rolls-Royce and RRESI in Nigeria, Indonesia and Russia along with the conduct of Rolls-Royce alone in Thailand, India, China and Malaysia. The DPA related to serious breaches of criminal law in the areas of bribery and corruption. These breaches included (but were not limited to) agreements to make corrupt payments to agents in connection with the sale of Trent aero engines for civil aircraft in Indonesia and Thailand between 1989 and 2006; an agreement to make corrupt payments to agents in connection with the supply of gas compression equipment in Russia between January 2008 and December 2009; failing to prevent the bribery by employees or intermediaries in conducting its energy business in Nigeria and Indonesia between the commencement of the Bribery Act 2010 and May 2013 and July 2013 respectively (with similar failures in relation to its civil business in Indonesia); failure to prevent the provision by Rolls-Royce employees, of inducements which constitute bribery in its civil business in China and Malaysia between the commencement of the Bribery Act 2010 and December 2013.

Source: Serious Fraud Office UK, https://www.judiciary.uk/wp-content/uploads/2017/01/sfo-v-rolls-royce.pdf.

Case Study 15.2: The following case study is an example of a large company with an international footprint being fined for the bribing of its customers through the use of external consultants. The nature and method of wrongdoing can be perpetrated by large and small businesses alike. Sometimes the scale of the wrongdoing

Case Study 15.2: Bribery

Case study concerning the criminal conduct of Airbus SE

In January 2020, the Serious Fraud Office entered into a record-breaking Deferred Prosecution Agreement (DPA) with the global aerospace company Airbus SE. Under the terms of the DPA, Airbus SE agreed to pay a fine and costs amounting to €991 million in the UK as part of a €3.6 billion global settlement for bribery involving authorities in France and the United States. The settlement came a little under four years after the SFO began investigating the company over allegations that it had used external consultants to bribe customers to buy its civilian and military aircraft. The indictment, which has been suspended for the term of the DPA, covers five counts of failure to prevent bribery. The conduct involves Airbus' Commercial and Defence & Space divisions. The conduct covered by the UK DPA took place across five jurisdictions: Sri Lanka, Malaysia, Indonesia, Taiwan and Ghana between 2011 and 2015. On 31 January 2020, at a public hearing at the Royal Courts of Justice, the Judge ruled that the total sum (€983.97 million plus the SFO's costs of €6.9 million) reflected the gravity of the conduct, the full cooperation of Airbus SE in the investigation, and the programme of corporate reform and compliance put in place by new leadership at the top of the company. As part of the DPA, the company agreed to full cooperation with the SFO and its law enforcement partners in any future investigations and prosecutions, and disclosure of any subsequent wrongdoing by the company or its employees, subject to applicable laws. If the company does not honour the conditions of the DPA, the prosecution may resume. Airbus SE has also reached a Convention Judiciaire d'Intérêt Public with the Parquet National Financier (PNF) and a Deferred Prosecution Agreement with the US Department of Justice and the US Department of State. In total, these agreements together with the SFO DPA require Airbus SE to pay approximately €3.6 billion (including €2,083,137,455 to the PNF and €525,655,000 to the US authorities) at the exchange rate at the time of payment. In her judgment, Dame Victoria Sharp said: 'bribery was endemic in two core business areas within Airbus'. Lisa Osofsky, Director of the SFO, said:

Airbus paid bribes through agents around the world to stack the decks in its favour and win contracts around the globe. Corruption like this undermines free trade and fair development and it is to Airbus's credit that it has admitted its culpability, cleaned its house and come forward to put this conduct to bed.

Source: Serious Fraud Office UK, https://www.sfo.gov.uk/2020/01/31/sfo-enters-into-e991m-deferred-prosecution-agreement-with-airbus-as-part-of-a-e3-6bn-global-resolution/.

is not the most pertinent issue, it is the damage to a business's reputation in the marketplace and the reluctance of buyers, suppliers, consultants and contractors to engage with the business in the future in that they do not want their reputation tarnished by association.

Red flags: A 'red flag' is a fact, event, or set of circumstances, or other information that may indicate a potential legal compliance concern for illegal or unethical business conduct, particularly with regard to corrupt practices. Sometimes the way people or organisations behave might suggest they are committing a fraud. The signs are referred to as 'red flags'. With procurement fraud the three main areas are internal accounting, tendering and contract award. These indicators should be used as part of the risk manager's 'toolkit' to understand both risk exposure and the mitigation measures to be put in place.

Poor reputation of a contractor (or other parties including sub-contractor, supplier or potential joint venture partner)

- The contractor/business has a poor reputation generally and specifically a reputation for suspicious, immoral, disreputable or unlawful conduct as well as its sub-agents and/or its employees.
- The contractor/business has a history of improper payment practices, such as prior or ongoing formal or informal investigations by law enforcement authorities or prior convictions.
- The contractor/business has been subject to criminal enforcement actions or civil actions for acts suggesting illegal, improper or unethical conduct.
- Allegations made concerning integrity, such as a reputation for illegal, improper, or unethical conduct.
- Other companies have terminated contracts with the contractor/business for improper conduct.
- The contractor/business does not have an adequate compliance process in place or code of conduct, or refuses to adopt one.

Plan to join forces with an overseas business ('Third Party')

- The Third Party is recommended by a public official, a member of his/her family, or his/her close associate.
- Third Party is a company with an owner, major shareholder or executive manager who is a public official.
- The Third Party has financial or business ties, relationships, or an association with public officials.
- The Third Party has previously worked in a government agency or state-owned company at a high level, or in an agency/department relevant to the work he/she will be performing.
- The Third Party has a close family member who is a public official or is closely associated with a public official or agency.
- The Third Party makes large or frequent political contributions, makes references to political or charitable donations as a way of influencing official action.
- The Third Party conducts private meetings with public officials, provides lavish gifts or hospitality to public officials, or insists on dealing with public officials without the participation of the business.

Questionable or suspicious behaviour by a public official

- A public official requests meals, alcohol, travel, entertainment, gifts, services, benefits, hiring of relatives, political or charitable contributions, or any other favour.
- A public official is reported to have engaged in suspicious, unethical, or unlawful behaviour.
- A public official requests, urges, insists or demands that a particular company, or individual (including agents, suppliers, contractors, sub-contractors or service providers) be selected/appointed.
- A public official requests unusual methods of payment for government services (for instance through a third party or in cash).

Questionable or suspicious behaviour by 'Third Party'

- Lack of written agreement or refusal to execute a written agreement or requests to perform services without a written agreement where one is sought.
- Failure to cooperate with a due diligence investigation or refusal to answer questions or make representations and warranties.
- Suspicious statements such as needing payments to 'secure the business' or 'make the necessary arrangements' or 'take care of things' or 'finalise the deal'.
- Pending or previous criminal charges.

- Refusal to accept audit clauses in contracts.
- Requests for anonymity or insistence that their identity remain confidential or that the relationship remain secret.
- Refusal to divulge the identity of owners, directors, officers or senior managers in a business.
- Any suggestion that anti-corruption compliance policies do not need to be followed.
- Any suggestion that illegal conduct is acceptable because it is the norm or customs in a particular country.
- Alleged performance of the third party is suspiciously higher than competitors or companies in related industries.

Questionable accounting practices or invoicing adopted by 'Third Party'

- Request for payments to be made in third countries or through third parties or shell companies, particularly requests for payment in a jurisdiction outside the home country that has no relationship to the transaction.
- Request that payments be made into two or more bank accounts.
- Request for payments in cash or other anonymous payments.
- Request for payment arrangements that would not comply with local laws, such as payment in another country's currency.
- Requests that a donation be made to a charity or for the donation of goods and services.
- Call for an advance payment to be made to employees or third parties, particularly insistence to receive payments urgently or ahead of schedule.
- Unrecorded or incorrectly recorded transactions and other failures to follow accounting procedures/policies.
- Requests for an invoice to be amended to reflect a higher amount than the actual price of goods provided.
- Invoices only vaguely describe the services provided or lack detail (e.g., 'services rendered').
- Poor or non-existent documentation for reimbursement for travel and expenses.
- Duplicate invoices.

Step 4B: Risk identification

Tackling bribery is complex as it can take place in such a multitude of different scenarios and circumstances; however, the underlying concepts are simple. A business wants to secure an advantage over its competitors and the facilitator wants to secure a financial inducement for bringing about the contract or appointment.

Table 15.1 Bribery threat event causes

Bribery (Cause → Threat → Impact)	
The **causes** or triggers behind the fraudulent activity	
Pressure	Pressure placed on sales executives to secure orders.
Culture	Pervasive culture within certain foreign countries where government officials expect rewards, inducements, up-front payments or non-financial benefits in return for contracts.
Incentives	Desire of sales personnel to secure lucrative bonuses and benefits.
Greed	Employees with sole responsibility for placing orders and contracts seek personal gain to support an improvement in lifestyle.

In general terms, a threat is broken into several components, how these components are articulated is critical to how that risk is viewed, understood and managed. 'Because of a [cause or causes], a [threat] may occur, which would lead to an [impact]'. The common 'cause' is the motivation of individuals to secure financial gain from a business activity, contract or project. It is a common phenomenon in the business environment and perpetually gives rise to uncertainty. The list of causes included in Table 15.1 is not exhaustive. Businesses operate in counties where norms and behaviours are different but where bribery and fraud legislation is the same the world over. Table 15.2 describes the common threat areas without going into substantial detail, as each business will have to tailor its schedule of risks to reflect its markets and method of operation. Table 15.3 describes how the incidence of bribery and corruption may impact a business.

Step 4C: Risk analysis

When examining the characteristics of a potential threat, it commonly involves estimating the likelihood, the impact (in cost and time together with other parameters when appropriate) and the proximity (when is the threat likely to materialise). Included in Table 15.4 is a descriptive analysis of the likelihood, impact and proximity; however, for actual assessments, approximate figures would be captured.

Step 5: Response actions

Specific response actions: governance, audits, systems and people

Included in Figure 15.3 are specific response actions that should be considered with regard to the topics of governance, audits, systems and people. The actions

Table 15.2 Bribery event threats

Threats (uncertain events)	
Country risk	The business has to operate in a country where there is a high prevalence of corruption, and the incidence of bribery is the norm rather than the exception. *Notes: This risk category relates to perceived high levels of corruption within a particular country where there is an absence of effectively implemented anti-bribery legislation and a failure of local and central governments, the professions, the local business community, media and civil society to effectively promote transparent procurement and investment policies. The Risk Advisory Group, an independent global risk consultancy firm, in their 2019 Corruption Challenges Index assessed 187 countries, assigning each an overall 'corruption challenge' score weighted against three factors: corruption threat, regime instability and accessibility of information.*
Counterparty risk	The business enters into a contract with an organisation which reneges on its contractual obligations. In simple terms, Company A agrees to goods or services from Company B, but Company A withdraws. When during the process Company A withdraws will generally influence the degree of damage caused. However, in terms of bribery, re-engaging on contractual obligations may relate specifically to not following pre-agreed anti-bribery practices. *Notes: Counterparty risk relates to the likelihood that an organisation that the business has entered into a contract with – who is a counterparty to the contract – defaults on its contractual obligations.*
Sector risk	The business is exposed to corrupt practices in excess of those anticipated due to the sector it is working in. *Notes: Certain business sectors typically have been associated with higher levels of bribery risk than others. The OECD Foreign Bribery Report 2014 found that two-thirds of the foreign bribery cases occurred in four sectors: extractive (19%), construction (15%), transportation and storage 15%), and information and communication (10%). These percentages should have a health warning attached, as a high-risk sector may well face low risk exposure because of the particular circumstances of its business; however, a company in a low-risk sector should not be lulled into thinking of itself as low risk – without proper analysis.*

(Continued)

Threats (uncertain events)	
Transaction risk	The ability to secure commodities at prices reflected in the business case is uncertain due to the volatility in regional prices compounded by the behaviour of buyers and sellers in the marketplace. *Notes: Transaction risk is the exposure to uncertainty factors that may impact the expected return from a deal or transaction. This could include but is not limited to foreign exchange risk, commodity and time risk. It essentially encompasses all negative events that can prevent a deal from happening.*
Business partnership risk	The working relationship with the business partner is difficult due to the partner's unwillingness to abide by the contract in terms of decision making, independently consulting government officials and undermining existing long-term relationships with suppliers. *Notes: Typically this risk category relates to a number of factors such as loss of autonomy (the challenge of shared decision-making processes and the need for securing agreement with a partner before action can be taken and the implications for existing arrangements with suppliers and consultants); conflicts of interest (where a decision or action that is right for the interests of the partnership but may be at odds with the business's interests); drain on resources (a significantly greater commitment to time and resources than anticipated to deliver the partnership's goals); implementation challenges (the day-to-day demands of participating in a collaborative venture, with all the additional management, tracking, reporting and evaluation of requirements that entails); and negative reputation impact (when partnerships go wrong causing damage to the reputation or track record of the individual partners). In this context, the risk relates to the partner not adhering to the terms of the partnership in, say, following anti-bribery guidelines, contacting foreign public officials, engaging intermediaries without prior agreement and not ensuring they are contracted to adhere to anti-bribery practices, forming relationships with politically exposed persons and placing contracts without prior agreement.*
Legal risks	Unanticipated significant variations in anti-bribery legislation and norms between neighbouring districts in the same country. *Notes: The legal and regulatory framework for jurisdictions in which the company operates can introduce additional risk exposure. Broadly speaking anti-bribery approaches are relatively similar across jurisdictions, but there can be significant local variations which may bring risks and will require tailoring of policies and procedures.*

Interaction with public officials	Foreign public officials insist on incentive payments to secure government contracts. *Notes: In many countries, any dealings with government officials are likely to carry a higher level of risk. The UK Bribery Act has explicit prohibitions on the bribery of foreign public officials. One of the challenges is to identify who is a government official. In European countries, this is typically straightforward. However, in some countries, there is a degree of uncertainty about whether particular organisations belong in the public or private sector. For any UK business, interaction with an overseas business must take account of the extent to which the overseas business has government contracts or other interactions with the government agencies.*
Third parties	The business discovers that sales agents have paid bribes to government officials to secure their sales commission/ bonus. *Notes: Many of the major bribery scandals have involved the use of third parties, especially sales agents and consultants. A decision needs to be made as to whether to continue to use sales agents because of their attached risks.*

Table 15.3 Bribery impact descriptions

Impact descriptions (if the threats were to materialise)	
Prosecution	The business is prosecuted under the UK Bribery Act.
Loss of reputation	The business suffers reputational damage from prosecutions under the Bribery Act and dissuades companies from trading or engaging with it.
Time	The directors spend far more time on the contract(s) than anticipated due to the need to manage the business partner, intermediaries or agents.
Cost	The business suffers penalties, fines and/or additional in-country expenses.
Relationships	Relationships are undermined by business partners, sales agents or consultants where they have made promises of bribes which the business refuses to pay.

Table 15.4 Bribery risk analysis

Analysis of bribery risks	
Likelihood	While businesses trading overseas are more likely to encounter situations that have to be carefully managed, particularly when facing the challenging behaviour of elected government officials, the letting of contracts in the UK can also require stringent control.
Financial impact	The financial impact can be severe in terms of penalties or fines; however, there may be a myriad of other costs such as solicitor fees; research costs; increase in insurance premiums; costs arising from revising policies, processes and contracts; rebuilding customer confidence; and changes to recruitment practices.
Time impact	If the business is prosecuted for fraud and acts of bribery, the whole process can be very time consuming before the case is even taken to court and may distract the business's director or directors for many months unravelling what has been undertaken by whom, when and what the potential defence may be.
Proximity	All sales activity is exposed to this risk, and hence, it is a 'here and now risk'.

that a business chooses to adopt from the proposed responses will depend on, for instance, its industry, the specific markets it operates in, the percentage of sales overseas, the number of intermediaries or consultancies it uses and the current level of maturity of its anti-bribery processes and procedures. The actions are written for those businesses that have just started out on the journey of ensuring that they comply with all legislation relating to bribery and corruption and play their part in ensuring there is a level playing field – for the benefit of all.

Step 6: Implementation of actions

The timing of the implementation of response actions will depend on an assessment of what's already in place, the business's current vulnerabilities, the prioritisation of business needs and the resources available to introduce change.

Your Governance	Your Audits
Commitment: The director(s) must document commitment to the principles behind the Bribery Act 2010 and foster a culture within the business where bribery is never acceptable.	**Compliance:** Assess compliance with the Bribery Act 2010. Conduct due diligence of the persons and companies who will be providing services to the business, particularly from overseas.
Procedures: The director(s) to ensure that procedures are proportional to the scale, nature and location of their business operations. A detailed anti-bribery policy mandating a zero tolerance to bribery may only be warranted for medium businesses operating in high-risk countries.	**Guidance:** Audit whether personnel are aware of the Ministry of Justice (MoJ) guidance published in 2012 on the procedures businesses can put into place to prevent persons associated with them from bribing.
Awareness: The director(s) to ensure that management, employees and any organisations the business engages with are aware of the need to comply with the Bribery Act.	**Policy:** Audit the business's anti-bribery and corruption policy for its adequacy in terms of the approach adopted to reducing and controlling the risks of bribery. It should describe rules about accepting gifts, hospitality or donations and provide guidance on how to conduct the negotiation of contracts and how to avoid or stop conflicts of interest.
Direction: The director(s) to establish the right 'tone at the top' by propagating clear anti-bribery practices rather than a tick-box system. In line with the principle of top-level commitment, there should be regular and documented communication with employees about bribery issues. Depending on the size of the business, organise training. Keep records of all communications and training.	**Audit:** Following Principle 3, 'Risk Assessment', of the MoJ Guidance, audit whether the business assesses the nature and extent of its exposure to potential external and internal risks of bribery likely to be committed by persons acting on its behalf. The assessment is periodic, informed and documented.
Empowerment: Employees and business partners must be given the information, skills and resources they need to comply with the policy and a zero tolerance to bribery.	**Review:** Examine whether the risks commonly described as Country, Sectoral, Transaction, Business Opportunity, Business Partnership, Legal, Interaction and Third-Party Relationships have been addressed.
Forgoing contracts: Directors make it clear to stakeholders/business partners that the business is prepared to forego contracts rather than pay bribes and will support employees in sales and marketing when faced with lose of sales owing to the refusal to pay bribes.	**Regular reviews:** Maintain evidence of a regular review of areas of the business which could be susceptible to becoming involved with bribery. In areas where the risk is higher, there should be detailed mechanisms for reporting and investigating cases of suspected bribery.

Figure 15.3 Bribery risk response actions

Intermediate

Establish a risk management process which captures the causes, threats and impact of bribery events and instigates risk response planning. Like quality and safety, risk management must be the responsibility of all employees.

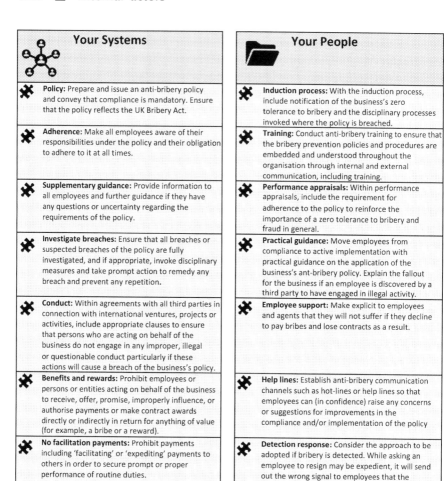

Your Systems

Policy: Prepare and issue an anti-bribery policy and convey that compliance is mandatory. Ensure that the policy reflects the UK Bribery Act.

Adherence: Make all employees aware of their responsibilities under the policy and their obligation to adhere to it at all times.

Supplementary guidance: Provide information to all employees and further guidance if they have any questions or uncertainty regarding the requirements of the policy.

Investigate breaches: Ensure that all breaches or suspected breaches of the policy are fully investigated, and if appropriate, invoke disciplinary measures and take prompt action to remedy any breach and prevent any repetition.

Conduct: Within agreements with all third parties in connection with international ventures, projects or activities, include appropriate clauses to ensure that persons who are acting on behalf of the business do not engage in any improper, illegal or questionable conduct particularly if these actions will cause a breach of the business's policy.

Benefits and rewards: Prohibit employees or persons or entities acting on behalf of the business to receive, offer, promise, improperly influence, or authorise payments or make contract awards directly or indirectly in return for anything of value (for example, a bribe or a reward).

No facilitation payments: Prohibit payments including 'facilitating' or 'expediting' payments to others in order to secure prompt or proper performance of routine duties.

Your People

Induction process: With the induction process, include notification of the business's zero tolerance to bribery and the disciplinary processes invoked where the policy is breached.

Training: Conduct anti-bribery training to ensure that the bribery prevention policies and procedures are embedded and understood throughout the organisation through internal and external communication, including training.

Performance appraisals: Within performance appraisals, include the requirement for adherence to the policy to reinforce the importance of a zero tolerance to bribery and fraud in general.

Practical guidance: Move employees from compliance to active implementation with practical guidance on the application of the business's ant-bribery policy. Explain the fallout for the business if an employee is discovered by a third party to have engaged in illegal activity.

Employee support: Make explicit to employees and agents that they will not suffer if they decline to pay bribes and lose contracts as a result.

Help lines: Establish anti-bribery communication channels such as hot-lines or help lines so that employees can (in confidence) raise any concerns or suggestions for improvements in the compliance and/or implementation of the policy

Detection response: Consider the approach to be adopted if bribery is detected. While asking an employee to resign may be expedient, it will send out the wrong signal to employees that the business is not stringent in applying sanctions.

Figure 15.3 (*Continued*)

Short term

In the short term, identify who within the business is best placed to review the needs of the business, understand its vulnerabilities and develop a plan of specific actions to be implemented.

- Prepare or revisit the anti-bribery and corruption policy.
- Make explicit the consequences for those that commit fraud.
- Re-examine the anti-bribery content of induction and periodic employee training; instigate employing e-learning where appropriate.

- Ensure partners, intermediaries, consultants and contractors clearly understand the anti-fraud policy of the business and the boundaries they are permitted to work within.
- Share anti-fraud and bribery contract clauses with potential partners at the outset.
- Make it explicit employees can withdraw from a potential sale or contract if securing the work is conditional upon making a bride.
- Move employees from awareness to implementation.

Long term

Consider the countries where the business wants and does not want to operate based on the norms, culture and behaviours of clients and government officials in those countries.

Summary

All SMEs operating in the UK need to consider their exposure to the risks of bribery and corruption and the measures needed to prevent wrongdoing. While a business may have the best policies, processes and systems in the world, it is the behaviour of its staff that will determine whether it avoids committing acts of fraud. Employees are the most effective control against bribery and corruption. The pattern and mechanics of bribery have been outlined to aid assimilation of this important subject. The case studies, while focusing on large organisations, are equally relevant to all businesses seeking business overseas and convictions can be very costly and damaging. Reputations can take years to build but can be destroyed in a matter of days. While a number of red flags have been recorded it is not an exhaustive list and requires development and tailoring to a business's unique operations. Businesses need to look at their governance, audits, systems and people in terms of the steps to be taken to embed an anti-bribery and corruption culture within their day-to-day operations. Policies and practices need to be integrated within induction processes, staff training and performance reviews as well as contracts with third parties supporting the business. The greatest exposure can come from consultants, intermediaries and joint venture partners working on behalf or with a business in their dealings with say government officials overseas.

Notes

1 https://www.gov.uk/government/publications/bribery-act-2010-guidance.
2 National Crime Agency: https://www.nationalcrimeagency.gov.uk/what-we-do/crime-threats/money-laundering-and-illicit-finance.

3 National Crime Agency: https://nationalcrimeagency.gov.uk/what-we-do/crime-threats/bribery-corruption-and-sanctions-evasion.

4 HMG (2015) "Insight into awareness and impact of the Bribery Act 2010 Among small and medium sized enterprises (SMEs)", Prepared for BIS and MoJ by IFF Research Ltd. https://assets.publishing.service.gov.uk/government/uploads/system/uploads/attachment_data/file/440661/insight-into-awareness-and-impact-of-the-bribery-act-2010.pdf.

Chapter 16

Procurement fraud

Structure of Chapter 16

Chapter 16 is subdivided into the following four sections. An overview of the fraud type is provided followed by an assessment of the threat posed by the fraud, suggested response actions and staged timing of implementation (Figure 16.1).

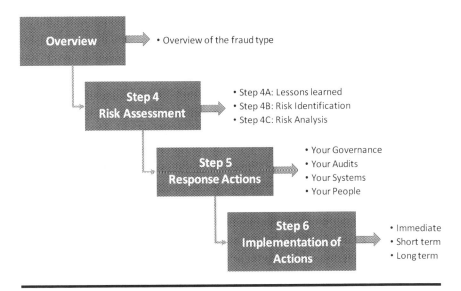

Figure 16.1 Structure of Chapter 16

DOI: 10.4324/9781003200383-19

Overview

Procurement is the process of acquiring goods or services in order to satisfy the needs of a business. It includes the purchase of small commodities such as machine parts or one-off services such as new security alarms through to the procurement of large-scale goods such as production machinery or establishing long-term maintenance contracts. The expression 'procurement fraud' (sometimes referred to as supply chain fraud) is adopted here to refer to all unlawful activity that occurs throughout the procurement cycle including the sourcing, letting and management of contracts. Procurement fraud is a complex problem. It is an unlawful practice relating to the purchase of goods or services or the placing of contracts. It is a deliberate deception intended to influence any stage of the procurement lifecycle in order to make a financial gain or cause a loss. Procurement fraud is difficult to detect. Cases are rarely reported and as a consequence, it is difficult to understand the scale of the problem. It takes a long time to come to light and can result in significant financial and reputational loss for a business. A lack of awareness, understanding and detection creates an environment where procurement fraud can flourish. If businesses are not considering the risk of fraud before they embark on procurement, then procurement fraud can go undetected. It can be perpetrated by staff within an organisation as well as by contractors and sub-contractors external to the organisation. The nature of procurement fraud differs between the two core stages of the procurement lifecycle, pre-contract award and post-contract award. Fraud in the pre-contract award phase is predominantly more complex and may involve activities such as collusion between bidders and corruption during the tender process when a tenderer secures an unfair advantage by paying an 'incentive' payment to an employee on the tender team. Fraud in the post-contract stage is considerably different. As contracts are already in place, most cases of fraud tend to involve overpayments to contractors through false or duplicate invoicing, payments for substandard work or work not completed under contract terms. Suppliers may overcharge for goods or services subsequent to agreeing to fixed prices. Where fraud is detected, any investigation is resource hungry and prosecution (typically very expensive) rarely ends in a conviction or the recovery of losses. A comprehensive approach to fraud risk management is required to ensure risk assessments are conducted: before embarking on procurement processes; during stage gate reviews (held at the intermediate project or activity stages); by auditors post-contract award; and at project/activity completion. In essence, there needs to be an acknowledgement that: fraud takes place, preventative measures need to be put in place and should it be detected, there needs to be a prompt response (which includes capturing as much hard evidence of the event or events as possible), as summarised in Figure 16.2.

Acknowledge	Prevent	Report
Acknowledge and understand procurement fraud	Preventing and detecting fraud	Reporting unearthed fraud to the police
• Understanding fraud risk and how it may be committed • Committing processes and support to combatting fraud • Maintaining a robust anti-fraud organisation	• Making better use of information technology • Enhancing fraud controls and processes • Developing a more effective anti-fraud culture	• Understanding who to report fraud to and their contact details • Pre-determining the information that will be required • Reporting fraud in a timely manner

Figure 16.2 Acknowledging, preventing and reporting fraud

Step 4: Risk assessment

Risk assessment consists of a sequence of activities which answer the questions: what are the possible problems my business may face? how likely are they? what impact will they have? and how soon will they impact? How well these questions can be answered depends on the research undertaken. A starting point is undertaking lessons learned. For large businesses operating over a number of years, they may have developed a database of events, recording how they were managed and what degree of success was achieved. However, for SMEs, they typically have to look outside of their business for lessons learned.

Step 4A: Lessons learned

To appreciate the vulnerabilities of a business to procurement fraud (as with other types of fraud) requires an appreciation of the sequence or pattern of these fraud events, the tools and techniques employed (described here as the mechanics), historical events (captured in case studies) together with 'red flags' or the 'alarm bells' over potential exposure, as illustrated in Figure 16.3. These activities contribute to Lessons Learned which in turn assist in deciding on the actions to be implemented, to thwart procurement fraud.

 Understanding the pattern of procurement fraud: One of the more well-known and understood aspects of procurement fraud is collusion. There are typically four simple steps in the perpetration of collusion between contractors at pre-tender stage as described below and illustrated in Figure 16.4.

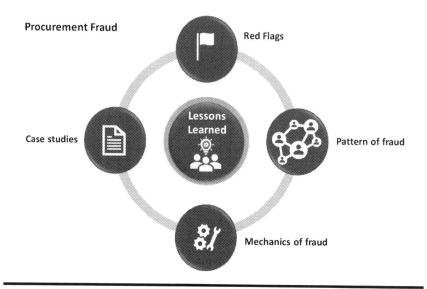

Figure 16.3 The lessons learned from prior events

Figure 16.4 The pattern of procurement fraud at the pre-tender stage prior to contract award

- A tender invitation is typically issued to a shortlist of contractors who have previously completed a prequalification questionnaire to ascertain their suitability for the contract. For certain specialist types of work, there may be a limited number of experienced contractors who are able to carry out the work and as a consequence, the same contractors are invited to tender over and over again. Through trade magazines, contractor signboards and new recruits as well as through their contacts in sub-contractors, plant hire companies and suppliers, contractors quickly learn who has won what contract and hence who the competition is.
- A group of contractors meets who are the recipients of the same tender invitation. They may hold a closed tender opening among themselves to see who would have won. The winner then adds a percentage to their price and the other tenderers increase their price to ensure it exceeds the price of the winning bid. Or, if the goal is for the winner to be the contractor geographically closest to the location of the project, bidders withdraw or increase their prices to ensure the contractor closest to the site is the favoured bid.
- The winning bid is agreed upon between the group of tenderers. Any compensation payments are also agreed to enable the 'chosen winner' to be successful.
- The winning tender is submitted as well as the tenders of the other colluding contractors.

Understanding the mechanics of procurement fraud: procurement fraud may be accomplished by the following; however, it should be recognised that this is not an exhaustive list.

- Contractor fraud
    - Collusion between participating tenderers.
    - Overcharging by contractors post award for variations and the substitution of materials for cheaper products.
    - Charging for fictitious: delays by third parties; increases in prices; or fuel duty increases.
    - Production of duplicate invoices.
    - Charging for work not completed.
    - Charging for work not yet completed at a contractual milestone.
- Employee fraud during pre- and post-tender
    - Taking a bribe to share commercially sensitive information.
    - Taking a bribe as part of supporting single tender action.
    - Taking a bribe to influence the tender panel's decision on contractor selection.
    - Taking a bribe to add a contractor's name to a list of bidders despite the contractor failing the pre-qualification process.

- Failure to keep and publish evaluation criteria.
- Failure to provide a rationale for the selection of certain bidders chosen to be invited to tender.
- Splitting contracts with no rationale.
- Negotiation of key contract issues post-award.
- Creation of false invoices for a legitimate company to receive payments in a personal bank account.
- Changing the bank details on legitimate invoices to divert funds.
- Creating invoices for fictitious companies and forwarding payments to a personal bank account.
- Manipulation of company records to cover up false accounting.
- Cybercriminal activity during pre- and post-tender
  - Theft of sensitive information such as the value of bids prior to contract award.
  - The interception and amendment of invoices diverting payments to a different bank account.
  - Issue a business with a fake invoice asking for immediate payment for goods or services. The invoice says the due date for payment has passed and threatens that if the business does not pay it will affect its credit rating. In fact, the invoice is fake and the business did not order or receive the goods or services described in the invoice.

Case study 16.1: The following case study is an example of the behaviour of an employee trusted with the role of approving invoices submitted by contractors and suppliers.

Case study 16.2: While it is the large-scale frauds that capture the news headlines such as the fraud committed by former employees of National Grid described below, procurement fraud occurs and is no less prevalent in small businesses and the damage caused to reputation is no less debilitating.

Case study 16.3: When the placing of contracts is in the control of a single individual where there is no management oversight or an effective audit function, fraud is more likely to take place.

Red flags: Sometimes the way people or organisations behave might suggest they are committing a fraud. The signs are referred to as 'red flags'. With procurement fraud, the five main areas are personnel behaviour, internal audit, tendering, supplier and contract award.

Case Study 16.1: Procurement Fraud

Fraudulent invoices

A member of the finance team in a government department created invoices for a non-existent supplier quoting a virtual office address and fictitious Companies House and VAT registrations. The employee created eight invoices for the supplier, five of which were paid. The employee was a registered approver of invoices and a senior member of the finance management team. The fraud came to light when the bank to which the funds had been diverted, contacted the department to notify them of unusually high funds and subsequent transactions passing through the individual's bank account. In total, the employee diverted £246,000 to his own bank account. An investigation ensued and found weaknesses in processes within the department relating to supplier set-up. New suppliers were found to be automatically set up on the payment system simply by submitting an invoice, with no checks being undertaken on the validity of the invoice and the company. The department put in place new controls including a process whereby new suppliers were only to be placed on the payment system when a member of the procurement team and finance team had approved this. All new suppliers are now approved by the Chief Accountant in the department.

Source: National Fraud Authority, Procurement Fraud in the Public Sector 2011.

Personnel behaviour red flags:

- Extravagant spending habits of a member of the procurement team which appear to be inconsistent with their salary.
- Large personal debts or financial losses of a member of the procurement team arising from say a gambling habit resulting in an urgent need for another source of income.
- A member of the procurement team has recently divorced resulting in the need to support two households and buy a partner out of their current shared property.
- Private meetings between a procurement team member and contractors or suppliers hoping to tender for contracts.
- Briefings made to just one of the tenderers (and not all).

Case Study 16.2: Procurement Fraud

Kickbacks from vendors

On 17 June 2021 John Pettigrew CEO of National Grid plc (part of one of the world's largest publicly listed utility companies focused on transmission and distribution of electricity and gas), announced that five former National Grid employees from the facilities department in New York were arrested on charges of federal fraud and bribery. He stated they were alleged to have intentionally evaded National Grid procurement processes and taken kickbacks from vendors in the form of cash and gifts. A kickback is a term commonly used in the US to describe an illegal payment intended as compensation for preferential treatment or any other type of improper services received. FBI Assistant Director-in-Charge William F Sweeney said in a statement 'crimes of this nature weaken the integrity of the bidding process and deny consumers the benefit of free and open competition in the market place'. Between 2013 and 2020 the former employees had accepted hundreds of thousands of dollars, international travel, hotel stays, home improvements, landscaping and a vehicle in return for the award of mostly facilities maintenance contracts.

Source: Adapted from National Grid, FBI, crownheights.info, energynews.us and newsday.com.

- Acceptance by one or more of the tendering team to attend lavish parties, night clubs, holiday homes, casinos, race meetings or trips overseas organised by one of the tenderers.

Internal audit red flags:

- Unexplained discrepancies in accounting records, particularly where there is a repetitive pattern.
- Missing documents, or only photocopied documents available.
- Inconsistent, vague or implausible responses to procurement inquiries.
- Unusual discrepancies between a contractor's records and the business's records.
- Inconsistencies between VAT receipts and VAT payments.
- Duplicate invoices.
- Common bank details on different contractors' invoices.
- A request for a change of bank details, supposedly from suppliers or contractors.

Case Study 16.3: Procurement Fraud

Bribes received in return for tailored tender documents

An electrical engineer favoured an electrical contractor in exchange for bribes. The engineer fixed tenders by tailoring specifications to ensure the contractor won a number of rewiring jobs. This was carried out by including a specific requirement for the installation of a fire alarm within all tender invitations except the invitation sent to the favoured contractor, allowing them to undercut the competing bids by £14,000 and thereby secure the work. The fraud was exposed by a shareholder of the favoured contractor who was uncomfortable with the behaviour of the company. The electrical engineer lost his job when it was evident that: private work had been carried out on his behalf at the expense of the contractor, he had regularly socialised with the contractor and attended hospitability events hosted by the contractor.

Source: Adapted from Ministry of Housing, Communities & Local Government, 8 June 2020. "Local Government Procurement: Fraud and Corruption Risk Review". A review into the risks of fraud and corruption in local government procurement as committed to in the UK anti-corruption strategy 2017 to 2022.

- Manual alterations on documents.
- Duplications (such as duplicate payments).
- One employee has control of a process from the start to finish with no segregation of duties.
- Invoices being agreed in excess of a contract price without a reasonable explanation.
- Payments being made through a third-party country – for example, goods or services supplied to country 'A' but payment usually being made to a shell company in country 'B'.

Tendering red flags:

- The options for cost savings submitted by tenderers shared with just one of the tenderers.
- Tender evaluation criteria shared with only one of the tenderers.
- Unexpected or illogical decisions made regarding the acceptance of tenders.
- Superficial tender evaluation.

- The addition on a contractor on a tender invitation list that had previously failed to pass the screening process in terms of experience, size, references or key staff.
- Abuse of the decision processes or delegated powers in specific cases.
- Agreeing contracts not favourable to the business either because of the terms or the time period.
- Bypassing normal tendering or contracting procedures.
- Missing documents or records regarding meetings or decisions.
- Missing tender submissions.
- Contractors that would normally tender fail to do so.
- Competitors' bids are received together.
- Identical irregularities in bids or similar wording.
- Identical prices.

Supplier red flags:

- A supplier has been awarded multiple sole-source packages without justification.
- Variations awarded have a high value when compared to the price of the original contract.
- There are a high number of variations awarded to a particular supplier.

Contract award red flags:

- Contract awarded to a contractor with inadequate experience, poor finance history, environmental track record or known breaches of health and safety legislation.
- A large difference between the price of the winning bid and other bids.
- Acceptance of a significant increase in price levels after receiving a bid from a new entrant.
- The same contractor is often the successful bidder.
- The lowest bidder not picked for the contract with no documented explanation.
- The winning bidder seems to rotate amongst several contractors.

Step 4B: Risk identification

The goal of any business is to improve employees' understanding of the risks of fraud but particularly how to spot fraud indicators across the procurement life-cycle and how to recognise and take action against collusion activity. This type of fraud can occur during both the pre-contract award and post-contract award phases of the procurement life cycle. There are numerous threat events that may materialise to undermine business performance.

As repeated throughout the book to reinforce the message, a risk is broken into several components, how these components are articulated is vital to how that risk is viewed, understood and managed. 'Because of a [cause or causes], a [threat] may occur, which would should it materialise would lead to an [impact] on the business's objectives'. The common 'cause' is the motivation of rogue businesses or individuals to secure financial gain at the expense of others. How well the threat is described will determine how appropriate the mitigation actions or actions will be.

The risk of fraud and corruption within procurement may stem from outside the organisation, inside the organisation or from collusion between staff members and external parties, such as suppliers. The impact of each threat, should it materialise, would be the same, with the business awarding the contract being commercially disadvantaged and paying a higher price than it should. The list of threats included in Tables 16.1 and 16.3 are not exhaustive. Businesses operate in a dynamic environment where methods of perpetrating fraud and procurement practices are changing all the time.

Given that there are distinct business activities pre- and post-contract award, each phase has its own set of risks. Hence the risk events included in Table 16.3

Table 16.1 Procurement fraud (pre-contract award) threats

Procurement fraud – pre-contract award *(Cause → Threat → Impact)*	
Risk events or threats (uncertain events)	
Outside: Collusion between contractors	
Price fixing	Contractors collude to fix the prices they will charge.
Market sharing	Contractors collude to divide up markets between them (e.g. geographical market share).
Bid rigging	Contractors collude to ensure a particular bidder wins the contract, for example, by reaching an agreement on the bids that will be submitted.
Bid suppression	One or several bidders withdraw their bid (or fail to bid) known as 'bid suppression'.
Cover pricing	Contractors collude in 'cover pricing' where high bids which are not intended to be successful make the favoured bid look more attractive, and may involve 'compensation payments' to those bidders that do not win.
Bid rotation	Contractors collude in 'bid rotation' where bidders take turns at submitting the lowest price.
Manipulation of procurement procedures	The procurement procedure is manipulated by the bidders to ensure a particular bidder is successful.

(Continued)

Procurement fraud – pre-contract award *(Cause → Threat → Impact)*	
Outside: contractor looking for an advantage	
Manipulation of contract content	Manipulation of specifications resulting from inappropriate involvement in the shaping of the requirement during preliminary market consultations.
Manipulation of specifications	Specifications are manipulated to favour a particular bidder. Or specifications not fully developed before contract award.
Tender document rooms	Tender document rooms containing submitted tenders are not locked and accessed by tenderer seeking to secure pricing information prior to negotiations.
Outside: cybercrime	
Hack	Hacking into business systems to obtain confidential and commercially sensitive information about bids received to secure commercial advantage.
Flash drive	Flash drive left in the office by a bidder during early briefings in the hope that it will be inserted into an office computer and malware is downloaded.
Eavesdropping	Placement of listening devices in meeting rooms being used as tender preparation and tender evaluation rooms to secure commercial advantage.
Inside: employee	
Payment for securing a contract	An employee accepts a payment or gifts to provide a contractor with a contract on a single source basis, i.e. there is no competitive tender.
Conflict of interest	An employee does not disclose a financial interest in a contract. This might be perceived to compromise their impartiality and independence in the context of the procurement or contract management process. An employee awards a contract to a business they are a director of and excludes other bidders.
Disclosure	An employee is incentivised to disclose confidential and commercially sensitive information about other bids to a particular bidder during negotiations.
Single source	An employee approaches a contractor with the offer of a single source contract in return for incentives.
Invoices	Employee creates duplicate invoices, additional invoices where he/she is the recipient of the payments, or organises 'uplifted' invoices from a supplier where the employee pockets the difference between the original and the uplifted invoices.
Payments	Sanctioning payments to a contractor for: work undertaken by 'ghost' sub-contractors, work never undertaken by genuine sub-contractors, unused materials, and charging for the removal of 'contaminated' material which was not and overstated work.

Table 16.2 Procurement fraud (pre-contract award) impact description

Impact description (if the threat were to materialise)	
Reduction in value for money	The business suffers from procurement fraud resulting in the business not receiving the most favourable price for a contract, affecting bottom-line performance.

Table 16.3 Procurement fraud (post-contract award) threats

Procurement fraud – post-contract award (Cause → Threat → Impact)	
Risk events or threats (uncertain events)	
Contractor	
Overbilling	Overbilling in relation to the goods and services which have already been delivered.
Non-delivery	Billing for goods or supplies that have not been delivered in full or in part.
Duplication	The company is billed twice for the same goods or services.
False claims and variations	Unjustified contractual claims (and payments) for contract variations. This type of fraud is often associated with under-priced bids (associated with 'no profit' bids).
Disruption	Excessive claims for disruption arising from unexpected events.
Price rises	Excessive claims for material price rises (where percentage increases are chargeable).
Milestones	Payment is claimed for target completion dates that have not been achieved.
Sub-standard materials	Cheaper materials are substituted for those specified in the contract. The use of sub-standard materials may introduce security, maintenance, health and safety or environmental risks.
External third-party behaviour	
Hack	Cyberattack leading to payment to a genuine supplier being diverted to a bank account controlled by a criminal.
Phantom suppliers	Payment to a fictitious company or a real company that does not have a genuine relationship with the business.

(*Continued*)

Procurement fraud – post-contract award *(Cause → Threat → Impact)*	
Misappropriation of assets	Cyberattacks leading to procurement processes being stolen or exploited illegitimately.
Employee behavior	
Diverted payment	Payment to a genuine supplier or contractor is diverted to a bank account controlled by an employee.
False invoices	False contractor invoices raised with payment made to a bank account controlled by an employee.
Procedures circumnavigated	Procurement procedures are not followed, for example, unjustified contract extension, scope increase without adequate pricing and second phase awarded without securing competitive prices.
Consultant behavior	
Overcharging	Unjustified billing of expenses claimed by consultants.
Overbilling	Inflated value of consultants' invoices which exceed contract arrangements.

Table 16.4 Procurement fraud (post-contract award) impact statement

Impact description (if the threats were to materialise)	
Increase in cost of projects impacting profitability	The business suffers from procurement fraud resulting in the business having to address overbilling, claims, materials substitution, false invoicing and/or cybercrime.

relate specifically to post-contract award, in other words after the contractor has been appointed and the contract signed.

Step 4C Risk analysis

When examining the characteristics of a potential threat it commonly involves estimating the likelihood, the impact (in cost and time together with other parameters when appropriate) and the proximity (when is the threat likely to materialise). Included in the Table 16.5 is a descriptive analysis of the likelihood, impact and proximity; however, for actual assessments figures would normally be provided.

Table 16.5 Procurement fraud risk analysis

Analysis of procurement risks (pre-contract award)	
Likelihood	As these risks have already been encountered by numerous other firms, the likelihood of their occurrence (in the absence of any mitigation actions being implemented) is very high.
Financial impact	The financial impact, should the risks materialise, will depend on a series of factors such as the contract (or contracts impacted), the scale of the fraud, whether it is a serial problem, the need to cancel existing contracts and engage a replacement contractor, and whether solicitors have to be engaged.
Time impact	The time impact, should the risks materialise, may relate to the time that specific resources have to be dedicated to resolving the fraud or the time taken to replace contractors or suppliers and complete specific contracts where fraud has been uncovered.
Proximity	Out of the course assessment of 'short', 'medium' and 'long' terms, all of these risks relate to the short term and need to be addressed at the earliest opportunity.

Step 5 Response actions

Specific response actions: governance, audits, systems and people

Included in Figure 16.5 are specific response actions that should be implemented with regard to governance, audits, your systems and your people.

Step 6: Implementation of actions

Immediate

If fraud has been committed, report it to Action Fraud which can be done at any time of the day or night using its online reporting tool. Reporting online is quick, easy and can be done on any device. Their tool will guide respondents through simple questions to identify what has happened and its advisers are available on web chat 24 hours a day to give businesses help and advice if needed. To access web chat just click on the red chat icon at the bottom of your device screen. It should be borne in mind the vast majority of fraud reported to the police via Action Fraud is not allocated to a police force for further investigation and

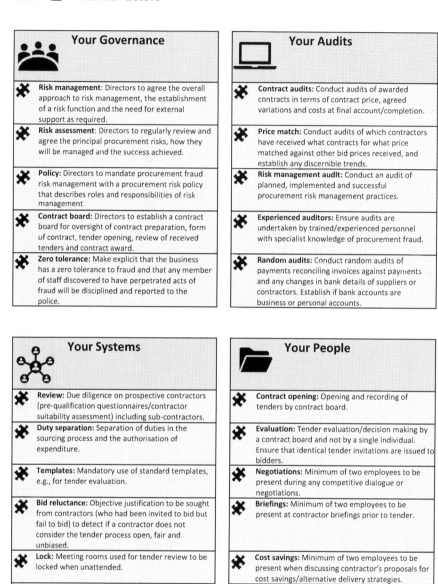

Figure 16.5 Response actions to tackle procurement fraud risk

✹ **Contract reviews:** Regular contract reviews to look at payments (against the contract sum) and the reason behind variations and an assessment of the costs against the contract sum.

✹ **Records:** Digital recording of all tenders issued, contract awards, prices, payments, variations and final settlement figures to provide a 'searchable' audit trail of selection and payment.

✹ **Update training:** Prepare and regularly update procurement fraud risk management training modules, ideally including changes in legislation and new case studies.

✹ **Zero tolerance:** Regularly reinforce the zero-tolerance policy towards procurement fraud.

✹ **Risk assessments:** Undertake procurement fraud risk identification and assessment on a regular basis.

✹ **Vigilance:** Ensure that the business is vigilant in understanding new procurement fraud risks and scams.

✹ **Counter measures:** Ensure that the right overall approach is adopted including the establishment of strategies, policies and plans which are effective in countering procurement fraud.

✹ **Internal controls:** Identify areas where internal controls are not working as well as intended and quickly take action to address any shortcomings discovered.

✹ **Matches:** Carry out proactive data set matches of your staff against suppliers, looking for shared bank accounts, address and telephone numbers.

✹ **Thresholds:** Ensure that payment thresholds are established with associated authorisation levels. Check that the thresholds are not being exceeded. Analyse business spend patterns with suppliers to ensure the business spending is as expected. Check that there isn't evidence of the splitting of orders to circumvent tender thresholds.

✹ **Red flags:** Ensure that red flags are not overlooked or ignored and are followed up. They are red flags for good reason. Long-standing staff assumed to be loyal to the business can just as readily commit fraud, particularly if their circumstances change.

✹ **Conflicts of interest:** Stress to employees and bidders alike that any conflicts of interest are to be declared immediately.

✹ **Authorisation:** Sign-off authorisation to be mandated for single sourcing and waivers.

✹ **Training:** Employees to undertake fraud risk management training, which is considered crucial to detecting, investigating and prosecuting fraudsters. Ensure that staff have clarity over how to conduct fraud risk assessments.

✹ **Staff:** Dedicate counter-fraud staff to review the procurement activity of the organisation, or periodically engage a third party to carry out a review.

✹ **Awareness:** Raise awareness of procurement fraud and associated risks with new staff (including agency staff), existing staff and suppliers.

✹ **Reporting:** Establish (and communicate) effective arrangements for recording and reporting procurement fraud.

✹ **Whistleblowing:** Set in place effective whistleblowing arrangements whereby staff are aware of them, confident in the confidentiality of them and reassured that any concerns raised will be addressed.

✹ **Intelligence:** Set up communication channels between staff and other organisations to ensure information is effectively shared about fraud and fraudsters.

✹ **Permissions:** Staff members often move to other departments within an organisation. If a staff member moves departments, remove all of their current permissions and authorities, and add the permissions applicable to their new role.

✹ **Duties:** Ensure that duties are segregated and the segregation is maintained especially after reorganisation or taking on new staff. In addition, implement a two-person system to define who can either add or delete a supplier from the approved supplier list or change a supplier's bank account number.

✹ **Directorships:** Check that employees (or their family members) are not a director of one of the supplier companies regularly used.

Figure 16.5 (*Continued*)

remains logged on a database for intelligence purposes. All fraud reports whether they relate to procurement fraud or not will be allocated to a police force or other agency for further investigation only when they meet certain criteria e.g. there are viable lines of enquiry such as known suspects who are based in the UK and include factors such as multiple victims; significant losses to individuals or organisations; organised criminal groups linked to terrorism, firearms, people trafficking and drugs; or regulated professionals such as solicitors, accountants and financial advisors.

Short term

In the short term make it clear to employees that the business has a zero tolerance to fraud. Consider whether anti-procurement fraud training is helpful or just arms employees with information on how to more be more successful in concealing fraud. Plan regular unannounced audits of payments made by the business over the last 12 months reconciling invoices against payments. Understand how money leaves your business, including methods of payment, who has authority to make those payments and who checks payments are legitimate. Where temporary or contract staff are engaged, ensure they are not part of the chain in sanctioning or orchestrating payments.

Medium term

Determine the steps to be taken if fraud is suspected or discovered. Take advice on how employees discovered to be involved in fraud are to be treated.

Long term

Establish those organisations providing procurement fraud prevention advice as well as those that provide guidance for when fraud is suspected or uncovered.

Cifas (UK's fraud prevention service)

Cifas is a not-for-profit company working to protect businesses, charities, public bodies and individuals from financial crime. They have more than 25 years of experience in fraud prevention and financial crime, working with a range of UK organisations to protect their customers and the public.

Experian

Experian is the leading global information services company, providing data and analytical tools. The company helps businesses to manage credit risk, prevent fraud, target marketing offers and automate decision-making. Experian also helps individuals to check their credit report and credit score, and protect against identity theft.

Action fraud

Action Fraud is the UK's national reporting centre for fraud and cybercrime where you should report fraud if you have been scammed, defrauded or experienced cybercrime in England, Wales and Northern Ireland.

Summary

As described in this chapter, procurement fraud is a deliberate deception intended to influence any stage of the procurement lifecycle in order to make a financial gain or cause a loss. A lack of awareness, understanding and detection creates an environment where procurement fraud can flourish. If businesses are not considering the risk of fraud before they embark on procurement, then procurement fraud may go undetected. It can be perpetrated by staff within an organisation as well as by contractors and sub-contractors external to the organisation. The nature of procurement fraud differs between the two core stages of the procurement lifecycle, pre-contract award and post-contract award. Fraud in the pre-contract award phase may involve activities such as collusion between bidders and corruption during the tender process when a tenderer secures an unfair advantage by paying an 'incentive' payment to an employee on the tender team. Fraud in the post-contract stage is different. As contracts are already in place, most cases of fraud tend to involve overpayments to contractors, through false or duplicate invoicing, and payments for work not completed under contract terms. A comprehensive approach to fraud risk management is required to understand the threats, their potential impact and the preventative measures that need to be put in place.

ADDITIONAL INFORMATION

Introduction to Section 4

The following appendices are intended to support readers in their journey into addressing cybercrime and fraud to support the profitability, growth and longevity of their businesses in a very complex and evolving business environment.

DOI: 10.4324/9781003200383-20   **291**

Appendix 1: Provides the terms and definitions employed in the fields of enterprise and project risk management. The glossary is broader than just the terms used in this book so that if readers widen their research, reading and exploration of the field of risk management beyond the scope of this book they will still be supported in expanding their comprehension of the subject.

Appendix 2: For those new to information technology, cybercrime and the deployment of malware it is hoped that readers will find the appendix helpful in navigating what at times can be a bewildering and expansive list of acronyms, terms and abbreviations which appears to expand almost by the day. Increasingly these terms are finding their way into the English dictionary. The list of terms is not intended to be exhaustive, (as it would swamp the book), but to provide sight of the most commonly used.

Appendix 3: There are a myriad of organisations involved in combatting fraud and cybercrime and this appendix is aimed at unravelling the primary organisations involved and what their role is. The UK government has yet to provide: a map of all of the UK government ministerial and non-ministerial departments and agencies involved in tackling cybercrime and fraud; a clear definition of the roles and responsibilities of each; and an unambiguous explanation of how they all work together, not just a few. It would appear that a significant co-ordination effort is required to ensure that their contributions are combined as effectively as possible in tackling what are very serious problems facing UK businesses and in turn the UK economy.

Appendix 4: Provides further reading on the subject of intellectual property fraud. The entrepreneurial talent of UK businesses is undermined by rogue employees, organised criminal groups and nation states intent on developing their economies to the detriment of others.

Appendix 1

Enterprise and project risk management terms and definitions

The vocabulary of enterprise risk management has expanded considerably over time. As new approaches, tools and techniques are developed, new terms and their definition are added to the risk management language. Included below are the more common terms and a description of their meaning. The descriptions are based on a number of publications, are in everyday use and have not been 're-invented' for this text (Table A1.1).

Risk Management terms and definitions

Table A1.1 Risk management terms and their definition

Term	Definition
Consequence	*See* impact.
Dependencies	Activities that must be completed for the business to complete specific tasks or actions.

(Continued)

Term	Definition
Impact	A measure of the effect of a threat on one or more of a project's objectives. Also known as a consequence.
Issue	A relevant event that has happened, was not planned and requires management action. It could be a risk that has materialised. Its resolution should be prioritised over risk response planning as it is an actual problem rather than a potential problem.
Issue response	A response to a known problem which may be a risk that has materialised.
Lessons learned	A record of events that had a positive or negative impact on more or more previous projects.
Mandate	A commitment by senior management to implement risk management which may be recorded in a Risk Policy and include the assignment of accountabilities and responsibilities.
Novel technology	A novel or new technology is one which is either still under development and has no history of proven performance or has a very short history of proven performance. A novel technology may be also described as one which has not been tested or evaluated to the same degree as proven technologies and or has not received regulatory approval.
Opportunity	A positive risk, an uncertain event that if successfully exploited would have a favourable impact on a project's objectives or benefits.
Project Life Cycle (PLC)	A PLC is composed of a series of inter-related (typically linear) phases which collectively provide a structure for governing the progression of the work. The phases may be interspersed by gate reviews which are go, no-go decision points. A typical project includes the phases: concept, design, procurement, execution, handover and closure.
Project Risk Management (PRM)	ISO 31000 defines 'Risk' as 'effect of uncertainty on objectives' whereas 'Project Risk Management' (PRM) refers to the management of that exposure in the pursuit of achieving predefined goals. Hence PRM has two primary functions. A management activity (the 'what') to drive down the exposure to threats and exploit opportunities, and a goal-seeking function to support the satisfaction of a project's aims or objectives (the 'why'). Consequently, PRM requires both a support management process and comprehension of the project objectives. (Typically, objectives include cost, time and quality however they may also include goals relating to cost-in-use, the environment, maintainability, reliability, reputation, safety, scope and sustainability). Reflecting on the primary aim of PRM a possible definition is as follows: PRM is the pro-active management process designed to exploit opportunities and treat threats to secure a project's agreed, defined and disseminated objectives.

Term	Definition
Project risk manager	In essence, the role of the Risk Manager (or similar named position) is to assist in defining and supporting the delivery of a project's risk management objectives. The role description needs to be tailored to the organisation's objectives, risk management maturity, frameworks, policies, plans, procedures, reporting requirements, audit processes and stakeholder (and or contractual) commitments. Typical duties involve preparing, reviewing and or approving the risk management framework, policy, plan and procedures, facilitating risk workshops and meetings, contributing to the preparation of the business case and feasibility studies, supporting the selection of the procurement route and the form of contract, carrying out quantitative risk analysis as required, overseeing the implementation of risk management in the supply chain and risk reporting. Each organisation, programme or project must make it abundantly apparent to its project personnel that risk management is everyone's responsibility, in just the same way that the delivery of quality and safety are.
Project sponsor	Individual or organisation that is authorising of providing the funding for a project respectively.
Quantitative analysis	The technique used to predict the likely project outcome based on the combined effect of the risks (threats and opportunities). Provides a numerical estimate of the overall effect of risk on the objectives of a project. Uses probability distributions to represent the probability and impact of individual risks.
RAG status	Threats are classified as red, amber or green depending on their potential impact on the project objectives, where red is the most severe and green is the least severe. It enables threats to be prioritised.
Relevant event	Events which have a direct bearing on the project objectives which have been defined as underpinning the project's business case.
Risk	An uncertain event that if it occurs would have a positive or negative effect on a project's objectives.
Risk Actionee	The individual responsible for a particular risk response activity. Given that there may be multiple actions to address a single risk, there may be multiple actionees for a single risk. The Actionee works under the direction of the Risk Owner.
Risk appetite	The type and extent of the principal risks an organisation's board is willing to accept in pursuit of its strategic objectives. The board must consider the risk exposure of individual projects within the context of the organisation's overall risk appetite to ensure that projects which appear profitable are not undertaken at the expense of projects with a greater likelihood of success or exposing the organisation to significant unmanageable risks.

(Continued)

Term	Definition
Risk appetite framework	Describes those aspects of the organisation that provide the context to enable a risk appetite statement to be prepared, such as the company's strategic objectives, the risk treatment categories, risk appetite scales, terms and their definition, the most significant areas of risk exposure, determining how much risk the board is willing to take and risk metrics.
Risk appetite scales	A matrix of appetite scales recorded against risk vs reward balance, risk treatment approach and response decision criteria.
Risk Breakdown Structure (RBS)	A hierarchical decomposition of the potential sources of risk to a project from the project environment through to project processes. Each descending level represents an increasingly detailed definition of the sources of risk to a project. Risk Breakdown Structures have their roots in project management Work Breakdown Structures (WBSs). The WBS is considered a key planning tool used to define projects in terms of their deliverables while providing a method for breaking these deliverables into meaningful subsets.
Risk capacity	The maximum amount and type of risk an organisation is able to bear in pursuit of its business objectives.
Risk cause	A description of the source of a risk, i.e. the event or situation that gives rise to the risk. It is not the description of the risk.
Risk effect	*See* risk impact.
Risk estimation	The estimation of the probability and impact of an individual risk where the impact is commonly described in terms of cost and or time.
Risk evaluation	The process undertaken to understand the combined net effect of the identified threats and opportunities on a project or sub-project when they are aggregated together, taking account of the relationship between the individual threats or opportunities.
Risk event	A description of a potential threat or opportunity.
Risk exposure	The aggregate amount of risk that an organisation is subject to at a given point in time.
Risk identification	The process of capturing and describing a list of potential threats and opportunities through the use of identification techniques.
Risk impact	A description of the impact a risk would have on an organisation, programme or project.
Risk improvement plan	A document describing planned improvements to support inculcating risk management within a project's culture ('way of doing things'). It describes specific activities (based on the findings of an assessment made when applying a risk maturity model), to be completed within a defined timeline by those assigned improvement responsibilities. Changes may be introduced as part of a change management initiative.

Term	Definition
Risk log	*See* risk register.
Risk management	The ongoing process of the identification, refinement and implementation of responses to identified threats and opportunities.
Risk management plan	A document that describes how project risk management will be implemented for a particular programme or project describing for instance the process, roles and responsibilities, glossary of terms, scales for estimating probability and impact, tools and techniques, risk register or database, how the evaluation will be implemented, how contingencies will be calculated, timing of risk management activities against the project life cycle, gate reviews, reporting requirements and escalation. A risk management plan is not the same as a risk register which contains a list of project risks.
Risk maturity	The risk maturity of a project is a measure of how well a project's risk management practices are working. The capability of a project to identify, assess and manage risks in a balanced and well-informed manner is fundamental to its decision-making processes.
Risk maturity model	A reference model or a framework of incremental mature practices for appraising a project's risk management competency. Typically structured as a matrix of maturity levels against risk categories/capabilities.
Risk mitigation	A risk treatment that deals with a negative consequence. The word 'mitigate' is described in the *Oxford Everyday Dictionary* (1981) as 'to make less intense or serious or severe'. Risk mitigation refers to reducing a threat but not removing it in its entirety.
Risk owner	An individual (or organisation) assigned to be responsible for the management of an individual threat or opportunity.
Risk policy	A high-level statement which records the mandate (directive) for implementing risk management prepared for an organisation or an individual programme or project. A policy may also stipulate the requirement for: risk management leadership; resources, assurance processes; continuous improvement; engagement; collaborative risk management practices; open, honest and factual representation of the threats and opportunities; adoption of lessons learned and support for embedding risk management.
Risk profile	Describes the types of risk faced by an organisation and its exposure to those risks.

(Continued)

Term	Definition
Risk register	A depository (either in the form of a spreadsheet or a database) containing both qualitative and quantitative risk analysis information together with details of the risk response plans. While each register will be tailored to the needs of a project it typically captures: the identified threats and opportunities, a unique identification number (or reference) for each threat and opportunity, the cause, impact (on objectives), risk owner, risk actionee, response type, response actions, date identified, project stage the risk relates to, the person that identified the risk, probability of occurrence, impact (commonly measured in time, money and quality), status (open or closed) and reason for closure if closed.
Risk response categories	A set of pre-determined and recorded response types or options from which a response may be selected for a particular risk.
Risk response	The specific action (or actions) selected to respond to previously identified threats or opportunities.
Risk tolerance	A risk response category where the project accepts to retain or accept the risk.
Risk transfer	A risk response category where a third party takes on responsibility for a specified risk.
Risk treatment	The development and implementation of responses to the identified threats and opportunities.
Risk window	The period (between two dates) during which the threat will materialise if it is to occur at all or the period during which an identified opportunity may be beneficially exploited.
Stage gate reviews	A stage gate review is a phase-driven 'go/no go' decision point to assure that the project is still aligned to the business case and that the scheduled activities for the phase have been completed satisfactorily. A project cannot proceed without a 'go' decision by senior management for each project phase.
Threat	An uncertain event that if it materialised could have a negative impact on a project's objectives and or benefits.
Uncertainty	Uncertain events where the probabilities of occurrence are unknown.

Appendix 2

Information technology, cyber security and cyberattacks terms and definitions

This is not intended to be an exhaustive list of terms, but those which follow are those which are most likely to be encountered by SMEs entering deeper into the world of information technology, cyber security and cybercrime (Table A2.1).

Table A2.1 IT and cyber security terms and their definition

Adware	Adware is plaguing users with unwanted advertising and degrading performance of the device or system being used. Adware is dissimilar to malware in that there is no malicious intent to harm users or their systems. Some adware can contain spyware-like features that collect information, such as browsing histories and personal information, without users' knowledge or consent.
Adwind	Adwind is a Remote Access Trojan (RAT) type of malware (also known as AlienSpy, JSocket, and jRat). The Trojan is a malware variant that targets the three major desktop operating systems (Linux, Windows and Mac OSX). Not only is the RAT able to collect PC information and keystrokes, as well as steal credentials and data submitted via web forms, the malware is also able to record video, sound, and take screenshots.

(Continued)

Boiler room scams	Share and bond scams are often run from 'boiler rooms' where fraudsters cold-call investors offering them worthless, overpriced or even non-existent shares or bonds. Boiler rooms use increasingly sophisticated tactics to approach investors, offering to buy or sell shares in a way that will bring a huge return. Source: Financial Conduct Authority.
Botnets	A botnet is a network of private computers infected with malicious software and controlled as a group without the owners' knowledge, e.g. to send spam. The word 'botnet' is a combination of the words 'robot' and 'network'. Each compromised device, known as a 'bot' is created when a device is penetrated by malicious software. Botnets can be used to perform DDoS attacks, steal data, send spam and allows the attacker to access the device and its connection. The owner can control the botnet using command and control (C&C) software.
Clone phishing	Attackers clone a legitimate email and then change the link or attachment.
Dark web	Effectively a marketplace to trade illegal goods and services, including drugs, firearms and malware. Anonymity emboldens people to break the law with platforms that enable dangerous crimes and appalling abuse.
DDoS	A Distributed Denial-of-Service (DDoS) attack is a cyber attack whereby the perpetrators seek to make a network resource unavailable. Typically the attacker's ultimate aim is to render a company's web site inoperable. Attacks may send so many requests to a server that legitimate users are unable to gain access. According to the software company Kaspersky, an attacker may request payment for stopping the attack. Hence it is described by Action Fraud as one of the methods adopted to defraud a company.
DNS	The DNS (Domain Name System) is a set of standards for how computers exchange data on the Internet. The DNS turns a user-friendly domain names like bbc.co.uk into an Internet Protocol (IP) address.
Internet	The Internet is a worldwide system of interconnected computer networks. When a computer is connected to the Internet via a user's Internet Service Provider (ISP) the user becomes part of the ISPs network which is connected to other networks that make up the Internet.
ISP	In simple terms an 'Internet Service Provider' provides their customers with access to the internet.
IP address	Computers use an IP address (Internet Protocol address) to identify each other. It's a bit like a postcode that is unique to each computer connected to the internet. An IP address is a set of numbers that might look like this: 175.188.87.12.

Malware	Malware is malicious software in the form of a program or file which is specifically designed to disrupt, damage, or gain authorized access to a computer system. Malware can be considered an umbrella or group term covering computer *viruses, worms, Trojan horses, spyware, ransomware, rootkit* and *RATs*. These malicious programs can perform a variety of functions, including stealing, encrypting or deleting sensitive data, altering or hijacking core computing functions and monitoring users' computer activity without their permission. The concept of malware took root in the technology industry, and examples of viruses and worms began to appear on Apple and IBM personal computers in the early 1980s before becoming popularized following the introduction of the *World Wide Web* and the commercial internet in the 1990s.
Mass market phishing	These emails go out to a large group of people and use a generic message to trick users into clicking a link or downloading a file. Attacks often use email spoofing, so that the message appears to come from a legitimate source.
NotPetya cyberattack	The UK's National Cyber Security Centre consider that the Russian military was almost certainly responsible for the 'NotPetya' cyber attack which occurred in June 2017 which particularly affected Ukraine's financial, energy and government institutions but its indiscriminate design caused it to spread beyond Ukraine.
Packets	When information is being sent from one computer to another it is broken down into small bits of data called 'packets'. Each packet includes information about where the data is going, where it is from and how to reassemble it.
Ransomware	Ransomware is a type of *malware* that encrypts files and folders, preventing access to important files. Ransomware attempts to extort money from victims by asking for money, usually in form of cryptocurrencies, in exchange for the decryption key. But cybercriminals won't always follow through and unlock the files they encrypted.
RAT	A RAT (Remote Access Trojan) is a type of *malware* program that secretly creates a backdoor into an infected system that allows threat actors to gain remote access to it without alerting the user or the system's security programs.
Router	A smart device that directs or routes information around the internet. When a data *packet* arrives, the router reads the IP address information and sends the packet along the best route to its destination.

(Continued)

Spoofing	The term 'spoofing' relates to falsifying the origin of internet communication in order to mislead the recipient. It's widely used to create trick emails or web pages in order to steal money, passwords or banking credentials. Email spoofing is the most commonly encountered. The apparent sender address of almost all spam emails is false. This is because the 'From' line in an email is not actually used to send it – it's just a piece of text. A specially-written email program can make it say anything at all, so you can't rely on it to find out where an email has really come from.
Social engineering	Social engineering fraud is a broad term that refers to the scams used by criminals to exploit a person's trust in order to obtain money directly or obtain confidential information to enable a subsequent crime. Social media is the preferred channel but it is not unusual for contact to be made by telephone.
Spear phishing	Spear phishing describes the fraudulent practice of sending emails to targeted individuals within an organisation or business (ostensibly from a known or trusted sender) for the purpose of distributing malware to extract sensitive information for financial gain. Spear phishing is a common method of attack and enabler for the vast majority of cybercrimes.
Untargeted	Untargeted phishing campaigns aim to reach as broad an audience as possible with the goal of tricking recipients into clicking a link, opening a malicious attachment, disclosing sensitive information or transferring funds.
Targeted	Targeted spear phishing attacks, relating to criminals utilising social engineering to glean a great deal of knowledge about the targets (and target environment) are far more effective than untargeted phishing. Although generally only a small proportion of victims click on the bait, the significant danger of phishing lies in the fact that one successful attempt can be enough to compromise a whole organisation. Source: Europol.[1]
Switch	A smart device that connects together many different devices so they can act as a network. Sometimes simpler devices called **'hubs'** are used.
Tabnapping	Tabnapping is a type of phishing scam that fraudsters use to get people's personal information. Tabnapping targets people who keep multiple tabs open in their browser, often for long periods of time. The fraudsters then use JavaScript to change the contents and label of an open, but not active, tab to resemble the login screen of a bank, email provider or online shopping store. When a user clicks back onto the tab to find the fake log-in screen, they assume that they have been logged out and re-enter their user information and password to log back in. When

	they enter these details, the personal information provided is sent straight to the fraudsters. Fraudsters can then use this personal information to commit fraud. The URL in the browser's address bar is not necessarily altered by tabnappers, so checking the URL is the legitimate URL of the service provider is not a sufficient precautionary measure. The fraudsters may even put an additional message on the fake log-in screen, saying that the session has timed out and the user needs to re-enter their log-in details. This is a message that appears on legitimate websites, particularly on banks, increasing the likelihood that the user thinks the log-in screen is trustworthy.
Trojan horse	A Trojan horse is a type of *malware* that is designed to appear as a legitimate program, however once unwittingly installed and activated, they are able to execute their malicious functions.
URL	Uniform Resource Locator. The URL structure is: Protocol + Domain Name + Port + Path to file. The protocol in this case http is the hypertext transfer protocol which is used by web browsers to get web pages and is the most common one you will encounter. The protocol is separated from the domain name with delimiters which are the colon plus two forward slashes: ://
Virus	A virus is the most common type of *malware* and is defined as a malicious program that can execute itself and spread by infecting other programs or files.
Vishing	Vishing is a phishing attempt using the phone. Victims are asked to call back and enter a PIN number or account number.
Water holing	Setting up a fake website or compromising a legitimate one in order to exploit visiting users.
WannaCry ransomware campaign	North Korean actors known as the Lazarus Group perpetrated the WannaCry ransomware campaign which was one of the most significant to hit the UK in terms of scale and disruption. It disrupted over a third of NHS trusts in England. Thousands of operations were cancelled, putting lives at risk.
Web browsers (commonly abbreviated to just browsers)	To access websites (and their web pages), a user must use a *web browser*, usually referred to as a *browser*. *Browsers* provide the software interface that enable individual users to use their mouse to click hyperlinked resources on the World Wide Web. The most used browsers include Google Chrome, Microsoft Edge and Firefox. Google Chrome has risen to pominence as it fast, secure, and has many features that other browsers don't have. Web browsers are used on a range of devices such as laptops, smartphones, tablets and desktops.

(Continued)

Whaling	These emails target someone on the executive team. Like spear phishing, these attacks start with research, which the attacker uses to write an email that appears legitimate.
WWW	The World Wide Web or the Web[2] as it is commonly referred to is a communications tool that enables users to find and exchange information over the internet. The web is based on several different technologies which include web browsers, Hypertext Markup Language (HTML) and Hypertext Transfer Protocol (HTTP) and Uniform Resource Locator (URLs).
Worm	A worm is a type of *malware* that can self-replicate without a host program; worms typically spread without any human interaction or directives from the malware authors.

Notes

1 Europol EC3 European Cybersecurity Centre. "Spear Phishing A Law Enforcement and Cross-Industry Perspective". The Hague, November 2019 https://www.europol.europa.eu/sites/default/files/documents/report_on_phishing_-_a_law_enforcement_perspective.pdf

2 It is commonly recognised that the Web was invented by Tim Berners-Lee. The date of the invention is recorded by different authors as either 1989 or 1991. It began as a project at the European Particle Physics Laboratory referred to as CERN. He was trying to find a new way for scientists to readily share the data from their experiments. Hypertext and the internet already existed but no one had thought of a way to use the internet to link one document directly to another. Berners-Lee, being familiar with hypertext (or linked words within text used to jump to other text or documents), proposed the idea of creating a global hypertext system. This system would allow individuals to link their documents together to create a web of interconnected documents. He named his system the World Wide Web. He suggested three main technologies so that all computers could understand each other (HTML, URL and HTTP). All of these remain in use today. Source: Bitesize, "What is the world wide web?". http://www.bbc.co.uk/guides/z2nbgk7.

Appendix 3

Glossary of organisations, government departments, agencies and external organisations together with their roles, terms and acronyms

Table A3.1 Government departments, agencies and external organisations

Organisation	Description
AAG	Accountancy Affinity Group: A meeting of all of UK accountancy professional body AML/CTF supervisors which aims to support the achievement of the UK's AML/CTF regime through the development of guidance, sharing best practices, input to national developments and liaison with government.
ACFE (US)	Association of Certified Fraud Examiners: Based in Austin, Texas, USA, the ACFE was founded in 1988. The ACFE describes itself as the world's largest anti-fraud organisation and premier provider of anti-fraud training and education. Its mission is to reduce the incidence of fraud and white-collar crime. Assistance to members: to assist in fraud detection and deterrence.

(*Continued*)

305

Organisation	Description
Action Fraud	The UK's National Fraud and Cyber Crime Reporting Centre hosted by the City of London Police, the national lead force for fraud. It receives crime and information reports on behalf of the police and gives advice and fraud prevention guidance. A dedicated line is available 24/7 for businesses suffering a live cyberattack. Businesses can report fraud and cybercrime 24/7, 365 days a year by visiting their website: actionfraud.police.uk. Note: Action Fraud does not have investigative powers and is unable to assist with the recovery of funds.
AGO	Attorney General's Office: Supports the Attorney General and the Solicitor General in their duty to provide legal advice to the UK government and to oversee the main prosecution authorities in England and Wales – the CPS and SFO.
BEIS	Department for Business, Energy and Industrial Strategy: Responsible for policy relating to business, including ensuring there is transparency around who ultimately owns and controls a company, which is an important part of the global fight against corruption, money laundering and terrorist financing.
Cabinet Office	The Cabinet Office supports the work of the National Security Council through the National Security Secretariat. The Cabinet Office is also the centre of the Government Counter Fraud Function, which brings together those working on fraud and economic crime across central government to set standards, develop capability and give expert advice. The Cabinet Office oversees the development of capability to counter fraud in the public sector, through the Government Counter Fraud Profession.
CIMA	Chartered Institute of Chartered Accountants: The Institute was founded in 1919 and claims on its website to be "the world's leading and largest professional body of management accountants". It helps individuals as well as businesses to succeed in the marketplace through the employment of management accounting. It offers a series of accounting qualifications which are recognised by employers in the UK and overseas. Assistance to members: Published guidance online.
City of London Police	Police the Square Mile is currently the world's leading international financial and business centre and is home to numerous multinational companies and small and medium-sized enterprises.

Organisation	Description
CoL ECA	The City of London Police Economic Crime Academy: Provides courses and advice for companies and individuals on how to fight economic crime.
Companies House	Companies House: Offers a range of digital services, the two primary ones being the filing of limited company details and providing a search engine for finding existing registered limited companies and their directors.
CPS	Crown Prosecution Service: Prosecutes serious and organised crime cases in England and Wales. CPS pursues all confiscation proceedings flowing from criminal investigations conducted by the NCA and HMRC and undertakes both criminal confiscation and civil recovery proceedings in conjunction with ROCUs and police forces.
DCMS	Department for Digital, Culture, Media and Sport: Leads the government's relations with the technology industry, including communications with service providers, while also overseeing data protection responsibilities.
DCPCU	Dedicated Card and Payment Crime Unit: A specialist police unit funded by the banking and cards industry which is comprised of officers from the City of London and Metropolitan Police as well as banking industry fraud investigators and support staff from UK Finance. It is in partnership with the Royal Mail and the telecommunications industry. It targets the criminal gangs responsible for fraud.
DFID	Department for International Development: Leads the UK's work to end extreme poverty and to deliver programmes to tackle insecurity and conflict in developing countries. This includes addressing underlying social and economic problems (such as corruption) that enable serious and organised crime to flourish.
Europol	The European Union's law enforcement agency. It is headquartered in the Netherlands and supports the EU Member States in their fight against terrorism, cybercrime and other serious crimes. It also works with many non-EU partner states and international organisations. It has identified the biggest security threats come from: organised fraud; terrorism; international drug trafficking and money laundering; the counterfeiting of euros; and trafficking in human beings. Help for businesses: If a business has been the victim of a crime it must contact its local or national police, not Europol.

(*Continued*)

Organisation	Description
FCA	Financial Conduct Authority: Regulates the financial sector and financial advisers, and will pursue criminal prosecutions, including for market manipulation. It is also an AML/CTF supervisor for financial institutions.
FCO	Foreign and Commonwealth Office: Responsible for delivering diplomatic and practical support to our priorities overseas, including on AML/CTF, serious and organised crime and corruption.
FIU	Financial Intelligence Unit: The FIU is sponsored by Europol and analyses the material it receives searching specifically for suspicious activity which may indicate potential money laundering or the financing of terrorism. When appropriate it forwards the intelligence it has gathered to the national authority responsible for prosecution.
FOS	Financial Ombudsman Service (www.financial-ombudsman.org.uk): Offers a free service to customers primarily looking to resolve a complaint. The complaint may emanate from one financial business concerning another or from a customer of a financial business. For small businesses (SMEs) that want to make a complaint they are directed to their dedicated small business website which provides more information about how they can help.
FSB	National Federation of Self Employed & Small Businesses Limited (www.fsb.org.uk): Provides a variety of guidance and support to its members with regard to tackling business fraud and cybercrime. Assistance to members: Provided through their legal advice line, partnership with the NCC and collaboration with NCSC and the PDSC. In particular through the issue of guides, telephone advice from lawyers and experts, documents, templates, training and webinars. Members are also provided with cyber insurance, the ability to purchase enhanced insurance. In specific circumstances, they are provided with Public Relations and Crisis Management. During Crisis Management they work closely with partners such as PDSC, NCSC and the Met Police.
FSCCC	Financial Sector Cyber Collaboration Centre: A partnership which identifies, investigates and coordinates the response to incidents that have potential consequences for the finance sector, by combining, analysing and distributing information from across the sector to produce timely outputs for the financial industry. The FSCCC currently includes around 40 firms but will continue to grow with the ambition of supporting other sectors in the future.

Organisation	Description
	FSCCC activities are coordinated by the Fusion Cell which works with partners from finance sector firms and other organisations, such as the Cyber Defence Alliance (CDA) and the Financial Services Information Sharing and Analysis Centre (FS-ISAC), analysing threats and corroborating intelligence from a range of sources. Since October 2019, the FSCCC briefed the sector on the latest developments in cyberattacks, such as DDoS extortion activity, and raised awareness of emerging threats enabling firms to refine defences. The Centre has convened incident management calls to share time-critical information on topics
Get Safe Online	The UK's most popular source of easy-to-understand information about online safety (https://getsafeonline.org/).
HMICFRS	HM Inspectorate of Constabulary, Fire Rescue Services: Independently assesses the effectiveness and efficiency of police forces and fire and rescue services. It assesses whether services are sufficient to meet the public interest and has a role to play in tackling corruption.
HMRC	HM Revenue and Customs: The UK's tax and customs authority, responsible for tackling fiscal fraud, with civil and criminal powers to investigate tax fraud. It is also an AML/CTF supervisor, including the money service, estate agency, trust and company service and accountancy businesses and high-value dealers.
HMT	HM Treasury: Responsible for regulating the financial and banking sectors, for the MLRs and overseeing AML/CTF supervision. HMT leads the UK's engagement with the FATF.
HO	The Home Office: Responsible for leading the UK's response to crime, working closely with the police, security and intelligence agencies and across government to do this. The Home Secretary and Minister of State for Security and Economic Crime have ministerial oversight at a policy level for the criminal justice aspects of the AML/CFT system, including national security and the counter-terrorism policy, as well as oversight of the NCA.
ICAEW	Institute of Chartered Accountants England and Wales: Is a professional membership organisation which provides accountancy qualifications, professional development and knowledge share and overall seeks to protect the integrity of the accountancy profession. The ICAEW was established by royal charter in 1880. Assistance to members: Provided through access to information resources, technical guidance, member offers and discounts, advisory services and local member networks.

(Continued)

Organisation	Description
Interpol	The International Criminal Police Organisation (www. interpol.int/): More well known by the abbreviation 'Interpol', has 194 member countries. Assistance to member countries: Provision of a range of policing expertise and capabilities to its member countries. Particularly: Toolkit to intercept fraudulent transfers called "Take Action: Urgent Stop-Payment Requests and Provisional Money-Freezing Orders" is available across INTERPOL's network of member countries. Coordinates its activities with Europol. Help for businesses: If a business has been the victim of a crime it must contact its local or national police, not Interpol.
JFT	Joint Fraud Taskforce: Set up in 2016, together with the private sector, law enforcement and government to protect the public from fraud.
JMLIT	Joint Money Laundering Intelligence Taskforce: Established in 2014 and launched as an operational pilot in 2015, the JMLIT has provided a mechanism for law enforcement and the financial sector to share information and work more closely together to detect, prevent and disrupt money laundering and wider economic crime. it is situated in the NECC.
MoJ	Ministry of Justice: Works to protect the public and reduce reoffending, and to provide a more effective, transparent and responsive criminal justice system for victims and the public. It is also responsible for ensuring that prison and probation services disrupt crime-related activity as part of a lifetime offender management approach.
MPS	Metropolitan Police Service: Its mission is to keep London safe for everyone. Ultimately, its vision is to be the most trusted police service in the world. Help for businesses: Provides helpful tips on preventing business fraud. Partnership with the TSB bank aimed at fraud prevention and tracking down fraudsters (announced in January 2019).
NCA	National Crime Agency: Leads and coordinates law enforcement's response to serious and organised crime in England and Wales and is responsible for developing a single authoritative view of the threat. Its key partners include the Serious Fraud Office, City of London Police (lead police force for fraud), Metropolitan Police Service, Financial Conduct Authority and the National Cyber Security Centre.

Organisation	Description
	The NCA also has a network of international liaison officers and is responsible for a number of national functions, including the responsibility for liaising with Europol, Interpol, the FBI and the US Secret Service. The NCA is led by a Director-General and overseen by the Home Secretary but is operationally independent. Help for businesses: Pursuit of sophisticated cybercriminals and the prevention of cybercrime in the first place. Other than fraud and cybercrime (including bribery, corruption and money laundering) the NCA is combatting: child sexual abuse; modern slavery and human trafficking, organised immigration crime; illegal drugs; illegal firearms; organised acquisitive crime; and sanctions evasion.
NCSC	National Cyber Security Centre (www.ncsc.gov.uk): Created in 2016 and forms part of GCHQ and is the UK's lead authority on cyber security. Preventing crime is the NCSC's priority, working in close partnership with law enforcement as well as the private and public sectors. The NCSC has created a 'Suspicious Email Reporting Service', established an 'Exercise in a Box' tool, and a 'Cyber Security Toolkit'. It has published advisory guidance for pharmaceutical companies supported by partners at the US Department for Homeland Security (DHS) Cybersecurity Infrastructure Security Agency (CISA) and National Security Agency (NSA), and the Canadian Communication Security Establishment (CSE). The toolkit has been used to support the retail sector as well as (for example) the construction, civil engineering and architectural sectors.
NECC	National Economic Crime Centre: Was set as a collaborative, multi-agency centre in 2018 with the core partners being the National Crime Agency (where it is based), City of London Police, Serious Fraud Office, Financial Conduct Authority, Crown Prosecution Service and Her Majesty's Revenue and Customs It was established to deliver a step change in the response to tackling serious and organised economic crime. The NECC sets threat priorities which informs operational coordination between partners and facilitates the exchange of data and intelligence between the public and private sectors.
NFIB	National Fraud Intelligence Bureau: A unit in the City of London Police, responsible for gathering and analysing intelligence relating to fraud and financially motivated cyber-crime.

(Continued)

Organisation	Description
No More Ransom	Aims to help victims of ransomware get back their encrypted data without having to pay the criminals (www.nomoreransom.org). The "No More Ransom" website was the initiative of the National High-Tech Crime Unit of the Netherlands' police, Europol's European Cybercrime Centre, Kaspersky and McAfee. Its goal is to help victims of ransomware retrieve their encrypted data without having to pay the criminals.
NPCC	National Police Chiefs' Council: The body responsible for the coordination of policing operations, reform, driving improvements and ensuring value for money.
OECD	Organisation for Economic Co-operation and Development (www.oecd.org): The OECD's website states it "is an international organisation that works to build better policies for better lives". Its goal is stated as being "to shape policies that foster prosperity, equality, opportunity and well-being for all".
OFSI	Office of Financial Sanctions Implementation: A part of HM Treasury that helps to ensure that financial sanctions are properly understood, implemented and enforced in the United Kingdom.
SAFO	Specified Anti-Fraud Organisations: An anti-fraud organisation specified in article 2 of the Serious Crime Act 2007. Under section 68(8), such an organisation is defined as any unincorporated association, body corporate or other people which enables or facilitates any sharing of information to prevent fraud.
SFO	Serious Fraud Office: A specialist prosecuting authority tackling the most serious complex fraud, bribery and corruption. It does **not** solely support combatting business fraud It is part of the UK criminal justice system covering England, Wales and NI. It takes on a small number of large economic crime cases that it selects itself based on the actual or intended harm that may be caused to the public, or the reputation and integrity of the UK as an international financial centre, or the economy and prosperity of the UK, and whether the complexity and nature of the suspected offence warrants the application of the SFO's specialist skills, powers and capabilities to investigate and prosecute. The SFO both investigates and prosecutes its cases. Help for businesses: It supports the maintenance of a 'level playing field' for businesses by prosecuting those businesses that seek an unfair advantage through bribery and corruption. While the SFO seeks to address the most

Organisation	Description
	serious cases typically with the corporate 'giants' it indirectly supports the SMEs who form the supply chain to the PLCs competing in the marketplace. The SFO works closely with: ■ the National Crime Agency's Economic Crime Command, International Corruption Unit and Bribery and Corruption Intelligence Unit ■ the City of London Police, including its Economic Crime Directorate, Action Fraud, and the National Fraud Intelligence Bureau ■ UK police forces and Regional Organised Crime Units, Regional Asset Recovery Teams and Regional Fraud Teams ■ HM Revenue & Customs ■ the Financial Conduct Authority
PDSC	Police Digital Security Centre (www.policedsc.com): A not-for-profit organisation, owned by the police, that works across the UK in partnership with industry, government, academia and law enforcement. Help for businesses: All their advice and guidance is consistent with the National Cyber Security Centre (NCSC). The PDSC believes that the majority of cybercrime can be prevented by organisations taking a few simple steps to protect their business.
PIPCU	The Police Intellectual Property Crime Unit: The following is an extract from https://assets.publishing.service.gov.uk/government/uploads/system/uploads/attachment_data/file/913644/ip-crime-report-2019-20.pdf: PIPCU is a department of the City of London Police, the national lead force for fraud. It was established in 2013 with the responsibility to investigate and deter serious and organised intellectual property crime in the United Kingdom. PIPCU is based in City of London Police's headquarters at Guildhall Yard East. Part of PIPCU's remit is to protect consumers from harm, focusing on intellectual property crime that has public safety implications. Since its inception, it has investigated intellectual property crime worth more than £700 million concerning counterfeit goods or digital piracy, and suspended more than 100,000 websites selling counterfeit goods. These websites have also been linked to identity theft.
POCA	Proceeds of Crime Act 2002: The goal of the Act is confiscation. In essence to deprive offenders of the proceeds of their criminal conduct, to deter criminals from committing further offences and to reduce the profits available to fund further criminal activity.

Organisation	Description
Police forces	Most of the operational work against crime in the UK is conducted by the 43 police forces in England and Wales at a regional and local level and by the Police Service of Scotland (Police Scotland) and Police Service Northern Ireland (PSNI). The Metropolitan Police Service and the City of London Police in particular have dedicated teams in place to combat terrorism, money laundering, fraud and other economic crimes and also provide an operational arm for other law enforcement agencies. Officers of the Police Service of Scotland are subject to the direction of the Lord Advocate and the Procurator Fiscal.
ROCUs	Regional Organised Crime Units: Regional police units that have a number of specialist capabilities used to investigate and disrupt serious and organised crime. There are nine ROCUs in England and in Wales and they are the principal interface between the NCA and police forces.
Royal Mail	Royal Mail Scam Mail Helpline: Support and advice if you've received items by post that you believe to be fraudulent (0845 611 3413).
SAR(s)	Suspicious Activity Report(s): They are provided by the private sector to the UK's Financial Intelligence Unit (UKFIU) to alert law enforcement to potential instances of money laundering or terrorist financing. SARs are made by professionals within financial institutions as well as solicitors, accountants and estate agents. They provide a vital source of intelligence on a wide range of criminal activities. Surprisingly, UKFIU receives more than 460,000 SARs a year.
National Fraud Intelligence Bureau	Receipt of reports from Action Fraud. Assessment of the level of risk and opportunities for investigation.
UKFIU	UK Financial Intelligence Unit: Housed within the NCA and is responsible for receiving and disseminating SARs and conducting analysis in line with its statutory mandate.
UNCAC	United Nations Convention Against Corruption: The only legally binding international anti-corruption multilateral treaty and has been entered into by the members of the UN. Within the preamble to the convention its states that it is "concerned about the seriousness of problems and threats posed by corruption to the stability and security of societies, undermining the institutions and values of democracy, ethical values and justice and jeopardising sustainable development and the rule of law".

Appendix 4

Further reading addressing intellectual property fraud

The UK Crown Prosecution Service

The Crown Prosecution Service (CPS) cites examples of criminal acts relating to intellectual property (IP) fraud as copyright infringement, intentional copying for registered designs and trademark infringement through counterfeiting. Under criminal law, certain uses of material subject to copyright, registered designs or trademarks, without the owner's permission can amount to a criminal offence. As defined by the CPS, IP results from any person's creativity or ideas. Such rights can exist in an invention, a product, a book, a brand, a design or a song. This list is not exhaustive. IP rights allow people to control the use that others can make of their works. The theft of IP can have a long-term impact on a business. Copyright law can be found in Part I of the Copyright, Designs and Patents Act 1988 as amended (known by the abbreviation CDPA). The CPDA creates criminal offences relating to articles which infringe copyright such as unauthorised copying, importing, possessing, selling, exhibiting, and distributing.

Government intellectual property system

Government IPO: The following description of the UK government's IPO office is drawn from their website: www.gov.uk/government/organisations/

315

intellectual-property-office/about. (This material is subject to Crown copyright under the terms of the Open Government Licence v3.0. See www.nationalar-chives.gov.uk/doc/open-government-licence/version/3/.)

> The website describes the Intellectual Property Office (IPO) as "the official UK government body responsible for intellectual property (IP) rights including patents, designs, trade-marks and copyright". It advises the IPO "is an executive agency, sponsored by the Department for Business, Energy & Industrial Strategy". The IPO sets out for clarity that it "is responsible for IP policy, educating businesses and consumers about IP rights and responsibilities, supporting IP enforcement and granting UK patents, trade-marks and design rights". In addition it's stated goal is to "operate and maintain a clear and accessible intellectual property system in the UK, which encourages innovation and helps the economy and society to benefit from knowledge and ideas". It strives to help people get the right type of protection for their creation or invention. The UK IPO has specialist IP attachés based in key economies around the world including China, India, Brazil and South East Asia. Their purpose is to support UK businesses operating overseas in exploiting their IP and navigating the issues involved in building their business.

Role of UK businesses: The UK government states it is a business's responsibility to defend its intellectual property (IP) and to take action if another business has used it without permission (known as 'infringement').

Examples of IP infringement include when someone:

- uses, sells or imports your patented product or process
- uses all or some of your work under copyright without your permission
- makes, offers or sells your registered design for commercial gain
- uses a trade mark that's identical or similar to one you've registered.

Anti-Copying in Design (ACID): is the leading UK design and intellectual property campaigning and membership organisation and advises on its website that it represents the views of thousands of designers spanning 25 different sectors within design. It is a not-for-profit trade association for designers and manufacturers funded by membership fees. It declares its aim is to provide cost effective tips, advice and guidelines to help its members protect their intellectual property to achieve growth through a proactive IP strategy. Most designers are micro and SME businesses and in 2018 the design economy gross value added (GVA)[1] grew at a faster rate than the UK average, and the value of exports where design had made a key contribution was £34 billion. Design's contribution to the UK economy is £85.2 billion in GVA equivalent to 7% of UK total GVA. ACID believes that collectively, design and design skills according to the Design Council, are worth £209 billion.

The threat from China

Chinese behaviour and ambitions: During the 2020 National Cybersecurity Summit in the US, FBI Director Christopher Wray[2] identified the Chinese government as one of the most significant threats to US business's intellectual property. Earlier in 2020[3] Wray identified that the Chinese had pioneered an expansive approach to stealing innovation through a wide range of actors, including not just Chinese intelligence services but also state-owned enterprises, seemingly private companies. In addition, the targets in the US were both diverse and extensive. Diverse in that Fortune 100 companies to Silicon Valley start-ups and from government and academia to high tech and agriculture were all being targeted. Extensive given that the FBI had ongoing investigations in all of its 56 field offices totalling some 1,000 cases involving China's attempted theft of U.S. based technology, spanning almost every industry and sector. The FBI is crystal clear that the Chinese government's ambition is to surpass the US's economic and technological leadership and to accomplish this, China is acquiring American intellectual property and innovation, by any means necessary. It is unclear how many other countries the Chinese are targeting to achieve their leadership goals.

Cooperation between China and the UK: The UK government website advises that the UK Intellectual Property Office (UKIPO) has cooperation relationships with a number of Chinese government agencies working on IP. In addition, the UKIPO and China's State Intellectual Property Office (SIPO) signed a cooperation agreement in 1996 covering patents and designs. The UKIPO signed a framework for cooperation on trademarks with China's State Administration for Industry & Commerce (SAIC) in 2009, and has operated a formal programme for cooperation with the National Copyright Administration of China (NCAC) since 2010. In addition, the UKIPO works with other UK Government partners and China's State Council Information Office to hold regular UK-China Internet Forums. These events look specifically at issues which both China and the UK face in managing copyright on the internet, including peer-to-peer file sharing.[4]

As far back as 2011, inventor Sir James Dyson warned China that it risked being expelled from the World Trade Organization (WTO) over copyright breaches including copies of the company's inventions. As reported in the *Telegraph*[5] Dyson said:

> They are running the risk of being expelled from the WTO.[6] They are creating an unlevel playing field by taking our technology and selling it all over the world.

The article reported that Dyson had observed that China benefits from strictly monitored IP regimes outside its own border, but has failed to crack down on domestic offenders as it pursues rapid economic growth. 'We had to put a private detective in their factory and take photos of them making the fans. Then we won the case and they were fined $7,500 but they didn't pay the fine and they just carried on', he said. Dyson is pursuing 20 design or patent cases around the world, many of them related to the distribution and sale of products made in China. The business has spent $3 million (£1.9 million) on legal fees. 'Under WTO regulations, each country is supposed to treat foreign patent applications with the same speed as local applications. But they are passing Chinese application in months and taking five years for ours'. He added: 'If we have someone copying our products in China, we cannot sue them until our patent is passed. This has not created a level playing field'.

Forms of intellectual property

To provide an accurate, up-to-date and factual description of the forms of intellectual property, the following descriptions are drawn directly from the UK government's websites: www.gov.uk/patent-your-invention, www.gov.uk/how-to-register-a-trade-mark, www.gov.uk/copyright and www.gov.uk/register-a-design. (This material is subject to Crown copyright under the terms of the Open Government Licence v3.0. See http://www.nationalarchives.gov.uk/doc/open-government-licence/version/3/.)

 Patent: A business can use a patent to protect its invention. It gives a business the right to take legal action against anyone who makes, uses, sells or imports it without your permission. To be granted a patent, a business's invention must be all of the following: something that can be made or used, new and inventive, not just a simple modification to something that already exists. Patents are expensive and difficult to obtain. Before an application is made, an assessment needs to be made to determine if a patent would be right for the business. The application process is complicated and typically only 1 in 20 applicants get a patent without professional help, they are expensive to obtain if professional help is sought and they usually take five years to obtain. If your business secures a patent, it will have to pay to renew it each year and finance the costs of legal action if it becomes necessary to defend it.

 Trademark: A business can register a trademark to protect its brand, for example, the name of its product or service. A trademark must be unique. A trademark can be something that allows consumers to distinguish a business's goods or services from those of another. It can include words, sounds, logos, colours or a combination of these. It cannot describe the goods or services it will relate to, for example, the word 'flour' cannot be a trademark for a flour mill company. In addition, it cannot be misleading or be too common and non-distinctive (for example be a simple statement like 'we are innovators' or look too similar to state symbols like flags or hallmarks. When a business registers a trademark, it will be able to take legal action against anyone who uses its brand without the business's permission, including counterfeiters. The ® symbol should be placed next to the brand to show that it's registered and warn others against using it. A registered trademark lasts ten years. A business can object to other business's trademarks, for example, if it is considered they are identical or similar to its own.

Copyright: Copyright protects a company's work and stops others from using it without a business's permission. Copyright protection is obtained automatically, it does not require an application or the payment of a fee. There isn't a register of copyright works in the UK. A business automatically obtains copyright protection when it creates: original literary, dramatic, musical and artistic work, including illustration and photography; original non-literary written work, such as software, web content and databases; sound and music recordings; film and television recordings; broadcasts; or the layout of published editions of written, dramatic and musical works. A business can mark its work with the copyright symbol (©), the company name and the year of creation. Whether a business marks its work (with the symbol) or not, it doesn't affect the level of protection a business has. Copyright prevents a business from: copying the work; distributing copies of it, whether free of charge or for sale; renting or lending copies of the work; performing, showing or playing the work in public; making an adaptation of the work; or putting it on the internet.

Design: A business can register the look of a product it has designed to stop other business's copying or stealing it. The look of a design includes the: appearance; physical shape; configuration (or how different parts of a design are arranged together); and decoration. Registering a design: protects any aspect of your design, for example, both the product's shape and decoration; gives a business the right to prevent others from using it for up to 25 years – a business has to renew its registered design every five years. Once registered a business can display its registration number on the design. To register a design, it cannot not be an invention or how a product works, for this a patent will be required.

UK Intellectual Property Crime Group: The UK IP Crime Group[7] within its 2019/2020 report[8] highlights the role of IP as crucial for legitimate businesses 'not merely as a form of protection, but also as a means of accessing the value creative production generates'. Within the context of an IP economy, the report says: 'criminals are drawn not to bank notes and bullion but to counterfeits and fakes' and seek to 'dupe the needy and profit from the unsuspecting'. The scale and scope of IP crime in the UK are overwhelming.

Notes

1 GVA is a measure of the increase in the value of the economy due to the production of goods and services. Its relationship to GDP is as follows: GVA = GDP + Subsidies − Taxes.

2 Source: FBI Director Christopher Wray delivered his remarks at the 2020 Cybersecurity and Infrastructure Security Agency (CISA) National Cybersecurity Summit on 16 September 2020.

3 Speech by FBI Director Christopher Wray 'Responding Effectively to the Chinese Economic Espionage Threat', Department of Justice China Initiative Conference, Centre for Strategic and International Studies, Washington, DC, February 6, 2020.

4 www.gov.uk/government/case-studies/uk-china-cooperation-on-intellectual-property.

5 The *Telegraph* (2011) 'China benefiting from flouting copyright and two-speed patent system that discriminates against foreign firms, says inventor', Dan Milmo, Industrial Editor, *The Sun*, 4 December 2011.

6 China joined the WTO, the body that enforces global trade rules, on 11 December 2001. It is still a member today.

7 The UK IP Crime Group was formed in 2004 and its membership consists of representatives from the private sector, enforcement agencies and government departments who are committed to reducing IP crime and infringement in the UK. The report draws together the experiences of key stakeholders in the IP crime prevention landscape and offers a unique insight into the nature of IP crime in the UK.

8 Page 5, the IP Crime and Enforcement Report 2019/2020 Editor Dan Anthony Published by the IP Crime Group, 2020.

Index

Note: **Bold** page numbers refer to tables; *italic* page numbers refer to figures.

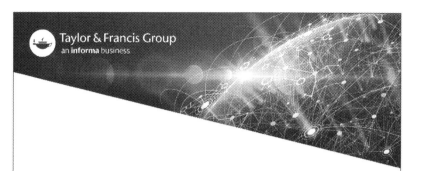

Printed in the United States
by Baker & Taylor Publisher Services